FREE Test Taking Tips Video/DVD Offer

To better serve you, we created videos covering test taking tips that we want to give you for FREE. **These videos cover world-class tips that will help you succeed on your test.**

We just ask that you send us feedback about this product. Please let us know what you thought about it—whether good, bad, or indifferent.

To get your **FREE videos**, you can use the QR code below or email freevideos@studyguideteam.com with "Free Videos" in the subject line and the following information in the body of the email:

a. The title of your product

b. Your product rating on a scale of 1-5, with 5 being the highest

c. Your feedback about the product

If you have any questions or concerns, please don't hesitate to contact us at info@studyguideteam.com.

Thank you!

GRE Prep 2022 - 2023 Review
3 Full-Length Practice Tests & GRE Study Book [12th Edition]

Joshua Rueda

Interested in buying more than 10 copies of our product? Contact us about bulk discounts:
bulkorders@studyguideteam.com

ISBN 13: 9781637759622
ISBN 10: 1637759622

Table of Contents

Quick Overview

As you draw closer to taking your exam, effective preparation becomes more and more important. Thankfully, you have this study guide to help you get ready. Use this guide to help keep your studying on track and refer to it often.

This study guide contains several key sections that will help you be successful on your exam. The guide contains tips for what you should do the night before and the day of the test. Also included are test-taking tips. Knowing the right information is not always enough. Many well-prepared test takers struggle with exams. These tips will help equip you to accurately read, assess, and answer test questions.

A large part of the guide is devoted to showing you what content to expect on the exam and to helping you better understand that content. In this guide are practice test questions so that you can see how well you have grasped the content. Then, answer explanations are provided so that you can understand why you missed certain questions.

Don't try to cram the night before you take your exam. This is not a wise strategy for a few reasons. First, your retention of the information will be low. Your time would be better used by reviewing information you already know rather than trying to learn a lot of new information. Second, you will likely become stressed as you try to gain a large amount of knowledge in a short amount of time. Third, you will be depriving yourself of sleep. So be sure to go to bed at a reasonable time the night before. Being well-rested helps you focus and remain calm.

Be sure to eat a substantial breakfast the morning of the exam. If you are taking the exam in the afternoon, be sure to have a good lunch as well. Being hungry is distracting and can make it difficult to focus. You have hopefully spent lots of time preparing for the exam. Don't let an empty stomach get in the way of success!

When travelling to the testing center, leave earlier than needed. That way, you have a buffer in case you experience any delays. This will help you remain calm and will keep you from missing your appointment time at the testing center.

Be sure to pace yourself during the exam. Don't try to rush through the exam. There is no need to risk performing poorly on the exam just so you can leave the testing center early. Allow yourself to use all of the allotted time if needed.

Remain positive while taking the exam even if you feel like you are performing poorly. Thinking about the content you should have mastered will not help you perform better on the exam.

Once the exam is complete, take some time to relax. Even if you feel that you need to take the exam again, you will be well served by some down time before you begin studying again. It's often easier to convince yourself to study if you know that it will come with a reward!

Test-Taking Strategies

1. Predicting the Answer

When you feel confident in your preparation for a multiple-choice test, try predicting the answer before reading the answer choices. This is especially useful on questions that test objective factual knowledge. By predicting the answer before reading the available choices, you eliminate the possibility that you will be distracted or led astray by an incorrect answer choice. You will feel more confident in your selection if you read the question, predict the answer, and then find your prediction among the answer choices. After using this strategy, be sure to still read all of the answer choices carefully and completely. If you feel unprepared, you should not attempt to predict the answers. This would be a waste of time and an opportunity for your mind to wander in the wrong direction.

2. Reading the Whole Question

Too often, test takers scan a multiple-choice question, recognize a few familiar words, and immediately jump to the answer choices. Test authors are aware of this common impatience, and they will sometimes prey upon it. For instance, a test author might subtly turn the question into a negative, or he or she might redirect the focus of the question right at the end. The only way to avoid falling into these traps is to read the entirety of the question carefully before reading the answer choices.

3. Looking for Wrong Answers

Long and complicated multiple-choice questions can be intimidating. One way to simplify a difficult multiple-choice question is to eliminate all of the answer choices that are clearly wrong. In most sets of answers, there will be at least one selection that can be dismissed right away. If the test is administered on paper, the test taker could draw a line through it to indicate that it may be ignored; otherwise, the test taker will have to perform this operation mentally or on scratch paper. In either case, once the obviously incorrect answers have been eliminated, the remaining choices may be considered. Sometimes identifying the clearly wrong answers will give the test taker some information about the correct answer. For instance, if one of the remaining answer choices is a direct opposite of one of the eliminated answer choices, it may well be the correct answer. The opposite of obviously wrong is obviously right! Of course, this is not always the case. Some answers are obviously incorrect simply because they are irrelevant to the question being asked. Still, identifying and eliminating some incorrect answer choices is a good way to simplify a multiple-choice question.

4. Don't Overanalyze

Anxious test takers often overanalyze questions. When you are nervous, your brain will often run wild, causing you to make associations and discover clues that don't actually exist. If you feel that this may be a problem for you, do whatever you can to slow down during the test. Try taking a deep breath or counting to ten. As you read and consider the question, restrict yourself to the particular words used by the author. Avoid thought tangents about what the author *really* meant, or what he or she was *trying* to say. The only things that matter on a multiple-choice test are the words that are actually in the question. You must avoid reading too much into a multiple-choice question, or supposing that the writer meant something other than what he or she wrote.

5. No Need for Panic

It is wise to learn as many strategies as possible before taking a multiple-choice test, but it is likely that you will come across a few questions for which you simply don't know the answer. In this situation, avoid panicking. Because most multiple-choice tests include dozens of questions, the relative value of a single wrong answer is small. As much as possible, you should compartmentalize each question on a multiple-choice test. In other words, you should not allow your feelings about one question to affect your success on the others. When you find a question that you either don't understand or don't know how to answer, just take a deep breath and do your best. Read the entire question slowly and carefully. Try rephrasing the question a couple of different ways. Then, read all of the answer choices carefully. After eliminating obviously wrong answers, make a selection and move on to the next question.

6. Confusing Answer Choices

When working on a difficult multiple-choice question, there may be a tendency to focus on the answer choices that are the easiest to understand. Many people, whether consciously or not, gravitate to the answer choices that require the least concentration, knowledge, and memory. This is a mistake. When you come across an answer choice that is confusing, you should give it extra attention. A question might be confusing because you do not know the subject matter to which it refers. If this is the case, don't eliminate the answer before you have affirmatively settled on another. When you come across an answer choice of this type, set it aside as you look at the remaining choices. If you can confidently assert that one of the other choices is correct, you can leave the confusing answer aside. Otherwise, you will need to take a moment to try to better understand the confusing answer choice. Rephrasing is one way to tease out the sense of a confusing answer choice.

7. Your First Instinct

Many people struggle with multiple-choice tests because they overthink the questions. If you have studied sufficiently for the test, you should be prepared to trust your first instinct once you have carefully and completely read the question and all of the answer choices. There is a great deal of research suggesting that the mind can come to the correct conclusion very quickly once it has obtained all of the relevant information. At times, it may seem to you as if your intuition is working faster even than your reasoning mind. This may in fact be true. The knowledge you obtain while studying may be retrieved from your subconscious before you have a chance to work out the associations that support it. Verify your instinct by working out the reasons that it should be trusted.

8. Key Words

Many test takers struggle with multiple-choice questions because they have poor reading comprehension skills. Quickly reading and understanding a multiple-choice question requires a mixture of skill and experience. To help with this, try jotting down a few key words and phrases on a piece of scrap paper. Doing this concentrates the process of reading and forces the mind to weigh the relative importance of the question's parts. In selecting words and phrases to write down, the test taker thinks about the question more deeply and carefully. This is especially true for multiple-choice questions that are preceded by a long prompt.

9. Subtle Negatives

One of the oldest tricks in the multiple-choice test writer's book is to subtly reverse the meaning of a question with a word like *not* or *except*. If you are not paying attention to each word in the question, you can easily be led astray by this trick. For instance, a common question format is, "Which of the following is…?" Obviously, if the question instead is, "Which of the following is not…?," then the answer will be quite different. Even worse, the test makers are aware of the potential for this mistake and will include one answer choice that would be correct if the question were not negated or reversed. A test taker who misses the reversal will find what he or she believes to be a correct answer and will be so confident that he or she will fail to reread the question and discover the original error. The only way to avoid this is to practice a wide variety of multiple-choice questions and to pay close attention to each and every word.

10. Reading Every Answer Choice

It may seem obvious, but you should always read every one of the answer choices! Too many test takers fall into the habit of scanning the question and assuming that they understand the question because they recognize a few key words. From there, they pick the first answer choice that answers the question they believe they have read. Test takers who read all of the answer choices might discover that one of the latter answer choices is actually *more* correct. Moreover, reading all of the answer choices can remind you of facts related to the question that can help you arrive at the correct answer. Sometimes, a misstatement or incorrect detail in one of the latter answer choices will trigger your memory of the subject and will enable you to find the right answer. Failing to read all of the answer choices is like not reading all of the items on a restaurant menu: you might miss out on the perfect choice.

11. Spot the Hedges

One of the keys to success on multiple-choice tests is paying close attention to every word. This is never truer than with words like almost, most, some, and sometimes. These words are called "hedges" because they indicate that a statement is not totally true or not true in every place and time. An absolute statement will contain no hedges, but in many subjects, the answers are not always straightforward or absolute. There are always exceptions to the rules in these subjects. For this reason, you should favor those multiple-choice questions that contain hedging language. The presence of qualifying words indicates that the author is taking special care with their words, which is certainly important when composing the right answer. After all, there are many ways to be wrong, but there is only one way to be right! For this reason, it is wise to avoid answers that are absolute when taking a multiple-choice test. An absolute answer is one that says things are either all one way or all another. They often include words like *every*, *always*, *best*, and *never*. If you are taking a multiple-choice test in a subject that doesn't lend itself to absolute answers, be on your guard if you see any of these words.

12. Long Answers

In many subject areas, the answers are not simple. As already mentioned, the right answer often requires hedges. Another common feature of the answers to a complex or subjective question are qualifying clauses, which are groups of words that subtly modify the meaning of the sentence. If the question or answer choice describes a rule to which there are exceptions or the subject matter is complicated, ambiguous, or confusing, the correct answer will require many words in order to be expressed clearly and accurately. In essence, you should not be deterred by answer choices that seem excessively long. Oftentimes, the author of the text will not be able to write the correct answer without offering some qualifications and modifications. Your job is to read the answer choices thoroughly and completely and to select the one that most accurately and precisely answers the question.

13. Restating to Understand

Sometimes, a question on a multiple-choice test is difficult not because of what it asks but because of how it is written. If this is the case, restate the question or answer choice in different words. This process serves a couple of important purposes. First, it forces you to concentrate on the core of the question. In order to rephrase the question accurately, you have to understand it well. Rephrasing the question will concentrate your mind on the key words and ideas. Second, it will present the information to your mind in a fresh way. This process may trigger your memory and render some useful scrap of information picked up while studying.

14. True Statements

Sometimes an answer choice will be true in itself, but it does not answer the question. This is one of the main reasons why it is essential to read the question carefully and completely before proceeding to the answer choices. Too often, test takers skip ahead to the answer choices and look for true statements. Having found one of these, they are content to select it without reference to the question above. Obviously, this provides an easy way for test makers to play tricks. The savvy test taker will always read the entire question before turning to the answer choices. Then, having settled on a correct answer choice, he or she will refer to the original question and ensure that the selected answer is relevant. The mistake of choosing a correct-but-irrelevant answer choice is especially common on questions related to specific pieces of objective knowledge. A prepared test taker will have a wealth of factual knowledge at their disposal, and should not be careless in its application.

15. No Patterns

One of the more dangerous ideas that circulates about multiple-choice tests is that the correct answers tend to fall into patterns. These erroneous ideas range from a belief that B and C are the most common right answers, to the idea that an unprepared test-taker should answer "A-B-A-C-A-D-A-B-A." It cannot be emphasized enough that pattern-seeking of this type is exactly the WRONG way to approach a multiple-choice test. To begin with, it is highly unlikely that the test maker will plot the correct answers according to some predetermined pattern. The questions are scrambled and delivered in a random order. Furthermore, even if the test maker was following a pattern in the assignation of correct answers, there is no reason why the test taker would know which pattern he or she was using. Any attempt to discern a pattern in the answer choices is a waste of time and a distraction from the real work of taking the test. A test taker would be much better served by extra preparation before the test than by reliance on a pattern in the answers.

FREE Videos/DVD OFFER

Doing well on your exam requires both knowing the test content and understanding how to use that knowledge to do well on the test. We offer completely FREE test taking tip videos. **These videos cover world-class tips that you can use to succeed on your test.**

To get your **FREE videos**, you can use the QR code below or email freevideos@studyguideteam.com with "Free Videos" in the subject line and the following information in the body of the email:

a. The title of your product

b. Your product rating on a scale of 1-5, with 5 being the highest

c. Your feedback about the product

If you have any questions or concerns, please don't hesitate to contact us at info@studyguideteam.com.

Thanks again!

Introduction to the GRE

Function of the Test

The **Graduate Record Examination** (GRE) General Test is a standardized test administered by the Educational Testing Service (ETS) and used as part of the admissions process by masters, doctoral, and business programs at various universities. Specifically, the test is accepted or required by virtually every graduate and business program in the United States as well as by many schools around the world. There are also seven GRE tests in specific subject areas, but "GRE" in common usage refers only to the General Test.

In recent years, around 500,000 people have taken the GRE annually. Because the GRE is exclusively used as an admissions exam, most test takers are seniors in undergraduate programs who are planning to attend graduate school or college graduates who are seeking a graduate degree.

Test Administration

In the United States, the GRE is administered by computer, year-round at Prometric testing centers and, from time to time, on specific dates at other testing centers. In the typical middle-sized city, a location to take the test will be available somewhere in town on most days of any given month. Outside the U.S., the GRE is administered by computer or, where computer-testing sites are not available, by paper.

The fee for taking the GRE is the same worldwide, with the exception of China, where fees are slightly higher. The computer-based version of the test can be taken up to five times within any rolling twelve-month window, although test takers must wait at least 21 days after an attempt to retake the exam. Note, however, that individual schools' rules about how they treat retest scores may vary. Reasonable accommodations are available for test takers with disabilities, provided requests are submitted to, and approved by, ETS before the test taker schedules a test date. Requests may be made through the test taker's electronic account with ETS.

Test Format

The computer-based GRE is "adaptive by section," meaning that the difficulty of the second verbal and second quantitative sections that the test taker receives will depend on their performance on the first of such sections completed. Test takers will have access to an on-screen calculator and may not use one of their own. Some questions provide multiple-choice answers, while others require test takers to fill in the blank.

The total test time is around 3 hours and 45 minutes, broken down as follows:

Section	Time	Description
Analytical Writing	60 minutes	Two 30-minute "issue" and "argument" writing tasks
Verbal Reasoning	2 30-minute sections	20 questions assessing reading comprehension, critical reasoning, and vocabulary usage
Quantitative Reasoning	2 35-minute sections	20 questions assessing quantitative comparisons, problem solving items, and data interpretation questions
Experimental/Research Section	1 30- or 35-minute unscored section	May be either Verbal Reasoning or Quantitative Reasoning

Scoring

On the Verbal and Quantitative Reasoning sections, students receive a raw score that is simply the total number of questions answered correctly. There is no penalty for guessing. The raw score is then scaled to a score that ranges from 130 to 170. This score is available upon completion of the test.

There is no set "passing" score on the GRE; rather, each school considers test takers' scores relative to the school's standards and to the scores of other applicants. The average score on the test is between 150 and 152, while average scores for applicants for elite programs might be around 160.

The writing sections are scored later, on a scale from 0 to 6 in 0.5-point increments. The average score is around a 3.5.

Recent and Future Developments

The GRE has undergone major revisions over the years, most recently with the introduction of the current "GRE revised" test in 2011. Prior to that revision, the test was adaptive from question to question (rather than from section to section) and was scored on a 1600-point scale. No substantial changes have been announced recently.

Study Prep Plan for the GRE

1   **Schedule -** Use one of our study schedules below or come up with one of your own.

2   **Relax -** Test anxiety can hurt even the best students. There are many ways to reduce stress. Find the one that works best for you.

3   **Execute -** Once you have a good plan in place, be sure to stick to it.

One Week Study Schedule

Day 1	Verbal Reasoning
Day 2	Quantitative Reasoning
Day 3	Analytical Writing
Day 4	Practice Test #1
Day 5	Practice Test #2
Day 6	Practice Test #3
Day 7	Take Your Exam!

Two Week Study Schedule

Day	Topic	Day	Topic
Day 1	Verbal Reasoning	Day 8	Practice Questions
Day 2	Integration of Ideas	Day 9	Analytical Writing
Day 3	Practice Questions	Day 10	Analytical Writing Example Prompts
Day 4	Quantitative Reasoning	Day 11	Practice Test #1
Day 5	Algebra	Day 12	Practice Test #2
Day 6	Data Analysis	Day 13	Practice Test #3
Day 7	Two-Way Tables	Day 14	Take Your Exam!

One Month Study Schedule							
Day 1	Verbal Reasoning	Day 11	Methods for Presenting Data	Day 21	Analyze an Issue Task
Day 2	Structure of Text	Day 12	Line Graphs	Day 22	Analyze an Argument Task
Day 3	Integration of Ideas	Day 13	Investigating Key Features of a Graph	Day 23	Analytical Writing Example Prompts
Day 4	Text Completion	Day 14	Two-Way Tables	Day 24	Practice Test #1
Day 5	Practice Questions	Day 15	Statistics	Day 25	Answer Explanations for Practice Test #1
Day 6	Quantitative Reasoning	Day 16	Set Notation	Day 26	Practice Test #2
Day 7	Order of Operations	Day 17	Describing a Set of Data	Day 27	Answer Explanations for Practice Test #2
Day 8	Algebra	Day 18	Practice Questions	Day 28	Practice Test #3
Day 9	Geometry and Measurement	Day 19	Analytical Writing	Day 29	Answer Explanations for Practice Test #3
Day 10	Data Analysis	Day 20	Conventions of Standard English	Day 30	Take Your Exam!

Verbal Reasoning

The **Verbal Reasoning** sections test a reader's ability to evaluate writing based on the logical development of points and sub-points, analyze and evaluate increasingly complex concepts, and understand the relationships of parts of the reading material to the whole in order to make comprehensive and meaningful sense out of texts. Therefore, it is wise for the reader to use several different study strategies to prepare for successful results when taking the Verbal Reasoning portion of the GRE exam.

Overall Question Structure

Several question structures are presented in the test. For example, in **Reading Comprehension**, test takers will be asked to read paragraphs and then will be presented with questions and possible answers that best support the meaning of the text. Another question structure, **Text Completion**, presents a statement with missing words. The reader will be asked to supply vocabulary words from a provided list to clarify the meaning of the sentence. The final question structure, **Sentence Equivalence**, is a single sentence with a missing word. The reader will select the two best possible missing words from a list of vocabulary words.

Reading and Vocabulary Preparation

The GRE Verbal Reasoning Exam tests one's ability to identify words used in context. Therefore, one of the best strategies to prepare for the test is to read high-level material. While reading, one should highlight challenging vocabulary words and their definitions on a separate document or on flashcards to review during the preparation stage. Because of effective reading preparation, the reader may have stronger recall during the test when they come across a word that is confusing. Readers must try to remember whether the word was used in a positive context or a negative context in their previous reading. This may help them make an educated guess during the test. Finally, as one studies word lists for the GRE, they should remember that the text completion and the sentence equivalence questions rely on understanding the words in context; therefore, it would be helpful for test takers to study synonyms and antonyms of vocabulary words.

Regarding the sentences in the GRE, note that the topics range from history to literature to geography. Test takers should read the sentences for cue words that will help determine the main idea the writer intended for the sentence as a whole and make relationships between the words selected in the sentence to the developing theme.

Reading Comprehension

Question Format

The GRE Reading Comprehension exercises vary in length from one to several paragraphs. Typically, shorter passages have one or two response questions, while longer passages have one to five associated questions.

First, one should read the passage carefully and look for clues as to how the development of the text completes the understanding of the paragraph. Signal words help determine the author's full intent. For example, words *like*, *moreover*, *although*, and *alternately* imply a comparison or contrast. Additionally, one should read thoroughly in order to understand the author's logic and recall significant points developed in the passage.

Multiple-Choice: Choose One Answer Choice

Readers will be faced with multiple-choice questions where they must pick a single answer. They should evaluate each multiple-choice question carefully before responding. The following are suggestions for readers who must select one answer choice:

- Readers should carefully review all of the options before selecting an answer. Ideas that are introduced in the choice selection (and therefore are not presented or inferred in the passage) are incorrect. One should read each answer choice slowly to decide whether or not it relates to the question.

- Readers should select the answer that is the best possible option. Other choices may seem reasonable, but readers must select the option that works best within the context of the information presented. It is wise for readers to take their time and to digest all the choices before making their selection.

- If a reader is not sure which option to choose, he or she should return to the main point of the question. Readers should try to select the answer option that fits the best with the information provided in the question and not get distracted by information beyond the selection in question. If readers have to return to the passage for more clues, they should read key points instead of the entire selection to keep within the time frame given.

Multiple-Choice: Choose One or More Answer Choices

Readers might be faced with questions where they will have to choose all the correct answers from a list of three options. The answer may include one, two, or all three options. Readers must select all of the correct answers to receive a positive score. Suggestions for this question format include the following:

- Readers can try to come up with correct answers before the answer options are read. That way, off-base answer options can quickly be eliminated. Rather than seeking connections between the options, each choice can be read with respect to the question. If a choice has a relationship to the question, test takers should mark it as a correct choice while they further consider other options.

- Readers should avoid rushing through the selection process. Instead, they should carefully select all the responses that work, whether that includes one, two, or three options. If readers make a rushed decision, they may miss the subtle ways that the author aligns the answers specifically to see if readers have used critical thinking strategies. Readers should practice using all their reading comprehension strategies before selecting choices.

Practice Examples

Questions 1–3 are based on this passage:

Most notably rooted in the Black musical experience, jazz music has been hailed as a true American art form. Responding to the late nineteenth- and twentieth-century influence of both European American and African American musical history, jazz music as a developing genre originated from pocket neighborhoods of New Orleans and offered a combination of traditional and popular musical influences. For over one hundred years, jazz incorporated the popular performance sounds of swing, improvisation, double discordant rhythms, and offbeat sounds. There are echoes of blues, big band sounds, and ragtime in the popular sounds of American jazz. During the jazz music evolution, other cultures added their musical styles to create a rich variety of subgenres, and later, fusion genres. The jazz musician's ability to improvise and use sounds to convey meaning offered a unique form of creative communication between the music maker and the listener. Because women jazz singers such as Billie Holiday and Ella Fitzgerald, and piano players like Lil Hardin Armstrong, attracted the applause of American audiences, the role of women gained a recognizable measure of social acceptance dating back to the 1920s. During the years of Prohibition in the United States, speakeasies furthered the jazz age culture of music, song, and dance, especially among the younger generation. Free jazz—a style of jazz that loosened the reins of meter, beat, and symmetry rules—was made popular by John Coltrane in the 1960s. Many other jazz styles emerged over the years including bebop—a musically challenging form of jazz; cool jazz—a Miles Davis favorite, noted for using long melody lines for a calming effect; soul jazz—taking some sounds from old gospel music; and smooth jazz—an early 1980s pop form of jazz. Finally, with the emergence of electronic music, jazz-rock music gained popularity in the early 2000s. Jazz will go down in history as a truly authentic American art form.

Select only one best answer choice.

1. Based on the information from the passage, which statement can be inferred to be true about the role of women and jazz?
    a. Women were not allowed to perform in American establishments where alcohol was served, which limited the success of female jazz singers and musicians during the 1920s.
    b. In the 1960s, women jazz singers and musicians first began to gain recognition as talented jazz entertainers, which garnered social recognition for them and subsequently gave them a respected place in American society.
    c. Billie Holiday and Ella Fitzgerald were members of an all-women jazz singing group; these all-female singing groups became popular because many of the men were enlisted in the armed forces during the wartime years.
    d. Female jazz artists, including both singers and jazz piano players, gained respect from American audiences long before the popular smooth jazz period emerged in the 1980s.
    e. European audiences accepted women jazz musicians because it was widely acknowledged that improvising skills, a trademark of jazz music, were more suited to women than men.

Explanation:

Choice *D* is correct based on the sentence that reads, "Because women jazz singers like Billie Holiday and Ella Fitzgerald, and piano players like Lil Hardin Armstrong, attracted the applause of American audiences, the role of women gained a recognizable measure of social acceptance dating back to the 1920s." Choice *A* is incorrect because there is no mention of women being allowed or not allowed in an establishment that served alcohol. Choice *B* is incorrect because the passage clearly states that the role of women and jazz was appealing to American audiences as early as the 1920s. Choice *C* is incorrect because the passage does not indicate that Billie Holiday and Ella Fitzgerald were members of an all-women jazz group. Choice *E* is incorrect because there is no statement in the passage regarding a connection between jazz improvisation and women in particular.

Consider each of the choices separately and select all that apply:

2. The passage suggests that jazz music, in all its forms, constitutes an authentic American art form for which of the following reasons?
    a. Jazz music emerged from small neighborhoods of New Orleans and preserved the basic features of purely traditional jazz sounds.
    b. Jazz music borrowed sounds from nineteenth- and twentieth-century European and African American musical history, which influenced the way jazz music evolved.
    c. Jazz music keeps its musical traditions consistent because, within the evolution of jazz music, there was never a time when meter, beat, and symmetry rules were dropped.
    d. During the jazz music evolution, other cultures added their musical styles to create a rich variety of subgenres, and later, fusion genres.
    e. Jazz musicians enjoyed improvising and using unique and creative sounds to convey meaning and communicate messages to the audience.

Explanation:

Choices *B*, *D*, and *E* are correct because the passage states that all three points contributed to the evolution of jazz music as an authentic American art form. Choice *A* is incorrect because it is only partially true; jazz music also borrowed sounds from popular music, not just traditional sounds. Choice *C* is incorrect because the passage states that free jazz loosened the rules of meter, beat, and symmetry.

Consider each of the choices separately and select all that apply:

3. According to the passage, which statements are accurate regarding each jazz artist mentioned and the time period in which their jazz style was popularized?
    a. Miles Davis was a favorite cool jazz player; he became popular for improvising with long melody lines, which gave the music a calming effect.
    b. Ella Fitzgerald was not a pianist, but her voice had deep, rich tones, which gained her acceptance with American audiences.
    c. Billie Holiday was both a jazz singer and a jazz piano player who was popular with both European and American audiences.
    d. John Coltrane created edgy sounds by dropping the rules of meter, beat, and symmetry. His jazz music was popularized during the 1960s and fell into the "free jazz" category.
    e. There are obvious sounds of blues, big band, and ragtime in the developing art of jazz music, which is another reason that jazz became known as authentic American music.

Explanation:

Choices *A* and *D* are correct based on the passage that states that Miles Davis became popular with cool jazz and John Coltrane loosened the rules of meter, beat, and symmetry. Choice *B* is incorrect because while it might be factually true, it contains details that are not stated in the passage. The choice mentions the "deep, rich tones" of Ella Fitzgerald's voice being the reason she gained acceptance with American audiences, but support of this assertion is not found in the passage; therefore, it is just a conjecture. Choice *C* is incorrect because the passage does not claim that Billie Holiday was both a jazz singer and a jazz pianist, nor does it note the role of European audiences in her popularity.

Choice *E* is incorrect because although the passage states that "there are echoes of blues, big band sounds, and ragtime in the popular sounds of American jazz," the question asks for statements that are true regarding jazz artists and the time period when their jazz style was popularized, and this answer choice is instead talking about the qualities that make jazz authentic American music. Therefore, Choice *E* is not a viable answer to this question since it is about neither jazz artists nor the time period when their jazz style was popularized.

Central Ideas and Details

Topic, Main Idea, Supporting Details, and Themes
The **topic** of a text is the overall subject, and the **main idea** more specifically builds on that subject. Consider a paragraph that begins with the following: "The United States government is made up of three branches: executive, judicial, and legislative." If this sentence is divided into its essential components, there is the topic (United States Government) and the main idea (the three branches of government).

A main idea must be supported with details, which usually appear in the form of quotations, paraphrasing, or analysis. Authors should connect details and analysis to the main point. Readers should always be cautious when accepting the validity of an argument and look for logical fallacies, such as slippery slope, straw man, and begging the question. It's okay for a reader to disagree with an author, because arguments may seem sound but be flawed upon further analysis.

It is important to remember that when most authors write, they want to make a point or send a message. The point, or message of a text, is known as the **theme**. Authors may state themes explicitly, like in *Aesop's Fables*. More often, especially in modern literature, readers must infer the theme based on textual details. Usually, after carefully reading and analyzing an entire text, the reader can identify the theme. Typically, the longer the piece, the more numerous its themes, though often one theme dominates the rest, as evidenced by the author's purposeful revisiting of it throughout the passage.

Cultural Differences in Themes
Regardless of culture, place, or time, certain themes are universal to the human condition. Because all humans experience certain feelings and engage in similar experiences—birth, death, marriage, friendship, finding meaning, etc.—certain themes span cultures. However, different cultures have different norms and general beliefs concerning these themes. For example, the theme of maturing and crossing from childhood to adulthood is a global theme; however, the literature from one culture might imply that this happens in someone's twenties, while another culture's literature might imply that it happens in the early teenage years.

It's important for the reader to be aware of these differences. Readers must avoid being **ethnocentric**, which means believing the aspects of one's own culture to be superior to those of other cultures.

Analyzing Topics and Summary Sentences
Good writers get to the point quickly. This is accomplished by developing a strong and effective topic sentence that details the author's purpose and answers questions such as *What does the author intend to explain or impress?* or *What does the author want the reader to believe?* The **topic sentence** is normally found at the beginning of a supporting paragraph and usually gives purpose to a single paragraph. Critical readers should find the topic sentence in each paragraph. If all information points back to one sentence, it's the topic sentence.

Summary sentences offer a recap of previously discussed information before transitioning to the next point or proceeding to the closing thoughts. Summary sentences can be found at the end of supporting paragraphs and in the conclusion of a text.

Identifying Logical Conclusions

Determining conclusions requires being an active reader, as a reader must make a prediction and analyze facts to identify a conclusion. A reader should identify key words in a passage to determine the logical conclusion from the information presented. Consider the passage below:

> Lindsay, covered in flour, moved around the kitchen frantically. Her mom yelled from another room, "Lindsay, we're going to be late!"

Readers can conclude that Lindsay's next steps are to finish baking, clean herself up, and head off somewhere with her baked goods. It's important to note that the conclusion cannot be verified factually. Many conclusions are not spelled out specifically in the text; thus, they have to be inferred and deduced by the reader.

Evaluating a Passage

Readers draw **conclusions** about what an author has presented. This helps them better understand what the writer has intended to communicate and whether they agree with what the author has offered. There are a few ways to determine a logical conclusion, but careful reading is the most important. It's helpful to read a passage a few times, noting details that seem important to the piece. Sometimes, readers arrive at a conclusion that is different than what the writer intended, or they may come up with more than one conclusion.

Textual evidence helps readers draw a conclusion about a passage. **Textual evidence** refers to information—facts and examples—that support the main point; it will likely come from outside sources and can be in the form of quoted or paraphrased material. In order to draw a conclusion from evidence, it's important to examine the credibility and validity of that evidence as well as how (and if) it relates to the main idea.

If an author presents a differing opinion or a **counterargument**, in order to refute it, the reader should consider how and why the information is being presented. It is meant to strengthen the original argument and shouldn't be confused with the author's intended conclusion, but it should also be considered in the reader's final evaluation.

Sometimes, authors explicitly state the conclusion that they want readers to understand. Alternatively, a conclusion may not be directly stated. In that case, readers must rely on the implications to form a logical conclusion:

> On the way to the bus stop, Michael realized his homework wasn't in his backpack. He ran back to the house to get it and made it back to the bus just in time.

In this example, although it's never explicitly stated, it can be inferred that Michael is a student on his way to school in the morning. When forming a conclusion from implied information, it's important to read the text carefully to find several pieces of evidence to support the conclusion.

Summarizing is an effective way to draw a conclusion from a passage. A **summary** is a shortened version of the original text, written by the reader in their own words. Focusing on the main points of the original text and including only the relevant details can help readers reach a conclusion. It's important to retain the original meaning of the passage.

Like summarizing, **paraphrasing** can also help a reader fully understand different parts of a text. Paraphrasing calls for the reader to take a small part of the passage and list or describe its main points. However, paraphrasing is more than rewording the original passage; paraphrases should be written in the reader's own words, while still retaining the meaning of the original source. This will indicate an understanding of the original source, yet still help the reader expand on their interpretation.

Structure of Text

Word and Phrase Meanings

Most experts agree that learning new words is worth the time it takes. It helps readers understand what they are reading, and it expands their vocabulary. An extensive vocabulary improves one's ability to think. When words are added to someone's vocabulary, they are better able to make sense of the world.

One of the fastest ways to decode a word is through context. **Context**, or surrounding words, gives clues about what unknown words mean. Take the following example: *When the students in the classroom teased Johnny, he was so discombobulated that he couldn't finish a simple math problem.* Even though a reader might be unfamiliar with the word *discombobulated*, he or she can use context clues in the sentence to make sense of the word. In this case, it can be deduced that *discombobulated* means confused or distracted.

Although context clues provide a rudimentary understanding of a word, using a dictionary can provide the reader with a more comprehensive meaning. Printed dictionaries list words in alphabetical order, and all versions—including those online—include a word's multiple meanings. Typically, the first definition is the most widely used or known. The second, third, and subsequent entries move toward the more unusual or archaic. Dictionaries also indicate the part(s) of speech of each word, such as noun, verb, adjective, etc.

Dictionaries are not fixed in time. The English language today looks nothing like it did in Shakespeare's time, and Shakespeare's English is vastly different from Chaucer's. The English language is constantly evolving, as evidenced by the deletion of old words and the addition of new ones. *Ginormous* and *bling-bling*, for example, can both be found in *Merriam-Webster's* latest edition, yet they were not found in prior editions.

Analyzing an Author's Rhetorical Choices

Authors utilize a wide range of techniques to tell a story or communicate information. Readers should be familiar with the most common of these techniques. Writing techniques are also known as **rhetorical devices**.

In nonfiction writing, authors employ argumentative techniques to present their opinions to readers in the most convincing way. Persuasive writing usually includes at least one type of **appeal**: an appeal to logic (**logos**), emotion (**pathos**), or credibility and trustworthiness (**ethos**). When writers appeal to logic, they are asking readers to agree with them based on research, evidence, and an established line of reasoning. An author's argument might also appeal to readers' emotions, perhaps by including personal stories and **anecdotes** (a short narrative of a specific event). A final type of appeal—appeal to authority—asks the reader to agree with the author's argument on the basis of their expertise or credentials. Three different approaches to arguing the same opinion are exemplified below:

Logic (Logos)

> Our school should abolish its current ban on campus cell phone use. The ban was adopted last year as an attempt to reduce class disruptions and help students focus more on their lessons. However, since the rule was enacted, there has been no change in the number of disciplinary problems in class. Therefore, the rule is ineffective and should be done away with.

The above is an example of an appeal to logic. The author uses evidence to disprove the logic of the school's rule (the rule was supposed to reduce discipline problems, but the number of problems has not been reduced; therefore, the rule is not working) and to call for its repeal.

Emotion (Pathos)

An author's argument might also appeal to readers' emotions, perhaps by including personal stories and anecdotes.

The next example presents an appeal to emotion. By sharing the personal anecdote of one student and speaking about emotional topics like family relationships, the author invokes the reader's empathy in asking them to reconsider the school rule.

> Our school should abolish its current ban on campus cell phone use. If students aren't able to use their phones during the school day, many of them feel isolated from their loved ones. For example, last semester, one student's grandmother had a heart attack in the morning. However, because he couldn't use his cell phone, the student didn't know about his grandmother's accident until the end of the day—when she had already passed away, and it was too late to say goodbye. By preventing students from contacting their friends and family, our school is placing undue stress and anxiety on students.

Credibility (Ethos)

Finally, an appeal to authority includes a statement from a relevant expert. In this case, the author uses a doctor in the field of education to support the argument. All three examples begin from the same opinion—the school's phone ban needs to change—but rely on different argumentative styles to persuade the reader.

> Our school should abolish its current ban on campus cell phone use. According to Dr. Bartholomew Everett, a leading educational expert, "Research studies show that cell phone usage has no real impact on student attentiveness. Rather, phones provide a valuable technological resource for learning. Schools need to learn how to integrate this new technology into their curriculum." Rather than banning phones altogether, our school should follow the advice of experts and allow students to use phones as part of their learning.

Rhetorical Questions

Another commonly used argumentative technique is asking **rhetorical questions**, which are questions that do not actually require an answer but that push the reader to consider the topic further.

> I wholly disagree with the proposal to ban restaurants from serving foods with high sugar and sodium contents. Do we really want to live in a world where the government can control what we eat? I prefer to make my own food choices.

Here, the author's rhetorical question prompts readers to put themselves in a hypothetical situation and imagine how they would feel about it.

Figurative Language

Similes and **metaphors** are types of figurative language that are used as rhetorical devices. Both are comparisons between two things, but their formats differ slightly. A simile says that two things are similar and makes a comparison using "like" or "as"—A is like B, or A is as [some characteristic] as B—whereas a metaphor states that two things are exactly the same—A is B. In both cases, similes and metaphors invite the reader to think more deeply about the characteristics of the two subjects and consider where they overlap. Sometimes the poet develops a complex metaphor throughout the entire poem; this is known as an **extended metaphor**. An example of metaphor can be found in the sentence: "His pillow was a fluffy cloud." An example of simile can be found in the first line of Robert Burns' famous poem:

> My love is like a red, red rose

This is comparison using "like," and the two things being compared are love and a rose. Some characteristics of a rose are that it is fragrant, beautiful, blossoming, colorful, vibrant—by comparing his love to a red, red rose, Burns asks the reader to apply these qualities of a rose to his love. In this way, he implies that his love is also fresh, blossoming, and brilliant.

Analyzing and Evaluating Text Structure

Depending on what the author is attempting to accomplish, certain formats or text structures work better than others. For example, a sequence structure might work for narration but not for identifying similarities and differences between concepts. Similarly, a comparison-contrast structure is not useful for narration. It's the author's job to put the right information in the correct format.

Readers should be familiar with the five main literary structures:

1. **Sequence** structure (sometimes referred to as the order structure) is when the order of events proceeds in a predictable manner. In many cases, this means the text goes through the plot elements: exposition, rising action, climax, falling action, and resolution. Readers are introduced to characters, setting, and conflict in the exposition. In the rising action, there's an increase in tension and suspense. The climax is the height of tension and the point of no return. Tension decreases during the falling action. In the resolution, any conflicts presented in the exposition are solved, and the story concludes. An informative text that is structured sequentially will often go in order from one step to the next.

2. In the **problem-solution** structure, authors identify a potential problem and suggest a solution. This form of writing is usually divided into two paragraphs and can be found in informational texts. For example, cell phone, cable, and satellite providers use this structure in manuals to help customers troubleshoot or identify problems with services or products.

3. When authors want to discuss similarities and differences between separate concepts, they arrange thoughts in a **comparison-contrast** paragraph structure. **Venn diagrams** are an effective graphic organizer for comparison-contrast structures because they feature two overlapping circles that can be used to organize and group similarities and differences. A comparison-contrast essay organizes one paragraph based on similarities and another based on differences. A comparison-contrast essay can also be arranged with the similarities and differences of individual traits

addressed within individual paragraphs. Words such as *however, but,* and *nevertheless* help signal a contrast in ideas.

4. The **descriptive** writing structure is designed to appeal to one's senses. Much like an artist who constructs a painting, good descriptive writing builds an image in the reader's mind by appealing to the five senses: sight, hearing, taste, touch, and smell. However, overly descriptive writing can become tedious, whereas sparse descriptions can make settings and characters seem flat. Good authors strike a balance by applying descriptions only to passages, characters, and settings that are integral to the plot.

5. Passages that use the **cause-and-effect** structure are simply asking *why* by demonstrating some type of connection between ideas. Words such as *if, since, because, then,* or *consequently* indicate relationship. By switching the order of a complex sentence, the writer can rearrange the emphasis on different clauses. Saying, *If Sheryl is late, we'll miss the dance,* is different from saying, *We'll miss the dance if Sheryl is late.* One emphasizes Sheryl's tardiness while the other emphasizes missing the dance. Paragraphs can also be arranged in a cause-and-effect format. Since the format—before and after—is sequential, it is useful when authors wish to discuss the impact of choices. Researchers often apply this paragraph structure to the scientific method.

Authorial Purpose and Perspective

No matter the genre or format, all authors are writing to persuade, inform, entertain, or express feelings. Often, these purposes are blended, with one dominating the rest. It's useful to learn to recognize the author's intent.

Persuasive writing is used to persuade or convince readers of something. It often contains two elements: the argument and the counterargument. The **argument** takes a stance on an issue, while the **counterargument** pokes holes in the opposition's stance. Authors rely on logic, emotion, and writer credibility to persuade readers to agree with them. If readers are opposed to the stance before reading, they are unlikely to adopt that stance. However, those who are undecided or committed to the same stance are more likely to agree with the author.

Informative writing tries to teach or inform. Workplace manuals, instructor lessons, statistical reports, and cookbooks are examples of informative texts. Informative writing is usually based on facts and does not use emotion and persuasion. Informative texts generally contain statistics, charts, and graphs. Although most informative texts lack a persuasive agenda, readers still must examine the text carefully to determine whether one exists within a given passage.

Stories or **narratives** are designed to entertain. When people go to the movies, they often want to escape for a few hours, not necessarily to think critically. **Entertaining** writing is designed to delight and engage the reader. However, sometimes this type of writing can be woven into more serious materials, such as persuasive or informative writing, to hook the reader before transitioning into a more scholarly discussion.

Emotional writing works to evoke the reader's feelings, such as anger, euphoria, or sadness. The connection between reader and author is an attempt to cause the reader to share the author's intended emotion or tone. Sometimes, in order to make a text more poignant, the author simply wants readers to feel the emotions that the author has felt. Other times, the author attempts to persuade or manipulate the reader into adopting their stance. While it's okay to sympathize with the author, readers should be aware of the individual's underlying intent.

Point of View

Point of view is another important writing device to consider. In fiction writing, **point of view** refers to who tells the story or from whose perspective readers are observing the story. In nonfiction writing, the **point of view** refers to whether the author refers to themselves, their readers, or neither. Whether fiction or nonfiction, the author carefully considers the impact the perspective will have on the purpose and main point of the writing.

- **First-person** point of view: The story is told from the writer's perspective. In fiction, this would mean that the main character is also the narrator. First-person point of view is easily recognized by the use of personal pronouns such as *I, me, we, us, our, my*, and *myself*.

- **Third-person** point of view: In a more formal essay, this would be an appropriate perspective because the focus should be on the subject matter, not the writer or the reader. Third-person point of view is recognized by the use of the pronouns *he, she, they*, and *it*. In fiction writing, third-person point of view has a few variations.

  - **Third-person limited** point of view refers to a story told by a narrator who has access to the thoughts and feelings of just one character.

  - In **third-person omniscient** point of view, the narrator has access to the thoughts and feelings of all the characters.

  - In **third-person objective** point of view, the narrator is like a fly on the wall and can see and hear what the characters do and say but does not have access to their thoughts and feelings.

- **Second-person** point of view: This point of view isn't commonly used in fiction or nonfiction writing because it directly addresses the reader using the pronouns *you, your*, and *yourself*. Second-person perspective is more appropriate in direct communication, such as business letters or emails.

Point of View	Pronouns used
First person	I, me, we, us, our, my, myself
Second person	You, your, yourself
Third person	He, she, it, they

Interpreting Authorial Decisions Rhetorically

There are a few ways for readers to engage actively with the text, such as making inferences and predictions. An **inference** refers to a point that is implied (as opposed to directly stated) by the evidence presented:

> Bradley packed up all of the items from his desk in a box and said goodbye to his coworkers for the last time.

From this sentence, although it is not directly stated, readers can infer that Bradley is leaving his job. It's necessary to use inference in order to draw conclusions about the meaning of a passage. When making an inference about a passage, it's important to rely only on the information that is provided in the text itself. This helps readers ensure that their conclusions are valid.

Readers will also find themselves making predictions when reading a passage or paragraph. **Predictions** are guesses about what's going to happen next. This is a natural tendency, especially when reading a good story or watching a suspenseful movie. It's fun to try to figure out how it will end. Authors intentionally use suspenseful language and situations to keep readers interested:

A cat darted across the street just as the car came careening around the curve.

One unfortunate prediction might be that the car will hit the cat. Of course, predictions aren't always accurate, so it's important to read carefully to the end of the text to determine the accuracy of one's predictions.

Readers should pay attention to the **sequence**, or the order in which details are laid out in the text, as this can be important to understanding its meaning as a whole. Writers will often use transitional words to help the reader understand the order of events and to stay on track. Words like *next, then, after,* and *finally* show that the order of events is important to the author. In some cases, the author omits these transitional words, and the sequence is implied. Authors may even purposely present the information out of order to make an impact or have an effect on the reader. An example might be when a narrative writer uses **flashback** to reveal information.

Drawing conclusions is also important when actively reading a passage. **Hedge phrases** such as *will, might, probably,* and *appear to be* are used by writers who want to cover their bases and show there are exceptions to their statements. **Absolute phrasing**, such as *always* and *never*, should be carefully considered, as the use of these words and their intended meanings are often incorrect.

Identifying the Appropriate Source for Locating Information

With a wealth of information at people's fingertips in this digital age, it's important to know not only the type of information one is looking for, but also in what medium one is most likely to find it. Information needs to be specific and reliable. For example, if someone is repairing a car, an encyclopedia would be mostly useless. While an encyclopedia might include information about cars, an owner's manual will contain the specific information needed for repairs. Information must also be credible, or trustworthy. A well-known newspaper may have reliable information, but a peer-reviewed journal article will have likely gone through a more rigorous check for validity. Determining **bias** can be helpful in determining credibility. If the information source (person, organization, or company) has something to gain from the reader forming a certain view on a topic, it's likely the information is skewed. For example, if trying to find the unemployment rate, the Bureau of Labor Statistics is a more credible source than a politician's speech.

Primary sources are best defined as records or items that serve as historical evidence. To be considered primary, the source documents or objects must have been created during the time period in which they reference. Examples include diaries, newspaper articles, speeches, government documents, photographs, and historical artifacts. In today's digital age, primary sources, which were once in print, are often embedded in secondary sources. **Secondary sources**—such as websites, history books, databases, or reviews—contain analysis or commentary on primary sources. Secondary sources borrow information from primary sources through the process of quoting, summarizing, or paraphrasing.

Today's students often complete research online through **electronic sources**. Electronic sources offer advantages over print and can be accessed on virtually any computer, while libraries or other research centers are limited to fixed locations and specific catalogs. Electronic sources are also efficient and yield massive amounts of data in seconds. The user can tailor a search based on key words, publication years, and article length. Lastly, many **databases** provide the user with instant citations, saving the user the trouble of manually assembling sources for a bibliography.

Although electronic sources yield powerful results, researchers must use caution. While there are many reputable and reliable sources on the internet, just as many are unreliable or biased sources. It's up to the researcher to examine and verify the reliability of sources. *Wikipedia*, for example, may or may not be accurate, depending on the contributor. Many databases, such as *EBSCO* or *SIRS*, offer peer-reviewed articles, meaning the publications have been reviewed for the quality and accuracy of their content.

Integration of Ideas

Understanding Authors' Claims

The goal of most persuasive and informative texts is to make a claim and support it with evidence. A **claim** is a statement made as though it is fact. Many claims are opinions; for example, "stealing is wrong." While this is generally true, it is arguable, meaning it is capable of being challenged. An initial reaction to "stealing is wrong" might be to agree; however, there may be circumstances in which it is warranted. If it is necessary for the survival of an individual or their loved ones (e.g., if they are starving and cannot afford to eat), then this assertion becomes morally ambiguous. While it may still be illegal, whether it is "wrong" is unclear.

When an assertion is made within a text, it is typically reinforced with supporting details as is exemplified in the following passage:

> The extinction of the dinosaurs has been a hot debate amongst scientists since the discovery of fossils in the eighteenth century. Numerous theories were developed in explanation, including extreme climate change, an epidemic of disease, or changes in the atmosphere. It wasn't until the late 1970s that a young geochemist, named Walter Alvarez, noticed significant changes in the soil layers of limestone he was studying in Italy. The layers contained fossilized remains of millions of small organisms within the layer that corresponded with the same period in which the dinosaurs lived. He noticed that the soil layer directly above this layer was suddenly devoid of any trace of these organisms. The soil layer directly above *this* layer was filled with an entirely new species of organisms. It seemed the first species had disappeared at the exact same time as the dinosaurs!

> With the help of his father, Walter Alvarez analyzed the soil layer between the extinct species and the new species and realized this layer was filled with an abnormal amount of *iridium*—a substance that is abundant in meteorites but almost never found on Earth. Unlike other elements in the fossil record, which take a long time to deposit, the iridium had been laid down very abruptly. The layer also contained high levels of soot, enough to account for all of the earth's forests burning to the ground at the same time. This led scientists to create the best-supported theory that the tiny organisms, as well as the dinosaurs and countless other species, had been destroyed by a giant asteroid that had slammed into Earth, raining tons of iridium down on the planet from a giant cosmic cloud.

Supporting Claims

Before beginning to answer questions, readers should summarize each paragraph. This will help in locating the supporting evidence. These summaries can be written down or completed mentally; full sentences are not necessary.

Paragraph 1: A layer of limestone shows that a species of organisms disappeared at the same time as the dinosaurs.

Paragraph 2: The layer had high amounts of iridium and soot—scientists believe the dinosaurs were destroyed by an asteroid.

Simply by summarizing the text, it has been plainly outlined where there will be answers to relevant questions. Although there are often claims already embedded within an educational text, a claim will most likely be given, but the evidence to support it will need to be located. Take this example question:

> Q: What evidence within the text best supports the theory that the dinosaurs became extinct because of an asteroid?

The claim here is that the <u>dinosaurs went extinct because of an asteroid</u>. Because the text is already outlined in the summaries, it is easy to see that the evidence supporting this theory is in the second paragraph:

> With the help of his father, they analyzed the soil layer between the extinct species and the new species and realized <u>this layer was filled with an abnormal amount of *iridium*</u>— a substance that is <u>abundant is meteorites</u> but almost never found on Earth. Unlike other elements in the fossil record, which takes a long time to deposit, the iridium had been laid down very abruptly. <u>The layer also contained high levels of soot</u>, enough to account for all of the earth's forests burning to the ground at the same time. <u>This led scientists to create the best-supported theory</u> that the tiny organisms, as well as the dinosaurs and countless other species, had been <u>destroyed by a giant asteroid</u> that had slammed into Earth, <u>raining tons of iridium down on the planet</u> from a giant cosmic cloud.

Now that the evidence within the text that best supports the theory has been located, the answer choices can be evaluated:
   a. Changes in climate and atmosphere caused an asteroid to crash into Earth.
   b. Walter and Luis Alvarez studied limestone with fossilized organisms.
   c. A soil layer lacking organisms that existed at the same time as the dinosaurs showed low levels of iridium.
   d. A soil layer lacking organisms that existed at the same time as the dinosaurs showed high levels of iridium.

Answer choice (a) is clearly false as there is nothing within the text that claims that climate changes caused an asteroid to crash into Earth. This kind of answer choice displays an incorrect use of detail. Although the passage may have contained the words "change," "climate," and "atmosphere," these terms were manipulated to form an erroneous answer.

Answer choice (b) is incorrect because while the scientists did study limestone with fossilized organisms, and in doing so they discovered evidence that led to the formation of the theory, this is not the actual evidence itself. This is an example of an out-of-scope answer choice: a true statement that may or may not have been in the passage, but that isn't the whole answer or isn't the point.

Answer choice (c) is incorrect because it is the opposite of the correct answer. Assuming the second paragraph was summarized correctly, it is already known that the soil layer contained *high* levels of iridium, not low levels. Even if the paragraph was not summarized that way, the final sentence states that "tons of iridium rained down on the planet." So, answer choice (c) is false.

Answer choice (d) is correct because it matches the evidence found in the second paragraph.

Fact and Opinion, Biases, and Stereotypes

It is important to distinguish between facts and opinions when reading a piece of writing. When an author presents **facts**, such as statistics or data, readers should be able to check those facts to verify that they are accurate. When authors share their own thoughts and feelings about a subject, they are expressing their **opinions**.

Authors often use words like *think, feel, believe,* or *in my opinion* when expressing an opinion, but these words won't always appear in an opinion piece, especially if it is formally written. An author's opinion may be backed up by facts, which gives it more credibility, but that opinion should not be taken as fact. A critical reader should be wary of an author's opinion, especially if it is only supported by other opinions.

Fact	Opinion
There are nine innings in a game of baseball.	Baseball games run too long.
James Garfield was assassinated on July 2, 1881.	James Garfield was a good president.
McDonald's® has stores in 118 countries.	McDonald's® has the best hamburgers.

Critical readers examine the facts used to support an author's argument. They check the facts against other sources to be sure those facts are correct. They also check the validity of the sources used to be sure those sources are credible, academic, and/or peer-reviewed. When an author uses another person's opinion to support their argument, even if it is an expert's opinion, it is still only an opinion and should not be taken as fact. A strong argument uses valid, measurable facts to support ideas. Even then, the reader may disagree with the argument.

An authoritative argument may use facts to sway the reader. For example, many experts differ in their opinions on whether or not homework should be assigned to elementary school students. Because of this, a writer may choose to only use the information and experts' opinions that supports their viewpoint. If the argument is that homework is necessary for reinforcing lessons taught in class, the author will use facts that support this idea. That same author may leave out relevant facts on excessive amounts of homework having a negative impact on grades and students' attitudes towards learning. The way the author uses facts can influence the reader, so it's important to consider the facts being used, how those facts are being presented, and what information might be left out.

Authors can also demonstrate **bias** if they ignore an opposing viewpoint or present their side in an unbalanced way. A strong argument considers the opposition and finds a way to refute it. Critical readers should look for an unfair or one-sided presentation of the argument and be skeptical, as a bias may be present. Even if this bias is unintentional, if it exists in the writing, the reader should be wary of the validity of the argument.

Readers should also look for the use of stereotypes that refer to specific groups. **Stereotypes** are often negative connotations about a person or place and should always be avoided. When a critical reader finds stereotypes in a piece of writing, he or she should immediately be critical of the argument and consider the validity of anything the author presents. Stereotypes reveal a flaw in the writer's thinking and may suggest a lack of knowledge or understanding about the subject.

Using Evidence to Make Connections Between Different Texts

When analyzing two or more texts, there are several different aspects that need to be considered, particularly the styles (or the artful way in which the authors use diction to deliver a theme), points of view, and types of argument. In order to do so, one should compare and contrast the following elements between the texts:

- Style: narrative, persuasive, descriptive, informative, etc.
- Tone: sarcastic, angry, somber, humorous, etc.
- Sentence structure: simple (1 clause) compound (2 clauses), complex-compound (3 clauses)
- Punctuation choice: question marks, exclamation points, periods, dashes, etc.
- Point of view: first person, second person, third person
- Paragraph structure: long, short, both, differences between the two
- Organizational structure: compare/contrast, problem/solution, chronological, etc.

The following two passages concern the theme of death and are presented to demonstrate how to evaluate the above elements:

Passage I

Death occurs in several stages. The first stage is the pre-active stage, which occurs a few days to weeks before death, in which the desire to eat and drink decreases, and the person may feel restless, irritable, and anxious. The second stage is the active stage, where the skin begins to cool, breathing becomes difficult as the lungs become congested (known as the "death rattle"), and the person loses control of their bodily fluids.

Once death occurs, there are also two stages. The first is clinical death, when the heart stops pumping blood and breathing ceases. This stage lasts approximately 4-6 minutes, and during this time, it is possible for a victim to be resuscitated via CPR or a defibrillator. After 6 minutes however, the oxygen stores within the brain begin to deplete, and the victim enters biological death. This is the point of no return, as the cells of the brain and vital organs begin to die, a process that is irreversible.

Passage II

It was her sister Josephine who told her, in broken sentences; veiled hints that revealed in half concealing. Her husband's friend Richards was there, too, near her. It was he who had been in the newspaper office when intelligence of the railroad disaster was received, with Brently Mallard's name leading the list of "killed." He had only taken the time to assure himself of its truth by a second telegram, and had hastened to forestall any less careful, less tender friend in bearing the sad message.

She did not hear the story as many women have heard the same, with a paralyzed inability to accept its significance. She wept at once, with sudden, wild abandonment, in her sister's arms.

When the storm of grief had spent itself, she went away to her room alone. She would have no one follow her.

There stood, facing the open window, a comfortable, roomy armchair. Into this she sank, pressed down by a physical exhaustion that haunted her body and seemed to reach into her soul.

Excerpt from "The Story of an Hour" by Kate Chopin

Now, using the outline above, the similarities and differences between the two passages are considered:

1. **Style:** Passage I is an expository style, presenting purely factual evidence on death, completely devoid of emotion. Passage II is a narrative style, where the theme of death is presented to us by the reaction of the loved ones involved. This narrative style is full of emotional language and imagery.

2. **Tone:** Passage I has no emotionally-charged words of any kind, and seems to view death simply as a process that happens, neither welcoming nor fearing it. The tone in this passage, therefore, is neutral. Passage II does not have a neutral tone—it uses words like "disaster," "killed," "sad," "wept," "wild abandonment," and "physical exhaustion," implying an anxiety toward the theme of death.

3. **Sentence Structure:** Passage I contains many complex-compound sentences, which are used to accommodate lots of information. The structure of these sentences contributes to the overall informative nature of the selection. Passage II has several compound sentences and complex sentences on their own. It's also marked by the use of many commas in a single sentence, separating modifying words. Perhaps this variety is meant to match the sporadic emotion of the character's discovery of her husband's death.

4. **Punctuation Choice:** Passage I uses only commas and periods, which adds to the overall neutral tone of the selection. Passage II mostly uses commas and periods, and then one semicolon. Again, the excess of commas and semicolon in the first sentence may be said to mirror the character's anxiety.

5. **Point of View:** Passage I uses third-person point of view, as it avoids any first- or second-person pronouns. Passage II also uses third-person point of view, as the story is being told by a narrator about characters separate from the narrator.

6. **Paragraph Structure:** The first passage is told in an objective way, and each paragraph is focused on the topic brought up in the first sentence. The second passage has no specific topic per paragraph. It is organized in a sequential way, so the paragraphs flow into the next in a chronological order.

7. **Organizational Structure:** The structure of Passage I is told in a very objective, organized way. The first paragraph tells of the stages before death, and the second paragraph tells of the stages after death. The second passage is told in chronological order, as a sequence of events, like in a fictional story.

When analyzing the different structures, it may be helpful to make a table and use single words to compare and contrast the texts:

Elements	Passage I	Passage II
Style	Expository	Narrative
Tone	Neutral	Emotional
Sentence Structure	Long	Long/Sporadic
Punctuation Choice	.	. and ,
Point of View	Third	Third
Paragraph Structure	Focused	Sequential
Organizational Structure	Objective/Logical	Chronological

The main differences between the two selections are style, tone, and structure. Possibly the most noticeable difference is the style and tone, as one tone is more neutral, and the other tone is more emotional. This is due to the word choice used and how each passage treats the topic of death. These are only a handful of the endless possible interpretations the reader could make.

Constructing Arguments Through Evidence

Using only one form of supporting evidence is not nearly as effective as using a variety to support a claim. Presenting only a list of statistics can be boring to the reader, but providing a true story that's both interesting and humanizing helps. In addition, one example isn't always enough to prove the writer's larger point, so combining it with other examples in the writing is extremely effective. Thus, when reading a passage, readers should not just look for a single form of supporting evidence.

For example, although most people can't argue with the statement, "Seat belts save lives," its impact on the reader is much greater when supported by additional content. The writer can support this idea by:

- Providing statistics on the rate of highway fatalities alongside statistics of estimated seat belt usage.

- Explaining the science behind car accidents and what happens to a passenger who doesn't use a seat belt.

- Offering anecdotal evidence or true stories from reliable sources on how seat belts prevent fatal injuries in car crashes.

Another key aspect of supporting evidence is a **reliable source**. Does the writer include the source of the information? If so, is the source well-known and trustworthy? Is there a potential for bias? For example, a seat belt study done by a seat belt manufacturer may have its own agenda to promote.

Logical Sequence

Even if the writer includes plenty of information to support their point, the writing is only effective when the information is in a logical order. **Logical sequencing** is really just common sense, but it's also an important writing technique. First, the writer should introduce the main idea, whether for a paragraph, a section, or the entire text. Then, they should present evidence to support the main idea by using transitional language. This shows the reader how the information relates to the main idea and to the sentences around it. The writer should then take time to interpret the information, making sure necessary connections are obvious to the reader. Finally, the writer can summarize the information in the closing section.

NOTE: Although most writing follows this pattern, it isn't a set rule. Sometimes writers change the order for effect. For example, the writer can begin with a surprising piece of supporting information to grab the reader's attention, and then transition to the main idea. Thus, if a passage doesn't follow the logical order, readers should not immediately assume it's wrong. However, most writing that has a nontraditional beginning usually settles into a logical sequence.

Text Completion

General Information

The **Text Completion** section of the GRE assesses the reader's ability to comprehend a passage by filling in missing words from a paragraph. The correct word choice(s) will clarify the meaning of the ideas that were organized and developed by the author. A critical reading of a passage means that the reader can break down complex concepts into accessible units. By evaluating the relationships of the parts to the whole, the skilled reader can determine the best word option that gives meaning to a sentence.

Question Format

Readers will see one to three blank columns, which contain options for the fill-in-the blank word. Unless otherwise stated, three answer choices will be provided for each blank. To receive full credit for the question, readers should be sure to select one option for each blank.

Readers may fill in the blanks in any order. If the answer to one blank is apparent, a previous blank (or a later blank) might be easier to fill in.

Suggestions

Reading and Understanding the Passage

- Readers should evaluate the sequence of main points, sub-points, and transitions to decipher the author's intended meaning.

- Another way for readers to better understand the passage is to practice reading more slowly if they cannot identify logical patterns and transitions from one point to the next. If readers do not comprehend the meaning and the context of what the writer intended to communicate, they will be at a disadvantage when selecting the correct answers to the questions.

- Readers should infer the main point of a sentence based on the information provided.

- Readers should always be ready to support their answer with information that is provided in the sentence. Answer choices that are too extreme or too simplistic should be avoided.

Filling in the Blanks with One's Own Words

Readers should fill in the meaning of the passage with their own words, then see if there are similar words in the list. If readers cannot create a reasonable summary in their mind, they should reread the relevant points to gain more comprehensive knowledge of the passage.

Practice Example

Select the best word from the corresponding column of choices that most clearly completes the passage.

1. With the constant growth of (i) _____, higher education curriculum design and delivery systems are transforming to adapt to a new community of learners. Potential students may choose from a menu of traditional, blended, and online delivery systems. To keep up with mobile technology, students may also select to engage in mLearning—learning from mobile devices—and uLearning, or (ii) _____ learning, meaning learning that can happen anywhere, inside or outside of a classroom, with or without teachers, and with or without fellow learners. Significantly, the pedagogical concern is that the learning units remain curriculum-based to ensure that learning objectives are created and met. As learning is unbundled from traditional delivery systems, it is important for curriculum designers to include models like Bloom's (iii) _____ of learning, the theory that learning begins as a repetition of facts and moves up the hierarchy to develop more complex critical thinking skills.

Blank (i)	Blank (ii)	Blank (iii)
a. Technology	d. Undulating	g. Taxonomy
b. Plagiarism	e. Ubiquitous	h. Anachronism
c. Resignations	f. Untenable	i. Panegyric

Explanation:

As one reads the passage for its broad meaning, it becomes obvious that a dominant theme of the piece focuses on learning in a higher education environment. As one considers the choices in the first blank, *plagiarism* (Choice B) and *resignation* (Choice C) both suggest a negative tone. The passage's sub-points, however, do not indicate a negative point of view. As one reads more about the introduction of mobile technology and higher education curriculum design, the term *uLearning* has a corresponding term that begins with the letter "u." All the words in column (ii) begin with the letter "u," so readers must use a process of elimination. Because *ubiquitous* means existing everywhere at the same time, completing the sentence with the word *ubiquitous* completes the definition of *uLearning*. Finally, if readers are familiar with the learning models in education, they will remember that Bloom's taxonomy of learning makes the best possible choice for the final blank. Therefore, *technology* (Choice A) is the correct answer for the first blank, *ubiquitous* (Choice E) is the correct answer for the second blank, and *taxonomy* (Choice G) is the correct answer for the third and final blank.

Select the best word from the corresponding column of choices that most clearly completes the passage.

2. Queen Elizabeth I was known for her (i) _____ passion for overcoming challenges; however, her competitors wished she was more (ii) _____ in governing.

Blank (i)	Blank (ii)
a. Wretched	d. Voracious
b. Pusillanimous	e. Obdurate
c. Sedulous	f. Tractable

Explanation:

Breaking down the larger concepts of overcoming challenges and competition, readers can quickly recognize that a word like *sedulous*—which means diligent, persevering, or persistent—is the best choice for the first blank. *Pusillanimous* means timid, which does not fit the theme of overcoming challenges, and *wretched* suggests pity or misfortune, which does not complement the notion of beating the odds. For the second blank, a word that denotes a characteristic that would be pleasing for Queen Elizabeth's competitors in governing should be considered. Therefore, *tractable* is the best choice for the sentence because it means she could be easily persuaded. The correct answer for blank (i) is *sedulous* (Choice *C*), and the correct answer for blank (ii) is *tractable* (Choice *F*).

Sentence Equivalence

General Information

The GRE **Sentence Equivalence** section tests a reader's ability to complete the full meaning of a sentence by supplying two of six possible word choices. Unlike traditional fill-in-the-blank tests, sentence equivalence questions ask for two words that are similar in meaning and that complete the meaning of the sentence. One note of caution: the meaning of the two words should be similar, but they do not necessarily have to be synonyms to be correct.

Checking for Logic, Grammar, and Style

Similar to the Text Completion section, readers should check the logic and grammar to determine which two best answer options fit the blank. To create a coherent sentence, each word should be tried in the blank to see which ones lend rational meaning to the sentence. The two words should relate to each other, and they also must each separately fit into the sentence's context in a logical manner.

It may also help for readers to be aware that the two correct answer choices will have grammatically similar parts of speech. Usually, the answer options will be made up of nouns, verbs, and adjectives. Again, test takers should pay attention to the context of the sentence to see which words precede or follow the blank in order to determine which answer options to rule out. Words should be chosen that fit within the blank stylistically as well.

Question Format

- The sentence will have one missing word indicated by a blank space.
- Readers will choose two similar words from a list of six options that best complete the sentence.
- Readers should make sure the two words not only share similar meanings, but that they also correctly complete the meaning of the sentence.

Suggestions

Reading and Understanding the Passage

Readers must be sure to develop a comprehensive, high-level vocabulary as a pretest strategy. Reading high-level material is the best way to come across relevant vocabulary in context. Also, readers should keep a running word list complete with definitions and synonym/antonym relationships. Looking for synonyms is one strategy for identifying correct choices on the Sentence Equivalence section of the test.

Readers should keep in mind during GRE study time that general and daily reading is essential if one intends to do well on the Verbal Reasoning section of the test. Readers can keep a list of GRE frequently used words and their definitions and practice memorizing these words for future use. Using flashcards is another way that one can speed up the learning experience.

Filling in the Blanks with One's Own Words

Readers should try to fill in the blank with their own word first. If a reader starts filling in the blank with the word choices supplied below the sentence, they may go off on the wrong track regarding the true meaning the writer intended. After a fill-in word is chosen, readers may look for similarities in the answer options. Remember that even though the words may not be synonyms, they should have similar meanings.

If readers know the definitions of all the answer options, another strategy is to plug sets of words into the blank in the sentence. If the selected words complete the overall meaning of the sentence, they are probably correct.

Practice Examples

Select two words that are similar in meaning to complete the sentence correctly and sensibly.

1. The lawyer, who began his presentation in a (an) _____ manner, faltered when new evidence was presented.
    a. Cogent
    b. Persuasive
    c. Ineffective
    d. Verbose
    e. Vacuous
    f. Phlegmatic

Explanation:

At first glance, several of the words could complete the sentence about the manner in which the lawyer presented his case. However, readers should select two words that are not only similar in meaning, but that also make the most sense in the context of the sentence. Readers will note that *ineffective* does not have a partner word. Yes, *verbose* makes sense, but it does not have a word of similar meaning, and *vacuous* and *phlegmatic* do not complete the sentence in a sensible way. Therefore, the correct pair is *cogent* and *persuasive*. They both mean "compelling," and they could be used interchangeably in the sentence.

The correct responses are Choice *A* (*cogent*), and Choice *B* (*persuasive*).

Select two words that are similar in meaning to complete the sentence correctly and sensibly.

2. If there is a remote possibility of winning the championship game, the players must practice without _____.

　　a. Apathy
　　b. Ardor
　　c. Fervor
　　d. Ennui
　　e. Vigor
　　f. Zeal

Explanation:

If readers understand the meaning of all the words, the best two words to complete the sentence stand out. Because players will need to increase their energy and power during practice, readers should select two words that suggest opposite ideas. It may be obvious that *zeal*, *fervor*, and *vigor* all share similar ideas. If readers are not sure what *ennui* means, they can make an educated guess that apathy and ardor are not synonyms. Therefore, the best words are *ennui* and *apathy* because they both suggest playing with a sense of boredom and detachment.

The correct responses are Choice *A* (*apathy*) and Choice *D* (*ennui*).

Verbal Reasoning Practice Quiz

Text Completion

Select the best word from the corresponding column of choices that most clearly completes the passage:

1. At one time, the Roman Empire was one of the most (i) _____b_____ military, economic, political, and cultural forces in the world. Around 100 BC, Rome was one of the largest and most (ii) _____d_____ cities in the world. It was an influential (iii) _____i_____ of the modern world.

Blank (i)	Blank (ii)	Blank (iii)
a. Acerbic	d. Potent	g. Acumen
b. Perspicacious	e. Obscure	h. Convention
c. Robust	f. Obsolete	i. Precursor

Sentence Equivalence

Select the two answer choices that can complete the sentence and create sentences that have complementary meaning.

2. Obviously, the new hires were motivated at the beginning of the day, but after a full week of training and evaluations, they acted _____ when asked to perform one more test.
  a. Lackadaisical
  b. Indefatigable
  c. Lethargic
  d. Energized
  e. Vigorous
  f. Enterprising

Reading Comprehension

Questions 3–5 are based on the following passage:

> Despite spending far more on health care than any other nation, the United States ranks near the bottom on key health indicators. This paradox has been attributed to underinvestment in addressing social and behavioral determinants of health. A recent Institute of Medicine (IOM) report linked the shorter overall life expectancy in the United States to problems that are either caused by behavioral risks (e.g., injuries and homicides, adolescent pregnancy and sexually transmitted infections (STIs), HIV/AIDS, drug-related deaths, lung diseases, obesity, and diabetes) or affected by social conditions (e.g., birth outcomes, heart disease, and disability).

> While spending more than other countries per capita on health care services, the United States spends less on average than do other nations on social services impacting social and behavioral determinants of health. Bradley, et al., found that Organization for Economic Co-operation and Development (OECD) nations with a higher ratio of spending on social services relative to health care services have better health and longer life expectancies than do those like the United States that have a lower ratio.

The Clinical & Translational Science Awards (CTSAs) established by the National Institutes of Health (NIH) have helped initiate interdisciplinary programs in more than sixty institutions that aim to advance the translation of research findings from "bench" to "bedside" to "community." Social and behavioral issues are inherent aspects of the translation of findings at the bench into better care and better health. Insofar as Clinical and Translational Science Institutes (CTSIs) will be evaluated for renewal—not only on the basis of their bench science discoveries, but also by their ability to move these discoveries into practice and improve individual and population health—the CTSIs should be motivated to include social and behavioral scientists in their work.

Population Health: Behavioral and Social Science Insights, Robert M. Kaplan et al. (2015), published by the Agency for Healthcare Research and Quality (National Institutes of Health), "Determinants of Health and Longevity" by Nancy E. Adler and Aric A. Prather, excerpted from pages 411 and 417

Consider each of the choices separately and select all that apply:

3. Which statement(s) describes how the United States differs in its approach to health care compared with other nations?
    a. On average, the United States spends less on social services impacting social and behavioral determinants of health than other nations.
    b. Compared with other nations, the United States has a higher ratio of spending on social services relative to health care services.
    c. Compared with other nations, the United States spends more per capita on health care services despite producing worse health outcomes.
    d. Compared with other nations, the United States has a lower life expectancy due to its lack of spending on health care services.
    e. Unlike other nations, the United States doesn't fund interdisciplinary programs that include behavioral and social science.

Select only one answer choice:

4. Based on the passage, which statement(s) describes the primary purpose of the Clinical and Translational Science Awards?
    a. The Clinical and Translational Science Awards advocate for the expansion of social services in the United States.
    b. The Clinical and Translational Science Awards seek to advance the translation of research findings from "bench" to "bedside" to "community."
    c. The Clinical and Translational Science Awards conduct research on how to mitigate the behavioral risks that have caused the decline in Americans' life expectancy.
    d. The Clinical and Translational Science Awards exclusively employ social and behavioral scientists, filling a void in the American health care system.
    e. The Clinical and Translational Science Awards calculate the optimal ratio for spending on social services relative to health care services.

Select only one answer choice:

5. Which statement(s) most accurately identifies the author's main thesis?

    a. Despite outspending other countries on health care, the United States performs poorly on key health indicators.

    b. The National Institutes of Health created the Clinical and Translational Science Awards to develop interdisciplinary programs in more than sixty institutions.

    c. Social and behavioral factors are an underappreciated aspect of health, and if they are better understood and properly addressed, health outcomes will improve.

    d. The United States has the shortest overall life expectancy in the world due to unaddressed behavioral risks and deteriorating social conditions.

    e. Life expectancy is the most important health care indicator because it encapsulates every other relevant factor.

Answer Explanations

Text Completion

1. C, D, I: If the Roman military was robust and potent, then it would have been influential economically and culturally, which could have been a logical precursor to the developing modern world. Thus, *robust*, *potent*, and *precursor* are the three choices that would fit best within the sentence.

Sentence Equivalence

2. A, C: The key word in this sentence is "but," a conjunction that signals that something will be contrasted with something else. In this sentence, the word "motivated" suggests a positive mood, so the answer words should be a switch from positive to negative. Therefore, because *energized*, *vigorous*, *indefatigable*, and *enterprising* are lively words, the best choices to complete the thought without changing the meaning are *lackadaisical* and *lethargic*.

Reading Comprehension

3. A, C: The first sentence of the second paragraph states, "While spending more than other countries per capita on health care services, the United States spends less on average than do other nations on social services impacting social and behavioral determinants of health." Thus, Choices *A* and *C* are the correct answers. Choice *B* is incorrect because it reverses the United States' ratio. The author argues that America's lower life expectancy is due to lower spending on social services, not insufficient funding for health care, so Choice *D* is incorrect. Choice *E* is incorrect because the United States does fund interdisciplinary programs that include behavioral and social science, like the Clinical and Translational Science Awards.

4. B: The Clinical and Translational Science Awards are mentioned in the third paragraph, and the author states that its interdisciplinary programs "aim to advance the translation of research findings from 'bench' to 'bedside' to 'community.'" Thus, Choice *B* is the correct answer. The Clinical and Translational Science Awards would likely support expanding social services, but advocating for that position isn't their purpose, so Choice *A* is incorrect. Similarly, the Clinical and Translational Science Awards likely conduct research on behavioral risks, but that's only part of the larger goal. So, Choice *C* is incorrect. Choice *D* is incorrect because employing social and behavioral scientists is not the Clinical and Translational Science Awards' primary purpose. It's unclear whether the Clinical and Translational Science Awards would even be involved in policy questions like calculating the optimal ratio for government spending, so Choice *E* isn't the primary purpose.

5. C: The author repeatedly mentions how the United States neglects social services. According to the author, this is why the United States performs poorly on key health indicators despite spending more per capita on health care than any other country. In addition, the author argues that the Clinical and Translational Science Awards should hire more social and behavioral scientists. Thus, Choice *C* is the correct answer. Choices *A* and *D* are premises that support the conclusion, not the main thesis, so they are both incorrect. Choice *B* is incorrect because it's only providing background information about the Clinical and Translational Science Awards. The author never asserts that life expectancy is the most important health care indicator, and, even if that were true, it wouldn't be the main thesis. Thus, Choice *E* is incorrect.

Quantitative Reasoning

Arithmetic

Numbers usually serve as an adjective representing a quantity of objects. They function as placeholders for a value. Numbers can be better understood by their type and related characteristics.

Integers

An **integer** is any number that doesn't have a fractional part. This includes all positive and negative **whole numbers** and zero. Fractions and decimals—which aren't whole numbers—aren't integers.

Prime Numbers

A **prime** number cannot be divided except by 1 and itself. A prime number has no other factors, which means that no other combination of whole numbers can be multiplied to reach that number. For example, the set of prime numbers between 1 and 27 is {2, 3, 5, 7, 11, 13, 17, 19, 23}.

The number 7 is a prime number because its only factors are 1 and 7. In contrast, 12 isn't a prime number, as it can be divided by other numbers like 2, 3, 4, and 6. Because they are composed of multiple factors, numbers like 12 are called **composite** numbers. All numbers greater than 1 that aren't prime numbers are composite numbers.

Even and Odd Numbers

An integer is **even** if one of its factors is 2, while those integers without a factor of 2 are **odd**. No numbers except for integers can have either of these labels. For example, 2, 40, -16, and 108 are all even numbers, while -1, 13, 59, and 77 are all odd numbers, since they are integers that cannot be divided by 2 without a remainder. Numbers like 0.4, $\frac{5}{9}$, π, and $\sqrt{7}$ are neither odd nor even because they are not integers.

Decimals

A **decimal** number is designated by a **decimal point**, which indicates that what follows the point is a value that is less than 1 and is added to the integer number preceding the decimal point. The digit immediately following the decimal point is in the tenths place, the digit following the tenths place is in the hundredths place, and so on.

For example, the decimal number 1.735 has a value greater than 1 but less than 2. The 7 represents seven tenths of the unit 1 (0.7 or $\frac{7}{10}$); the 3 represents three hundredths of 1 (0.03 or $\frac{3}{100}$); and the 5 represents five thousandths of 1 (0.005 or $\frac{5}{1000}$).

Rational and Irrational Numbers

Rational numbers include all numbers that can be expressed as a fraction; in other words, rational numbers encompass all integers and all numbers with terminating or repeating decimals. That is, any rational number either will have a countable number of nonzero digits or will end with an ellipsis or a bar (3.6666... or 3.$\overline{6}$) to depict repeating decimal digits.

Some examples of rational numbers include 12, -3.54, $110.\overline{256}$, $\frac{-35}{10}$, and $4.\overline{7}$.

Irrational numbers include all real numbers that aren't rational. It can be thought of as any number with endless non-repeating digits to the right of the decimal point. They can be expressed as an endless decimal but never as a fraction. The most common irrational number is π, which has an endless and non-repeating decimal, but there are other well-known irrational numbers like e and $\sqrt{2}$.

Real Numbers

Defined by Descartes in the seventeenth century, **real numbers** include all numbers found on an infinite number line. All irrational and rational numbers are real numbers. Nonterminating decimal numbers and π are also real numbers. As the range of real numbers extends to both negative and positive infinity, the set of real numbers is complete and uncountable. This set is known as the **complete ordered field of numbers.**

Rounding Numbers

It's often convenient to **round** a number, which means to give an approximate figure to make it easier to compare amounts or perform mental math. When rounding to a certain place value, consider the next digit after that place value. When that digit is 5 or more, the digit in the selected place value gets rounded up. The digit used to determine the rounding, and all subsequent digits, become 0, and the selected place value is increased by 1. Here are some examples:

75 rounded to the nearest ten is 80

380 rounded to the nearest hundred is 400

22.697 rounded to the nearest hundredth is 22.70

When rounding to a certain place value, again consider the next digit after that place value. When that digit is below 5, the digit in the selected place value stays the same. The digit used to determine the rounding, and all subsequent digits, become 0.

Here are some examples:

92 rounded to the nearest ten is 90

839 rounded to the nearest hundred is 800

22.64 rounded to the nearest hundredth is 22.60

Addition

Addition is the combination of two numbers so their quantities are added together cumulatively. The sign for an addition operation is the + symbol. For example, $9 + 6 = 15$. The 9 and 6 combine to achieve a cumulative value, called a **sum**.

Addition holds the commutative property, which means that the order of the numbers in an addition equation can be switched without altering the result. The formula for the commutative property is $a + b = b + a$. The following examples can demonstrate how the commutative property works:

$$7 = 3 + 4 = 4 + 3 = 7$$

$$20 = 12 + 8 = 8 + 12 = 20$$

Addition also holds the **associative property**, which means that the grouping of numbers does not matter in an addition problem. In other words, the presence or absence of parentheses is irrelevant. The formula for the associative property is $(a + b) + c = a + (b + c)$. Here are some examples of the associative property at work:

$$30 = (6 + 14) + 10 = 6 + (14 + 10) = 30$$

$$35 = 8 + (2 + 25) = (8 + 2) + 25 = 35$$

Subtraction

Subtraction is taking away one number from another, so their quantities are reduced. The sign designating a subtraction operation is the $-$ symbol, and the result is called the **difference.** For example, $9 - 6 = 3$. The number 6 detracts from the number 9 to reach the difference 3.

Unlike addition, subtraction follows neither the commutative nor associative properties. The order and grouping in subtraction impact the result.

$$15 = 22 - 7 \neq 7 - 22 = -15$$

$$3 = (10 - 5) - 2 \neq 10 - (5 - 2) = 7$$

When working through subtraction problems involving larger numbers, it's necessary to regroup the numbers. The following practice problem uses regrouping:

$$\begin{array}{r} 3\ 2\ 5 \\ -\ 7\ 7 \\ \hline \end{array}$$

Here, it is clear that the ones and tens columns for 77 are greater than the ones and tens columns for 325. To subtract this number, one needs to borrow from the tens and hundreds columns. When borrowing from a column, subtracting 1 from the lender column will add 10 to the borrower column:

$$\begin{array}{ccc} 3\text{-}1 & 10\text{+}2\text{-}1 & 10\text{+}5 \\ - & 7 & 7 \end{array} = \begin{array}{ccc} 2 & 11 & 15 \\ - & 7 & 7 \\ \hline 2 & 4 & 8 \end{array}$$

After ensuring that each digit in the top row is greater than the digit in the corresponding bottom row, subtraction can proceed as normal, and the answer is found to be 248.

Multiplication

Multiplication involves adding together multiple copies of a number. It is indicated by an × symbol or a number immediately outside of a parenthesis. For example:

$$5(8 - 2)$$

The two numbers being multiplied together are called **factors**, and their result is called a **product**. For example, $9 \times 6 = 54$. This can be shown alternatively by expansion of either the 9 or the 6:

$$9 \times 6 = 9 + 9 + 9 + 9 + 9 + 9 = 54$$

$$9 \times 6 = 6 + 6 + 6 + 6 + 6 + 6 + 6 + 6 + 6 = 54$$

Like addition, multiplication holds the commutative and associative properties:

$$115 = 23 \times 5 = 5 \times 23 = 115$$

$$84 = 3 \times (7 \times 4) = (3 \times 7) \times 4 = 84$$

Multiplication also follows the **distributive property**, which allows the multiplication to be distributed through parentheses. The formula for distribution is $a \times (b + c) = ab + ac$. This is clear after the examples:

$$45 = 5 \times 9 = 5(3 + 6) = (5 \times 3) + (5 \times 6) = 15 + 30 = 45$$

$$20 = 4 \times 5 = 4(10 - 5) = (4 \times 10) - (4 \times 5) = 40 - 20 = 20$$

Multiplication becomes slightly more complicated when multiplying numbers with decimals. The easiest way to answer these problems is to ignore the decimals and multiply as if they were whole numbers. After multiplying the factors, a decimal gets placed in the product. The placement of the decimal is determined by taking the cumulative number of decimal places in the factors.

For example:

0.7	2.6	1.5
x 3	x 4.2	x 6.4
2.1	10.92	9.60

Starting with the first example, the first step is to ignore the decimal and multiply the numbers as though they were whole numbers, which results in a product of 21. The next step is to count the number of digits that follow a decimal (one, in this case). Finally, the decimal place gets moved that many positions to the left, because the factors have only one decimal place. The second example works the same way, except that there are two total decimal places in the factors, so the product's decimal is moved two places over. In the third example, the decimal should be moved over two digits, but the digit zero is no longer needed, so it is erased, and the final answer is 9.6.

Division

Division and multiplication are inverses of each other in the same way that addition and subtraction are opposites. The signs designating the division operation are the ÷ and / symbols. In division, the second number divides into the first.

The number before the division sign is called the **dividend** or, if expressed as a fraction, the **numerator.** For example, in $a \div b$, a is the dividend, while in $\frac{a}{b}$, a is the numerator.

The number after the division sign is called the **divisor** or, if expressed as a fraction, the **denominator.** For example, in $a \div b$, b is the divisor, while in $\frac{a}{b}$, b is the denominator.

Like subtraction, division doesn't follow the commutative property, as it matters which number comes before the division sign, and division doesn't follow the associative or distributive properties for the same reason. For example:

$$\frac{3}{2} = 9 \div 6 \neq 6 \div 9 = \frac{2}{3}$$

$$2 = 10 \div 5 = (30 \div 3) \div 5 \neq 30 \div (3 \div 5) = 30 \div \frac{3}{5} = 50$$

$$25 = 20 + 5 = (40 \div 2) + (40 \div 8) \neq 40 \div (2 + 8) = 40 \div 10 = 4$$

If a divisor doesn't divide into a dividend an integer number of times, whatever is left over is termed the **remainder**. The remainder can be further divided out into decimal form by using long division; however, this doesn't always give a **quotient** with a finite number of decimal places, so the remainder can also be expressed as a fraction over the original divisor.

Division with decimals is similar to multiplication with decimals in that when dividing a decimal by a whole number, one should ignore the decimal and divide as if it was a whole number.

Upon finding the answer, or quotient, the decimal point is inserted at the decimal place equal to that in the dividend.

$$15.75 \div 3 = 5.25$$

When the divisor is a decimal number, both the divisor and dividend get multiplied by 10. This process is repeated until the divisor is a whole number, then one needs to complete the division operation as described above.

$$17.5 \div 2.5 = 175 \div 25 = 7$$

Exponents

An **exponent** is an operation used as shorthand for a number multiplied or divided by itself for a defined number of times.

$$3^7 = 3 \times 3 \times 3 \times 3 \times 3 \times 3 \times 3$$

In this example, the 3 is called the **base**, and the 7 is called the **exponent**. The exponent is typically expressed as a superscript number near the upper right side of the base but can also be identified as the number following a caret symbol (^). This operation is verbally expressed as "3 to the 7th power" or "3 raised to the power of 7." Common exponents are 2 and 3. A base raised to the power of 2 is referred to as having been "squared," while a base raised to the power of 3 is referred to as having been "cubed."

Several special rules apply to exponents. First, the **Zero Power Rule** finds that any number raised to the zero power equals 1. For example, 100^0, 2^0, $(-3)^0$ and 0^0 all equal 1 because the bases are raised to the zero power.

Second, exponents can be negative. With negative exponents, the equation is expressed as a fraction, as in the following example:

$$3^{-7} = \frac{1}{3^7} = \frac{1}{3 \times 3 \times 3 \times 3 \times 3 \times 3 \times 3}$$

Third, the **Power Rule** concerns exponents being raised by another exponent. When this occurs, the exponents are multiplied by each other:

$$(x^2)^3 = x^6 = (x^3)^2$$

Fourth, when multiplying two exponents with the same base, the **Product Rule** requires that the base remains the same, and the exponents are added. For example, $a^x \times a^y = a^{x+y}$. Since addition and multiplication are commutative, the two terms being multiplied can be in any order.

$$x^3 x^5 = x^{3+5} = x^8 = x^{5+3} = x^5 x^3$$

Fifth, when dividing two exponents with the same base, the **Quotient Rule** requires that the base remains the same, but the exponents are subtracted. So, $a^x \div a^y = a^{x-y}$. Since subtraction and division are not commutative, the two terms must remain in order.

$$x^5 x^{-3} = x^{5-3} = x^2 = x^5 \div x^3 = \frac{x^5}{x^3}$$

Additionally, 1 raised to any power is still equal to 1, and any number raised to the power of 1 is equal to itself. In other words, $a^1 = a$ and $14^1 = 14$.

Exponents play an important role in scientific notation to present extremely large or small numbers as follows: $a \times 10^b$. To write the number in scientific notation, the decimal is moved until there is only one digit on the left side of the decimal point, indicating that the number a has a value between 1 and 10. The number of times the decimal moves indicates the exponent to which 10 is raised, here represented by b. If the decimal moves to the left, then b is positive, but if the decimal moves to the right, then b is negative. The following examples demonstrate these concepts:

$$3,050 = 3.05 \times 10^3$$

$$-777 = -7.77 \times 10^2$$

$$0.000123 = 1.23 \times 10^{-4}$$

$$-0.0525 = -5.25 \times 10^{-2}$$

Roots

The **square root** symbol is expressed as $\sqrt{}$ and is commonly known as the radical. Taking the root of a number is the inverse operation of multiplying that number by itself some number of times. For example, squaring the number 7 is equal to 7×7, or 49. Finding the square root is the opposite of finding an exponent, as the operation seeks a number that when multiplied by itself, equals the number in the square root symbol.

For example, $\sqrt{36} = 6$ because 6 multiplied by 6 equals 36. Note, the square root of 36 is also -6 since $-6 \times -6 = 36$. This can be indicated using a **plus/minus** symbol like this: ±6. However, square roots are often just expressed as a positive number for simplicity, with it being understood that the true value can be either positive or negative.

Perfect squares are numbers with whole number square roots. The list of perfect squares begins with 0, 1, 4, 9, 16, 25, 36, 49, 64, 81, and 100.

Determining the square root of imperfect squares requires a calculator to reach an exact figure. It's possible, however, to approximate the answer by finding the two perfect squares that the number fits between. For example, the square root of 40 is between 6 and 7 since the squares of those numbers are 36 and 49, respectively.

Square roots are the most common root operation. If the radical doesn't have a number to the upper left of the symbol $\sqrt{}$, then it's a **square root**. Sometimes a radical includes a number in the upper left, like $\sqrt[3]{27}$, as in the other common root type—the **cube root**. Complicated roots, like the cube root, often require a calculator.

Parentheses

Parentheses separate different parts of an equation, and operations within them should be thought of as taking place before the outside operations take place. Practically, this means that the distinction between what is inside and outside of the parentheses decides the order of operations that the equation follows. Failing to solve operations inside the parentheses before addressing the part of the equation outside of the parentheses will lead to incorrect results.

For example, in $5 - (3 + 25)$, addition within the parentheses must be solved first. So $3 + 25 = 28$, leaving $5 - (28) = -23$. If this was solved using the incorrect order of operations, the solution might be found to be $5 - 3 + 25 = 2 + 25 = 27$, which would be incorrect.

Equations often feature multiple layers of parentheses. To differentiate them, **square brackets** [ ] and **braces** { } are used in addition to parentheses. The innermost parentheses must be solved before working outward to larger brackets. For example, in $\{2 \div [5 - (3 + 1)]\}$, solving the innermost parentheses $(3 + 1)$ leaves $\{2 \div [5 - (4)]\}$. $[5 - (4)]$ is now the next smallest, which leaves $\{2 \div [1]\}$ in the final step, and 2 as the answer.

Order of Operations

When solving equations with multiple operations, special rules apply. These rules are known as the **Order of Operations**. The order is as follows: Parentheses, Exponents, Multiplication and Division from left to right, and Addition and Subtraction from left to right. A popular mnemonic device to help remember the order is Please Excuse My Dear Aunt Sally (PEMDAS). Evaluating the following two problems can help with understanding the Order of Operations:

$$4 + (3 \times 2)^2 \div 4$$

First, the operation within the parentheses must be completed, yielding: $4 + 6^2 \div 4$.

Second, the exponent is evaluated: $4 + 36 \div 4$.

Third, the division is conducted: $4 + 9$.

Fourth, addition is completed, giving the answer: 13.

$$2 \times (6 + 3) \div (2 + 1)^2$$
$$2 \times 9 \div (3)^2$$
$$2 \times 9 \div 9$$
$$18 \div 9$$
$$2$$

Positive and Negative Numbers

Signs
Aside from 0, numbers can be either positive or negative. The sign for a positive number is the plus sign or the + symbol, while the sign for a negative number is the minus sign or the − symbol. If a number has no designation, then it's assumed to be positive.

Absolute Values
Both positive and negative numbers are valued according to their distance from 0. Both +3 and -3 can be considered using the following number line:

Both 3 and -3 are three spaces from 0. The distance from 0 is called its **absolute value**. Thus, both -3 and 3 have an absolute value of 3 since they're both three spaces away from 0.

An absolute number is written by placing | | around the number. So, |3| and |−3| both equal 3, as that's their common absolute value.

Implications for Addition and Subtraction

For addition, if all numbers are either positive or negative, they are simply added together. For example, $4 + 4 = 8$ and $-4 + -4 = -8$. However, things get tricky when some of the numbers are negative, and some are positive.

For example, with $6 + (-4)$, the first step is to take the absolute values of the numbers, which are 6 and 4. Second, the smaller value is subtracted from the larger. The equation becomes $6 - 4 = 2$. Third, the sign of the original larger number is placed on the sum. Here, 6 is the larger number, and it's positive, so the sum is 2.

Here's an example where the negative number has a larger absolute value: $(-6) + 4$. The first two steps are the same as the example above. However, on the third step, the negative sign must be placed on the sum, because the absolute value of (-6) is greater than 4. Thus, $-6 + 4 = -2$.

The absolute value of numbers implies that subtraction can be thought of as flipping the sign of the number following the subtraction sign and simply adding the two numbers. This means that subtracting a negative number will, in fact, be adding the positive absolute value of the negative number. Here are some examples:

$$-6 - 4 = -6 + -4 = -10$$

$$3 - -6 = 3 + 6 = 9$$

$$-3 - 2 = -3 + -2 = -5$$

Implications for Multiplication and Division

For multiplication and division, if both numbers are positive, then the product or quotient is always positive. If both numbers are negative, then the product or quotient is also positive. However, if the numbers have opposite signs, the product or quotient is always negative.

Simply put, the product in multiplication and quotient in division is always positive, unless the numbers have opposing signs, in which case it's negative. Here are some examples:

$$(-6) \times (-5) = 30$$

$$(-50) \div 10 = -5$$

$$8 \times |-7| = 56$$

$$(-48) \div (-6) = 8$$

If there are more than two numbers in a multiplication or division problem, then whether the product or quotient is positive or negative depends on the number of negative numbers in the problem. If there is an odd number of negatives, then the product or quotient is negative. If there is an even number of negative numbers, then the result is positive.

Here are some examples:

$$(-6) \times 5 \times (-2) \times (-4) = -240$$

$$(-6) \times 5 \times 2 \times (-4) = 240$$

Factorization

Factors are the numbers multiplied to achieve a product. Thus, every product in a multiplication equation has, at minimum, two factors. Of course, some products will have more than two factors. For the sake of most discussions, one can assume that factors are positive integers.

To find a number's factors, one should start with 1 and the number itself. The next step is to divide the number by 2, 3, 4, and so on, to see if any divisors can divide the number without a remainder. A list should be kept of those that do. This process can be stopped upon reaching either the number itself or another factor.

For example, to find the factors of 45, the first step is to start with 1 and 45. The next step is to try to divide 45 by 2, which fails. After this, 45 gets divided by 3. The answer is 15, so 3 and 15 are now factors. Dividing by 4 doesn't work and dividing by 5 leaves 9. Lastly, dividing 45 by 6, 7, and 8 all don't work. The next integer to try is 9, but this is already known to be a factor, so the factorization is complete. The factors of 45 are 1, 3, 5, 9, 15 and 45.

Prime Factorization

Prime factorization involves an additional step after breaking a number down to its factors: breaking down the factors until they are all prime numbers. A **prime number** is any number that can only be divided by 1 and itself. The prime numbers between 1 and 20 are 2, 3, 5, 7, 11, 13, 17, and 19. As a simple test, numbers that are even or end in 5 are not prime.

When attempting to break 129 down into its prime factors, the factors are found first: 3 and 43. Both 3 and 43 are prime numbers, so that means the prime factorization is complete. If 43 was not a prime number, then it would also need to be factorized until all of the factors were expressed as prime numbers.

Common Factor

A **common factor** is a factor shared by two numbers. The following examples demonstrate how to find the common factors of 45 and 30:

- The factors of 45 are: 1, 3, 5, 9, 15, and 45.
- The factors of 30 are: 1, 2, 3, 5, 6, 10, 15, and 30.
- The common factors are 1, 3, 5, and 15.

Greatest Common Factor

The **greatest common factor** is the largest number among the shared, common factors. From the factors of 45 and 30, the common factors are 3, 5, and 15. Thus, 15 is the greatest common factor, as it's the largest number.

Least Common Multiple

The **least common multiple** is the smallest number that's a multiple of two numbers. For example, to find the least common multiple of 4 and 9, the multiples of 4 and 9 are found first. The multiples of 4 are 4, 8, 12, 16, 20, 24, 28, 32, 36, and so on. For 9, the multiples are 9, 18, 27, 36, 45, 54, etc. Thus, the least common multiple of 4 and 9 is 36, the lowest number where 4 and 9 share multiples.

If two numbers share no factors besides 1 in common, then their least common multiple will be simply their product. If two numbers have common factors, then their least common multiple will be their product divided by their greatest common factor. This can be visualized by the formula $LCM = \frac{x \times y}{GCF}$, where x and y are some integers, and LCM and GCF are their least common multiple and greatest common factor, respectively.

Fractions

A **fraction** is an equation that represents a part of a whole but can also be used to present ratios or division problems. An example of a fraction is $\frac{x}{y}$. In this example, x is called the **numerator**, while y is the **denominator**. The numerator represents the number of parts, and the denominator is the total number of parts. They are separated by a line or slash, known as a fraction bar. In simple fractions, the numerator and denominator can be nearly any integer. However, the denominator of a fraction can never be zero because dividing by zero is a function which is undefined.

To visualize the basic idea of fractions, one can imagine that an apple pie has been baked for a holiday party, and the full pie has eight slices. After the party, there are five slices left. How could the amount of the pie that remains be expressed as a fraction? The numerator is 5 since there are five parts left, and the denominator is 8, since there were eight total slices in the whole pie. Thus, expressed as a fraction, the leftover pie totals $\frac{5}{8}$ of the original amount.

Fractions come in three different varieties: proper fractions, improper fractions, and mixed numbers. **Proper fractions** have a numerator less than the denominator, such as $\frac{3}{8}$, but **improper fractions** have a numerator greater than the denominator, such as $\frac{15}{8}$. **Mixed numbers** combine a whole number with a proper fraction, such as $3\frac{1}{2}$. Any mixed number can be written as an improper fraction by multiplying the integer by the denominator, adding the product to the value of the numerator, and dividing the sum by the original denominator. For example, $3\frac{1}{2} = \frac{3 \times 2 + 1}{2} = \frac{7}{2}$. Whole numbers can also be converted into fractions by placing the whole number as the numerator and making the denominator 1. For example, $3 = \frac{3}{1}$.

One of the most fundamental concepts of fractions is their ability to be manipulated by multiplication or division. This is possible since $\frac{n}{n} = 1$ for any non-zero integer. As a result, multiplying or dividing by $\frac{n}{n}$ will not alter the original fraction since any number multiplied or divided by 1 doesn't change the value of that number. Fractions of the same value are known as equivalent fractions. For example, $\frac{2}{4}, \frac{4}{8}, \frac{50}{100}$, and $\frac{75}{150}$ are equivalent, as they all equal $\frac{1}{2}$.

Although many equivalent fractions exist, they are easier to compare and interpret when reduced or simplified. The numerator and denominator of a simple fraction will have no factors in common other than 1. When reducing or simplifying fractions, the numerator and denominator are divided by the greatest common factor. A simple strategy is to divide the numerator and denominator by low numbers, like 2, 3, or 5 until arriving at a simple fraction, but the same thing could be achieved by determining the greatest common factor for both the numerator and denominator and dividing each by it. Using the first method is preferable when both the numerator and denominator are even, end in 5, or are obviously a multiple of another number. However, if no numbers seem to work, it will be necessary to factor the numerator and denominator to find the GCF.

The following problems provide examples:

Simplify the fraction $\frac{6}{8}$:

Dividing the numerator and denominator by 2 results in $\frac{3}{4}$, which is a simple fraction.

Simplify the fraction $\frac{12}{36}$:

Dividing the numerator and denominator by 2 leaves $\frac{6}{18}$. This isn't a simplified fraction, as both the numerator and denominator have factors in common. Dividing each by 3 results in $\frac{2}{6}$, but this can be further simplified by dividing by 2, to get $\frac{1}{3}$. This is the simplest fraction, as the numerator is 1. In cases like this, multiple division operations can be avoided by determining the greatest common factor between the numerator and denominator.

Simplify the fraction $\frac{18}{54}$ by dividing by the greatest common factor:

The first step is to determine the factors of the numerator and denominator. The factors of 18 are 1, 2, 3, 6, 9, and 18. The factors of 54 are 1, 2, 3, 6, 9, 18, 27, and 54. Thus, the greatest common factor is 18. Dividing $\frac{18}{54}$ by 18 leaves $\frac{1}{3}$, which is the simplest fraction. This method takes slightly more work, but it definitively arrives at the simplest fraction.

A **ratio** is a comparison between the relative sizes of two parts of a whole, separated by a colon. It's different from a fraction because, in a ratio, the second number represents the number of parts that aren't currently being referenced, while in a fraction, the second or bottom number represents the total number of parts in the whole. For example, if 3 pieces of an 8-piece pie were eaten, the number of uneaten parts expressed as a ratio to the number of eaten parts would be 5:3.

Equivalent ratios work just like equivalent fractions. For example, both 3:9 and 20:60 are equivalent ratios to 1:3 because both can be simplified to 1:3.

Operations with Fractions

Of the four basic operations that can be performed on fractions, the one that involves the least amount of work is multiplication. To multiply two fractions, the numerators are multiplied, the denominators are multiplied, and the products are placed together as a fraction. Whole numbers and mixed numbers can also be expressed as a fraction, as described above, which more easily facilitates multiplication with another fraction. The following problems provide examples:

1. $\frac{2}{5} \times \frac{3}{4} = \frac{6}{20} = \frac{3}{10}$

2. $\frac{4}{9} \times \frac{7}{11} = \frac{28}{99}$

Dividing fractions is similar to multiplication with one key difference. To divide fractions, the numerator and denominator of the second fraction are flipped, and then one proceeds as if it were a multiplication problem:

$$1. \frac{7}{8} \div \frac{4}{5} = \frac{7}{8} \times \frac{5}{4} = \frac{35}{32}$$

$$2. \frac{5}{9} \div \frac{1}{3} = \frac{5}{9} \times \frac{3}{1} = \frac{15}{9} = \frac{5}{3}$$

Addition and subtraction require more steps than multiplication and division, as these operations require the fractions to have the same denominator, also called a **common denominator**. It is always possible to find a common denominator by multiplying the denominators. However, when the denominators are large numbers, this method is unwieldy, especially if the answer must be provided in its simplest form. Thus, it's beneficial to find the least common denominator of the fractions—the least common denominator is incidentally also the least common multiple.

Once equivalent fractions have been found with common denominators, the numerators are simply added or subtracted to arrive at the answer:

$$1. \frac{1}{2} + \frac{3}{4} = \frac{2}{4} + \frac{3}{4} = \frac{5}{4}$$

$$2. \frac{3}{12} + \frac{11}{20} = \frac{15}{60} + \frac{33}{60} = \frac{48}{60} = \frac{4}{5}$$

$$3. \frac{7}{9} - \frac{4}{15} = \frac{35}{45} - \frac{12}{45} = \frac{23}{45}$$

$$4. \frac{5}{6} - \frac{7}{18} = \frac{15}{18} - \frac{7}{18} = \frac{8}{18} = \frac{4}{9}$$

Order of Rational Numbers

A common question type on the GRE asks test takers to order rational numbers from least to greatest or greatest to least. The numbers will come in a variety of formats, including decimals, percentages, roots, fractions, and whole numbers. These questions test for knowledge of different types of numbers and the ability to determine their respective values.

Whether the question asks to order the numbers from greatest to least or least to greatest, the crux of the question is the same—convert the numbers into a common format. Generally, it's easiest to write the numbers as whole numbers and decimals so they can be placed on a number line. The following examples illustrate this strategy:

1. Order the following rational numbers from greatest to least:

$$\sqrt{36}, 0.65, 78\%, \frac{3}{4}, 7, 90\%, \frac{5}{2}$$

Of the seven numbers, the whole number (7) and decimal (0.65) are already in an accessible form, so test takers should concentrate on the other five.

First, the square root of 36 equals 6. (If the test asks for the root of a non-perfect root, determine which two whole numbers the root lies between.) Next, the percentages should be converted to decimals. A percentage means "per hundred," so this conversion requires moving the decimal point two places to the left, leaving 0.78 and 0.9. Lastly, the fractions are evaluated: $\frac{3}{4} = \frac{75}{100} = 0.75; \frac{5}{2} = 2\frac{1}{2} = 2.5$

Now, the only step left is to list the numbers in the requested order:

$$7, \sqrt{36}, \frac{5}{2}, 90\%, 78\%, \frac{3}{4}, 0.65$$

2. Order the following rational numbers from least to greatest:

$$2.5, \sqrt{9}, -10.5, 0.853, 175\%, \sqrt{4}, \frac{4}{5}$$

$\sqrt{9} = 3$

$175\% = 1.75$

$\sqrt{4} = 2$

$\frac{4}{5} = 0.8$

From least to greatest, the answer is: $-10.5, \frac{4}{5}, 0.853, 175\%, \sqrt{4}, 2.5, \sqrt{9}$,

Algebra

Solving for X in Proportions

Proportions are commonly used in word problems to find unknown values, such as x, that are some percent or fraction of a known number. Proportions are solved by cross-multiplying and then dividing to arrive at x. The following examples show how this is done:

1. $\frac{75\%}{90\%} = \frac{25\%}{x}$

To solve for x, the fractions must be cross-multiplied: ($75\%x = 90\% \times 25\%$). To make things easier, the percentages can be converted to decimals: ($0.9 \times 0.25 = 0.225 = 0.75x$). To get rid of the coefficient of x, each side must be divided by that same coefficient to get the answer $x = 0.3$. The question could ask for the answer as a percentage or fraction in lowest terms, which are 30% and $\frac{3}{10}$, respectively.

2. $\frac{x}{12} = \frac{30}{96}$

Cross-multiply: $96x = 30 \times 12$

Multiply: $96x = 360$

Divide: $x = 360 \div 96$

Answer: $x = 3.75$

3. $\frac{0.5}{3} = \frac{x}{6}$

Cross-multiply: $3x = 0.5 \times 6$

Multiply: $3x = 3$

Divide: $x = 3 \div 3$

Answer: $x = 1$

Observant test takers may have noticed there's a faster way to arrive at the answer. If there is an obvious operation being performed on the proportion, the same operation can be used on the other side of the proportion to solve for x. For example, in the first practice problem, 75% became 25% when divided by 3, and upon doing the same to 90%, the correct answer of 30% would have been found with much less legwork. However, these questions aren't always so intuitive, so it's a good idea for test takers to work through the steps, even if the answer seems apparent from the onset.

Translating Words into Math

In word problems, test takers should look for key words indicating addition, subtraction, multiplication, or division:

- *Addition*: add, altogether, together, plus, increased by, more than, in all, sum, and total
- *Subtraction*: minus, less than, difference, decreased by, fewer than, remain, and take away
- *Multiplication*: times, twice, of, double, and triple
- *Division*: divided by, cut up, half, quotient of, split, and shared equally

If a question asks to give words to a mathematical expression and says "equals," then an = sign must be included in the answer. Similarly, "less than or equal to" is expressed by the inequality symbol ≤, and "greater than or equal" to is expressed as ≥. Furthermore, "less than" is represented by <, and "greater than" is expressed by >.

Word Problems

Word problems can appear daunting, but prepared test takers shouldn't let the verbiage psyche them out. No matter the scenario or specifics, the key to answering them is to translate the words into a math problem. It is critical to keep in mind what the question is asking and what operations could lead to that answer. The following word problem resembles one of the question types most frequently encountered on the exam.

Working with Money

Walter's Coffee Shop sells a variety of drinks and breakfast treats.

Price List	
Hot Coffee	$2.00
Slow Drip Iced Coffee	$3.00
Latte	$4.00
Muffins	$2.00
Crepe	$4.00
Egg Sandwich	$5.00

Costs	
Hot Coffee	$0.25
Slow Drip Iced Coffee	$0.75
Latte	$1.00
Muffins	$1.00
Crepe	$2.00
Egg Sandwich	$3.00

Walter's utilities, rent, and labor costs him $500 per day. Today, Walter sold 200 hot coffees, 100 slow drip iced coffees, 50 lattes, 75 muffins, 45 crepes, and 60 egg sandwiches. What was Walter's total profit today? To accurately answer this type of question, the first step is to determine the total cost of making his drinks and treats, then determine how much revenue he earned from selling those products. After arriving at these two totals, the profit is measured by deducting the total cost from the total revenue. Walter's costs for today:

200 hot coffees	× $0.25	= $50
100 slow drip iced coffees	× $0.75	= $75
50 lattes	× $1.00	= $50
75 muffins	× $1.00	= $75
45 crepes	× $2.00	= $90
60 egg sandwiches	× $3.00	= $180
Utilities, Rent, and Labor		= $500
Total costs		= $1,020

Walter's revenue for today:

200 hot coffees	× $2.00	= $400
100 slow drip iced coffees	× $3.00	= $300
50 lattes	× $4.00	= $200
75 muffins	× $2.00	= $150
45 crepes	× $4.00	= $180
60 egg sandwiches	× $5.00	= $300
Total revenue		= $1,530

Walter's $Profit = Revenue - Costs = \$1,530 - \$1,020 = \$510$

This strategy can be applied to other question types. For example, calculating salary after deductions, balancing a checkbook, and calculating a dinner bill are common word problems similar to business planning. In all cases, the most important step is remembering to use the correct operations. When a balance is increased, addition is used. When a balance is decreased, the problem requires subtraction. Common sense and organization are one's greatest assets when answering word problems.

Unit Rate

Unit rate word problems ask test takers to calculate the rate or quantity of something in a different value. For example, a problem might say that a car drove a certain number of miles in a certain number of minutes and then ask how many miles per hour the car was traveling. These questions involve solving proportions. Consider the following examples:

1. Alexandra made $96 during the first 3 hours of her shift as a temporary worker at a law office. She will continue to earn money at this rate until she finishes in 5 more hours. How much does Alexandra make per hour? How much money will Alexandra have made at the end of the day?

This problem can be solved in two ways. The first is to set up a proportion, as the rate of pay is constant. The second is to determine her hourly rate, multiply the 5 hours by that rate, and then add the $96.

To set up a proportion, the money already earned (numerator) is placed over the hours already worked (denominator) on one side of an equation. The other side has x over 8 hours (the total hours worked in the day). It looks like this: $\frac{96}{3} = \frac{x}{8}$. Now, cross-multiply yields $768 = 3x$. To get x, the 768 is divided by 3, which leaves $x = 256$. Alternatively, as x is the numerator of one of the proportions, multiplying by its denominator will reduce the solution by one step. Thus, Alexandra will make $256 at the end of the day. To calculate her hourly rate, the total is divided by 8, giving $32 per hour.

Alternatively, it is possible to figure out the hourly rate by dividing $96 by 3 hours to get $32 per hour. Now her total pay can be figured by multiplying $32 per hour by 8 hours, which comes out to $256.

2. Jonathan is reading a novel. So far, he has read 215 of the 335 total pages. It takes Jonathan 25 minutes to read 10 pages, and the rate is constant. How long does it take Jonathan to read one page? How much longer will it take him to finish the novel? Express the answer in time.

To calculate how long it takes Jonathan to read one page, 25 minutes is divided by 10 pages to determine the page per minute rate. Thus, it takes 2.5 minutes to read one page.

Jonathan must read 120 more pages to complete the novel. (This is calculated by subtracting the pages already read from the total.) Now, his rate per page is multiplied by the number of pages. Thus, $120 \times 2.5 = 300$. Expressed in time, 300 minutes is equal to 5 hours.

3. At a hotel, $\frac{4}{5}$ of the 120 rooms are booked for Saturday. On Sunday, $\frac{3}{4}$ of the rooms are booked. On which day are more of the rooms booked, and by how many more?

The first step is to calculate the number of rooms booked for each day. This is done by multiplying the fraction of the rooms booked by the total number of rooms.

$$\text{Saturday:} \frac{4}{5} \times 120 = \frac{4}{5} \times \frac{120}{1} = \frac{480}{5} = 96 \text{ rooms}$$

$$\text{Sunday:} \frac{3}{4} \times 120 = \frac{3}{4} \times \frac{120}{1} = \frac{360}{4} = 90 \text{ rooms}$$

Thus, more rooms were booked on Saturday by 6 rooms.

4. In a veterinary hospital, the veterinarian-to-pet ratio is 1:9. The ratio is always constant. If there are 45 pets in the hospital, how many veterinarians are currently in the veterinary hospital?

A proportion is set up to solve for the number of veterinarians: $\frac{1}{9} = \frac{x}{45}$

Cross-multiplying results in $9x = 45$, which works out to 5 veterinarians.

Alternatively, as there are always 9 times as many pets as veterinarians, it is possible to divide the number of pets (45) by 9. This also arrives at the correct answer of 5 veterinarians.

5. At a general practice law firm, 30% of the lawyers work solely on tort cases. If 9 lawyers work solely on tort cases, how many lawyers work at the firm?

The first step is to solve for the total number of lawyers working at the firm, which will be represented here with x. The problem states that 9 lawyers work solely on torts cases, and they make up 30% of the total lawyers at the firm. Thus, 30% multiplied by the total, x, will equal 9. Written as equation, this is: $30\% \times x = 9$.

It's easier to deal with the equation after converting the percentage to a decimal, leaving $0.3x = 9$. Thus, $x = \frac{9}{0.3} = 30$ lawyers working at the firm.

6. Xavier was hospitalized with pneumonia. He was originally given 35mg of antibiotics. Later, after his condition continued to worsen, Xavier's dosage was increased to 60mg. What was the percent increase of the antibiotics? Round the percentage to the nearest tenth.

An increase or decrease in percentage can be calculated by dividing the difference in amounts by the original amount and multiplying by 100. Written as an equation, the formula is:

$$\frac{new\ quantity - old\ quantity}{old\ quantity} \times 100$$

Here, the question states that the dosage was increased from 35mg to 60mg, so these values are plugged into the formula to find the percentage increase.

$$\frac{60 - 35}{35} \times 100 = \frac{25}{35} \times 100 = .7142 \times 100 = 71.4\%$$

FOIL Method

FOIL is a technique for generating polynomials through the multiplication of binomials. A **polynomial** is an expression of multiple variables (for example, x, y, z) in at least three terms involving only the four basic operations and exponents. FOIL is an acronym for First, Outer, Inner, and Last. "First" represents the multiplication of the terms appearing first in the binomials. "Outer" means multiplying the outermost terms. "Inner" means multiplying the terms inside. "Last" means multiplying the last terms of each binomial.

After completing FOIL and solving the operations, **like terms** are combined. To identify like terms, test takers should look for terms with the same variable and the same exponent. For example, in $4x^2 - x^2 + 15x + 2x^2 - 8$, the $4x^2, -x^2$, and $2x^2$ are all like terms because they have the variable (x) and exponent (2). Thus, after combining the like terms, the polynomial has been simplified to $5x^2 + 15x - 8$.

The purpose of FOIL is to simplify an equation involving multiple variables and operations. Although it sounds complicated, working through some examples will provide some clarity:

1. Simplify $(x + 10)(x + 4) =$

$$\underset{\text{First}}{(x \times x)} \quad + \quad \underset{\text{Outer}}{(x \times 4)} \quad + \quad \underset{\text{Inner}}{(10 \times x)} \quad + \quad \underset{\text{Last}}{(10 \times 4)}$$

After multiplying these binomials, it's time to solve the operations and combine like terms. Thus, the expression becomes: $x^2 + 4x + 10x + 40 = x^2 + 14x + 40$.

2. Simplify $2x (4x^3 - 7y^2 + 3x^2 + 4)$

Here, a monomial $(2x)$ is multiplied into a polynomial $(4x^3 - 7y^2 + 3x^2 + 4)$. Using the distributive property, the monomial gets multiplied by each term in the polynomial. This becomes:

$$2x(4x^3) - 2x(7y^2) + 2x(3x^2) + 2x(4)$$

Now, each monomial is simplified, starting with the coefficients:

$$(2 \times 4)(x \times x^3) - (2 \times 7)(x \times y^2) + (2 \times 3)(x \times x^2) + (2 \times 4)(x)$$

When multiplying powers with the same base, their exponents are added. Remember, a variable with no listed exponent has an exponent of 1, and exponents of distinct variables cannot be combined. This produces the answer:

$$8x^{1+3} - 14xy^2 + 6x^{1+2} + 8x = 8x^4 - 14xy^2 + 6x^3 + 8x$$

3. Simplify $(8x^{10}y^2z^4) \div (4x^2y^4z^7)$

The first step is to divide the coefficients of the first two polynomials: $8 \div 4 = 2$. The second step is to divide exponents with the same variable, which requires subtracting the exponents. This results in:

$$2(x^{10-2}y^{2-4}z^{4-7}) = 2x^8y^{-2}z^{-3}$$

However, the most simplified answer should include only positive exponents. Thus, $y^{-2}z^{-3}$ needs to be converted into fractions, respectively $\frac{1}{y^2}$ and $\frac{1}{z^3}$. Since the $2x^8$ has a positive exponent, it is placed in the numerator, and $\frac{1}{y^2}$ and $\frac{1}{z^3}$ are combined into the denominator, leaving $\frac{2x^8}{y^2z^3}$ as the final answer.

Rational Expressions

A **rational expression** is a fraction where the numerator and denominator are both polynomials. Some examples of rational expressions include the following: $\frac{4x^3y^5}{3z^4}$, $\frac{4x^3+3x}{x^2}$, and $\frac{x^2+7x+10}{x+2}$. Since these refer to expressions and not equations, they can be simplified but not solved. Using the rules in the previous

Exponents and *Roots* sections, some rational expressions with monomials can be simplified. Other rational expressions such as the last example, $\frac{x^2+7x+10}{x+2}$, require more steps to be simplified. First, the polynomial on top can be factored from $x^2 + 7x + 10$ into $(x + 5)(x + 2)$. Then the common factors can be canceled, and the expression can be simplified to $(x + 5)$.

The following problem is an example of using rational expressions:

Reggie wants to lay sod in his rectangular backyard. The length of the yard is given by the expression $4x + 2$, and the width is unknown. The area of the yard is $20x + 10$. Reggie needs to find the width of the yard. Knowing that the area of a rectangle is length multiplied by width, an expression can be written to find the width: $\frac{20x+10}{4x+2}$, area divided by length. Simplifying this expression by factoring out 10 on the top and 2 on the bottom leads to this expression: $\frac{10(2x+1)}{2(2x+1)}$. Cancelling out the $2x + 1$ results in $\frac{10}{2} = 5$. The width of the yard is found to be 5 by simplifying the rational expression.

Rational Equations

A **rational equation** can be as simple as an equation with a ratio of polynomials, $\frac{p(x)}{q(x)}$, set equal to a value, where $p(x)$ and $q(x)$ are both polynomials. A rational equation has an equal sign, which is different from expressions. This leads to solutions, or numbers that make the equation true.

It is possible to solve rational equations by trying to get all of the x terms out of the denominator and then isolating them on one side of the equation. For example, to solve the equation $\frac{3x+2}{2x+3} = 4$, both sides get multiplied by $(2x + 3)$. This will cancel on the left side to yield $3x + 2 = 4(2x + 3)$, then:

$$3x + 2 = 8x + 12$$

Now, subtract $8x$ from both sides, which yields:

$$-5x + 2 = 12$$

Subtracting 2 from both sides results in $-5x = 10$. Finally, both sides get divided by -5 to obtain $x = -2$.

Sometimes, when solving rational equations, it can be easier to try to simplify the rational expression by factoring the numerator and denominator first, then cancelling out common factors. For example, to solve $\frac{2x^2-8x+6}{x^2-3x+2} = 1$, the first step is to factor:

$$2x^2 - 8x + 6 = 2(x^2 - 4x + 3)$$

$$2(x - 1)(x - 3)$$

Then, factor $x^2 - 3x + 2$ into $(x - 1)(x - 2)$. This turns the original equation into:

$$\frac{2(x - 1)(x - 3)}{(x - 1)(x - 2)} = 1$$

The common factor of $(x - 1)$ can be canceled, leaving:

$$\frac{2(x - 3)}{x - 2} = 1$$

Now the same method used in the previous example can be followed. Multiplying both sides by $x - 1$ and performing the multiplication on the left yields $2x - 6 = x - 2$, which can be simplified to $x = 4$.

Rational Functions

A **rational function** is similar to an equation, but it includes two variables. In general, a rational function is in the form: $f(x) = \frac{p(x)}{q(x)}$, where $p(x)$ and $q(x)$ are polynomials. Refer to the *Functions* section (which follows) for a more detailed definition of functions. Rational functions are defined everywhere except where the denominator is equal to zero. When the denominator is equal to zero, this indicates either a hole in the graph or an asymptote. An example of a function with an asymptote is shown below.

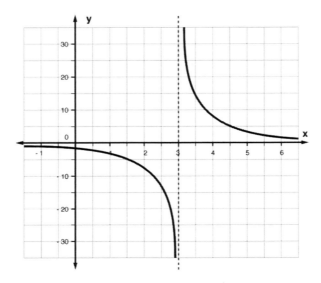

Algebraic Functions

A function is called **algebraic** if it is built up from polynomials by adding, subtracting, multiplying, dividing, and taking radicals. This means that, for example, the variable can never appear in an exponent. Thus, polynomials and rational functions are algebraic, but exponential functions are not algebraic. It turns out that logarithms and trigonometric functions are not algebraic either.

A function of the form $f(x) = a_n x^n + a_{n-1} x^{n-1} + a_{n-2} x^{n-2} + \cdots + a_1 x + a_0$ is called a **polynomial function**. The value of n is called the **degree** of the polynomial. In the case where $n = 1$, it is called a **linear function**. In the case where $n = 2$, it is called a **quadratic function**. In the case where $n = 3$, it is called a **cubic function**.

When n is even, the polynomial is called **even**, and not all real numbers will be in its range. When n is odd, the polynomial is called **odd**, and the range includes all real numbers.

The graph of a quadratic function $f(x) = ax^2 + bx + c$ will be a **parabola**. To see whether or not the parabola opens up or down, it's necessary to check the coefficient of x^2, which is the value a. If the coefficient is positive, then the parabola opens upward. If the coefficient is negative, then the parabola opens downward.

The quantity $D = b^2 - 4ac$ is called the **discriminant** of the parabola. If the discriminant is positive, then the parabola has two real zeros. If the discriminant is negative, then it has no real zeros. If the discriminant is zero, then the parabola's highest or lowest point is on the x-axis, and it has a single real zero.

The highest or lowest point of the parabola is called the **vertex**. The coordinates of the vertex are given by the point $(-\frac{b}{2a}, -\frac{D}{4a})$. The roots of a quadratic function can be found with the quadratic formula, which is:

$$x = \frac{-b \pm \sqrt{b^2 - 4ac}}{2a}$$

A **rational function** is a function $f(x) = \frac{p(x)}{q(x)}$, where p and q are both polynomials. The domain of f will be all real numbers except the (real) roots of q. At these roots, the graph of f will have a **vertical asymptote,** unless they are also roots of p. Here is an example to consider:

$$p(x) = p_n x^n + p_{n-1} x^{n-1} + p_{n-2} x^{n-2} + \cdots + p_1 x + p_0$$

$$q(x) = q_m x^m + q_{m-1} x^{m-1} + q_{m-2} x^{m-2} + \cdots + q_1 x + q_0$$

When the degree of p is less than the degree of q, there will be a **horizontal asymptote** of $y = 0$. If p and q have the same degree, there will be a horizontal asymptote of $y = \frac{p_n}{q_n}$. If the degree of p is exactly one greater than the degree of q, then f will have an oblique asymptote along the line:

$$y = \frac{p_n}{q_{n-1}} x + \frac{p_{n-1}}{q_{n-1}}$$

Geometry and Measurement

Shapes and Solids

Perimeter is the distance measurement around something. It can be thought of as the length of the boundary, like a fence. In contrast, **area** is the space occupied by a defined enclosure, like a field enclosed by a fence.

The perimeter of a square is measured by adding together all of the sides. Since a square has four equal sides, its perimeter can be calculated by multiplying the length of one side by 4. Thus, the formula is $P = 4 \times s$, where s equals one side. The area of a square is calculated by squaring the length of one side, which is expressed as the formula $A = s^2$.

Like a square, a rectangle's perimeter is measured by adding together all of the sides. But as the sides are unequal, the formula is different. A rectangle has equal values for its lengths (long sides) and equal values for its widths (short sides), so the perimeter formula for a rectangle is $P = l + l + w + w = 2l + 2w$, where l equals length and w equals width. The area is found by multiplying the length by the width, so the formula is $A = l \times w$.

A triangle's perimeter is measured by adding together the three sides, so the formula is $P = a + b + c$, where $a, b,$ and c are the values of the three sides. The area is calculated by multiplying the length of the base times the height times ½, so the formula is:

$$A = \frac{1}{2} \times b \times h = \frac{bh}{2}$$

The base is the bottom of the triangle, and the height is the distance from the base to the peak. If a problem asks one to calculate the area of a triangle, it will provide the base and height.

A circle's perimeter—also known as its **circumference**—is measured by multiplying the **diameter** (the straight line measured from one side, through the center, to the direct opposite side of the circle) by π, so the formula is $\pi \times d$. This is sometimes expressed by the formula $C = 2 \times \pi \times r$, where r is the **radius** of the circle. These formulas are equivalent, as the radius equals half of the diameter. The area of a circle is calculated with the formula:

$$A = \pi \times r^2$$

The test will indicate either to leave the answer with π attached or to calculate to the nearest decimal place, which means multiplying by 3.14 for π.

The perimeter of a parallelogram is measured by adding the lengths and widths together. Thus, the formula is the same as for a rectangle:

$$P = l + l + w + w = 2l + 2w$$

However, the area formula differs from the rectangle. For a parallelogram, the area is calculated by multiplying the length by the height: $A = h \times l$

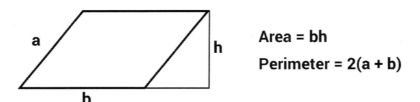

Area = bh

Perimeter = 2(a + b)

The perimeter of a trapezoid is calculated by adding the two unequal bases and two equal sides, so the formula is $P = a + b_1 + c + b_2$. Although unlikely to be a test question, the formula for the area of a trapezoid is $A = \frac{b_1 + b_2}{2} \times h$, where h equals height, and b_1 and b_2 equal the bases.

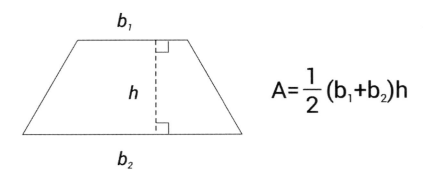

Congruence and Similarity

Triangles are similar if they have the same angle measurements, and their sides are proportional to one another. Triangles are **congruent** if the angles of the triangles are equal in measurement and the sides of the triangles are equal in measurement.

There are five ways to show that triangles are congruent:

1. SSS (Side-Side-Side Postulate) – when all three corresponding sides are equal in length, then the two triangles are congruent.

2. SAS (Side-Angle-Side Postulate) – if a pair of corresponding sides and the angle in between those two sides are equal, then the two triangles are congruent.

3. ASA (Angle-Side-Angle Postulate) – if a pair of corresponding angles are equal and the side lengths within those angles are equal, then the two triangles are equal.

4. AAS (Angle-Angle-Side Postulate) – when a pair of corresponding angles for two triangles and a non-included side are equal, then the two triangles are congruent.

5. HL (Hypotenuse-Leg Theorem) – if two right triangles have the same hypotenuse length, and one of the other sides in each triangle are of the same length, then the two triangles are congruent.

If two triangles are discovered to be similar or congruent, this information can assist in determining unknown parts of triangles, such as missing angles and sides.

The example below involves the question of congruent triangles. The first step is to examine whether the triangles are congruent. If the triangles are congruent, then the measure of a missing angle can be found.

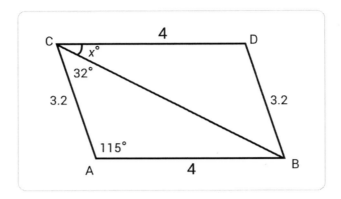

The above diagram provides values for angle measurements and side lengths in triangles *CAB* and *CDB*. Note that side *CA* is 3.2 and side *DB* is 3.2. Side *CD* is 4 and side *AB* is 4. Furthermore, line *CB* is congruent to itself by the reflexive property. Therefore, the two triangles are congruent by SSS (Side-Side-Side). Because the two triangles are congruent, all of the corresponding parts of the triangles are also congruent. Therefore, angle x is congruent to the inside of the angle for which a measurement is not provided in triangle *CAB*. Thus, $115º + 32º = 147º$. A triangle's angles sum to $180º$, therefore, $180º - 147º = 33º$. Angle $x = 33º$, because the two triangles are reversed.

Surface Area and Volume

Surface area and volume are two- and three-dimensional measurements. **Surface area** measures the total surface space of an object, like the six sides of a cube. Questions about surface area will ask how much of something is needed to cover a three-dimensional object, like wrapping a present. **Volume** is the measurement of how much space an object occupies, like how much space is in the cube. Volume questions will ask how much of something is needed to completely fill the object. The most common surface area and volume questions deal with spheres, cubes, and rectangular prisms.

The formula for a cube's surface area is $SA = 6 \times s^2$, where s is the length of a side. A cube has 6 equal sides, so the formula expresses the area of all the sides. Volume is simply measured by taking the cube of the length, so the formula is $V = s^3$.

The surface area formula for a rectangular prism or a general box is SA = $2(lw + lh + wh)$, where l is the length, h is the height, and w is the width. The volume formula is $V = l \times w \times h$, which is the cube's volume formula adjusted for the unequal lengths of a box's sides.

The formula for a sphere's surface area is $SA = 4\pi r^2$, where r is the sphere's radius. The surface area formula is the area for a circle multiplied by four. To measure volume, the formula is $V = \frac{4}{3}\pi r^3$.

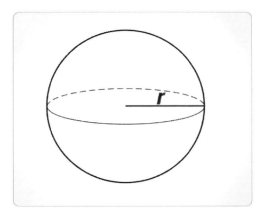

A **rectangular pyramid** is a figure with a rectangular base and four triangular sides that meet at a single vertex. If the rectangle has sides of lengths x and y, then the volume will be given by $V = \frac{1}{3}xyh$.

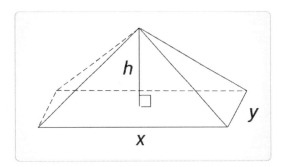

To find the surface area, the dimensions of each triangle must be known. However, these dimensions can differ depending on the problem in question. Therefore, there is no general formula for calculating total surface area.

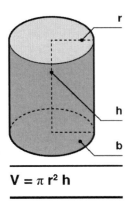

$$V = \pi r^2 h$$

The formula to find the volume of a cylinder is $\pi r^2 h$. This formula contains the formula for the area of a circle (πr^2) because the base of a cylinder is a circle. To calculate the volume of a cylinder, the slices of circles needed to build the entire height of the cylinder are added together. For example, if the radius is 5 feet and the height of the cylinder is 10 feet, the cylinder's volume is calculated by using the following equation: $\pi 5^2 \times 10$. Substituting 3.14 for π, the volume is 785 ft³.

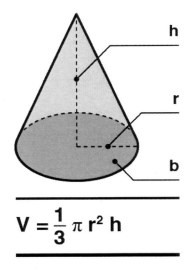

$$V = \frac{1}{3} \pi r^2 h$$

The formula used to calculate the volume of a cone is $\frac{1}{3}\pi r^2 h$. Essentially, the area of the base of the cone is multiplied by the cone's height. In a real-life example where the radius of a cone is 2 meters, and the height of a cone is 5 meters, the volume of the cone is calculated by utilizing the formula:

$$\frac{1}{3}\pi 2^2 \times 5 = 21 \text{ m}^3$$

Solving for Missing Values in Triangles

Suppose that Lara is 5 feet tall and is standing 30 feet from the base of a light pole, and her shadow is 6 feet long. How high is the light on the pole? To figure this out, it helps to make a sketch of the situation:

The light pole is the left side of the triangle. Lara is the 5-foot vertical line. Test takers should notice that there are two right triangles here, and that they have all the same angles as one another. Therefore, they form similar triangles. So, the ratio of proportionality between them must be found.

The bases of these triangles are known. The small triangle, formed by Lara and her shadow, has a base of 6 feet. The large triangle formed by the light pole along with the line from the base of the pole out to the end of Lara's shadow is $30 + 6 = 36$ feet long. So, the ratio of the big triangle to the little triangle is $\frac{36}{6} = 6$. The height of the little triangle is 5 feet. Therefore, the height of the big triangle will be $6 \times 5 = 30$ feet, meaning that the light is 30 feet up the pole.

The Pythagorean Theorem

The **Pythagorean theorem** states that for right triangles, the sum of the squares of the two shorter sides is equal to the square of the longest side (also called the **hypotenuse**). The longest side will always be the side opposite to the 90° angle. If this side is called c, and the other two sides are a and b, then the Pythagorean theorem states that $c^2 = a^2 + b^2$. Since lengths are always positive, this also can be written as $c = \sqrt{a^2 + b^2}$. A diagram to show the parts of a triangle using the Pythagorean theorem is below.

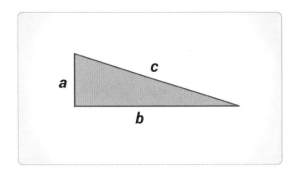

As an example of the theorem, suppose that Shirley has a rectangular field that is 5 feet wide and 12 feet long, and she wants to split it in half using a fence that goes from one corner to the opposite corner. How long will this fence need to be? To figure this out, note that this makes the field into two right triangles, whose hypotenuse will be the fence dividing it in half. Therefore, the fence length is given by:

$$\sqrt{5^2 + 12^2} = \sqrt{169} = 13 \text{ feet long}$$

Data Analysis

Ratios, Rates, and Proportions

Ratios are used to show the relationship between two quantities. The ratio of oranges to apples in the grocery store may be 3 to 2. That means that for every 3 oranges, there are 2 apples. This comparison can be expanded to represent the actual number of oranges and apples, such as 36 oranges to 24 apples. Another example may be the number of boys to girls in a math class. If the ratio of boys to girls is given as 2 to 5, that means there are 2 boys to every 5 girls in the class. Ratios can also be compared if the units in each ratio are the same. The ratio of boys to girls in the math class can be compared to the ratio of boys to girls in a science class by stating which ratio is higher and which is lower.

Rates are used to compare two quantities with different units. **Unit rates** are the simplest form of rate. With unit rates, the denominator in the comparison of two units is one. For example, if someone can type at a rate of 1000 words in 5 minutes, then their unit rate for typing is $\frac{1000}{5} = 200$ words in one minute or 200 words per minute. Any rate can be converted into a unit rate by dividing to make the denominator one. 1000 words in 5 minutes has been converted into the unit rate of 200 words per minute.

Ratios and rates can be used together to convert rates into different units. For example, if someone is driving 50 kilometers per hour, that rate can be converted into miles per hour by using a ratio known as the **conversion factor**. Since the given value contains kilometers and the final answer needs to be in miles, the ratio relating miles to kilometers needs to be used. There are 0.62 miles in 1 kilometer. This, written as a ratio and in fraction form, is

$$\frac{0.62 \text{ miles}}{1 \text{ km}}$$

To convert 50km/hour into miles per hour, the following conversion needs to be set up:

$$\frac{50 \text{ km}}{\text{hour}} \times \frac{0.62 \text{ miles}}{1 \text{ km}} = 31 \text{ miles per hour}$$

The ratio between two similar geometric figures is called the **scale factor**. For example, a problem may depict two similar triangles, A and B. The scale factor from the smaller triangle A to the larger triangle B is given as 2 because the length of the corresponding side of the larger triangle, 16, is twice the corresponding side on the smaller triangle, 8. This scale factor can also be used to find the value of a missing side, x, in triangle A. Since the scale factor from the smaller triangle (A) to larger one (B) is 2, the larger corresponding side in triangle B (given as 25) can be divided by 2 to find the missing side in A ($x = 12.5$). The scale factor can also be represented in the equation $2A = B$ because two times the lengths of A gives the corresponding lengths of B. This is the idea behind similar triangles.

Much like a scale factor can be written using an equation like $2A = B$, a **relationship** is represented by the equation $Y = kX$. X and Y are proportional because as values of X increase, the values of Y also increase. A relationship that is inversely proportional can be represented by the equation $Y = \frac{k}{X}$, where the value of Y decreases as the value of X increases and vice versa.

Proportional reasoning can be used to solve problems involving ratios, percentages, and averages. Ratios can be used in setting up proportions and solving them to find unknowns. For example, if a student completes an average of 10 pages of math homework in 3 nights, how long would it take the student to complete 22 pages? Both ratios can be written as fractions. The second ratio would contain the unknown.

The following proportion represents this problem, where x is the unknown number of nights:

$$\frac{10 \text{ pages}}{3 \text{ nights}} = \frac{22 \text{ pages}}{x \text{ nights}}$$

Solving this proportion entails cross-multiplying and results in the following equation: $10x = 22 \times 3$. Simplifying and solving for x results in the exact solution: $x = 6.6$ nights. The result would be rounded up to 7 because the homework would actually be completed on the 7th night.

The following problem uses ratios involving percentages:

If 20% of the class is girls and 30 students are in the class, how many girls are in the class?

To set up this problem, it is helpful to use the common proportion:

$$\frac{\%}{100} = \frac{is}{of}$$

Within the proportion, % is the percentage of girls, 100 is the total percentage of the class, *is* is the number of girls, and *of* is the total number of students in the class. Most percentage problems can be written using this language. To solve this problem, the proportion should be set up as $\frac{20}{100} = \frac{x}{30}$ and then solved for x. Cross-multiplying results in the equation $20 \times 30 = 100x$, which results in the solution $x = 6$. There are 6 girls in the class.

Problems involving volume, length, and other units can also be solved using ratios. A problem may ask for the volume of a cone that has a radius, $r = 7m$ and a height, $h = 16m$.

Referring to the formulas provided on the test, the volume of a cone is given as:

$$V = \pi r^2 \frac{h}{3}$$

r is the radius
h is the height

Plugging $r = 7$ and $h = 16$ into the formula, the following is obtained:

$$V = \pi(7^2)\frac{16}{3}$$

Therefore, the volume of the cone is found to be approximately 821m³. Sometimes, answers in different units are sought. If this problem wanted the answer in liters, 821m³ would need to be converted.

Using the equivalence statement 1m³ = 1000L, the following ratio would be used to solve for liters:

$$821 \text{ m}^3 \times \frac{1000 \text{ L}}{1 \text{ m}^3}$$

Cubic meters in the numerator and denominator cancel each other out, and the answer is converted to 821,000 liters, or 8.21×10^5 L.

Other conversions can also be made between different given and final units. If the temperature in a pool is 30°C, what is the temperature of the pool in degrees Fahrenheit? To convert these units, an equation is used relating Celsius to Fahrenheit. The following equation is used:

$$T_{°F} = 1.8T_{°C} + 32$$

Plugging in the given temperature and solving the equation for T yields the result:

$$T_{°F} = 1.8(30) + 32 = 86°F$$

Units in both Units in both the metric system and U.S. customary system are widely used.

Percentages

The word **percent** comes from the Latin phrase for "per one hundred." A percent is a way of writing out a fraction. It is a fraction with a denominator of 100. Thus, $65\% = \frac{65}{100}$.

To convert a fraction to a percent, the denominator is written as 100. For example, $\frac{3}{5} = \frac{60}{100} = 60\%$.

In converting a percent to a fraction, the percent is written with a denominator of 100, and the result is simplified. For example:

$$30\% = \frac{30}{100} = \frac{3}{10}$$

The basic percent equation is the following:

$$\frac{is}{of} = \frac{\%}{100}$$

The placement of numbers in the equation depends on what the question asks.

Example 1
Find 40% of 80.

Basically, the problem is asking, "What is 40% of 80?" The 40% is the percent, and 80 is the number to find the percent "of." The equation is:

$$\frac{x}{80} = \frac{40}{100}$$

After cross-multiplying, the problem becomes $100x = 80(40)$. Solving for x produces the answer: $x = 32$.

Example 2
What percent of 100 is 20?

20 fills in the "is" portion, while 100 fills in the "of." The question asks for the percent, so that will be x, the unknown. The following equation is set up:

$$\frac{20}{100} = \frac{x}{100}$$

Cross-multiplying yields the equation $100x = 20(100)$. Solving for x gives the answer: 20%.

Example 3
30% of what number is 30?

The following equation uses the clues and numbers in the problem:

$$\frac{30}{x} = \frac{30}{100}$$

Cross-multiplying results in the equation $30(100) = 30x$. Solving for x produces the answer: $x = 100$.

Methods for Presenting Data

Data in Tables

One of the most common ways to express data is in a table. The primary reason for plugging data into a table is to make interpretation more convenient. It's much easier to look at the table than to analyze results in a narrative paragraph. When analyzing a table, pay close attention to the title, variables, and data.

Let's analyze a theoretical antibiotic study. The study has 6 groups, named A through F, and each group receives a different dose of medicine. The results of the study are listed in the table below.

Results of Antibiotic Studies		
Group	**Dosage of Antibiotics in milligrams (mg)**	**Efficacy (% of participants cured)**
A	0 mg	20%
B	20 mg	40%
C	40 mg	75%
D	60 mg	95%
E	80 mg	100%
F	100 mg	100%

Tables generally list the title immediately above the data. The title should succinctly explain what is listed below. Here, "Results of Antibiotic Studies" informs the audience that the data pertains to the results of a scientific study on antibiotics.

Identifying the variables at play is one of the most important parts of interpreting data. Remember, the independent variable is intentionally altered, and its change is independent of the other variables. Here, the dosage of antibiotics administered to the different groups is the independent variable. The study is intentionally manipulating the strength of the medicine to study the related results. Efficacy is the dependent variable since its results *depend* on a different variable, the dose of antibiotics. Generally, the independent variable will be listed before the dependent variable in tables.

Also, pay close attention to the variables' labels. Here, the dose is expressed in milligrams (mg) and efficacy in percentages (%). Keep an eye out for questions referencing data in a different unit measurement or questions asking for a raw number when only the percentage is listed.

Now that the nature of the study and variables at play have been identified, the data itself needs be interpreted. Group A did not receive any of the medicine. As discussed earlier, Group A is the control, as it reflects the amount of people cured in the same timeframe without medicine. It's important to see that efficacy positively correlates with the dosage of medicine. A question using this study might ask for the lowest dose of antibiotics to achieve 100% efficacy. Although Group E and Group F both achieve 100% efficacy, it's important to note that Group E reaches 100% with a lower dose.

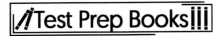

Bar Graph

A **bar graph** is a diagram in which the quantity of items within a specific classification is represented by the height of a rectangle. Each type of classification is represented by a rectangle of equal width. Here is an example of a bar graph:

Histograms

A set of data can be visually displayed in various forms allowing for quick identification of characteristics of the set. **Histograms**, such as the one shown below, display the number of data points (vertical axis) that fall into given intervals (horizontal axis) across the range of the set. The histogram below displays the heights of black cherry trees in a certain city park. Each rectangle represents the number of trees with heights between a given five-point span. For example, the furthest bar to the right indicates that two trees are between 85 and 90 feet. Histograms can describe the center, spread, shape, and any unusual characteristics of a data set.

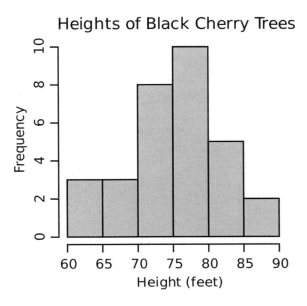

Scatterplots

A **scatter plot** is a mathematical diagram that visually displays the relationship or connection between two variables. The independent variable is placed on the x-axis, or horizontal axis, and the dependent variable is placed on the y-axis, or vertical axis. When visually examining the points on the graph, if the points model a linear relationship, or a **line of best-fit** can be drawn through the points with the points relatively close on either side, then a correlation exists. If the line of best-fit has a positive slope (rises from left to right), then the variables have a positive correlation. If the line of best-fit has a negative slope (falls from left to right), then the variables have a negative correlation. If a line of best-fit cannot be drawn, then no correlation exists. A positive or negative correlation can be categorized as strong or weak, depending on how closely the points are graphed around the line of best-fit.

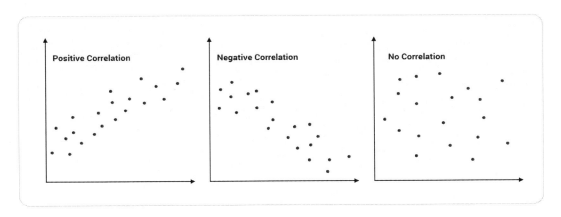

Line Graphs

Like a scatter plot, a **line graph** compares variables that change continuously, typically over time. Paired data values (ordered pair) are plotted on a coordinate grid with the x- and y-axis representing the variables. A line is drawn from each point to the next, going from left to right. The line graph below displays cell phone use for given years (two variables) for men, women, and both sexes (three data sets).

Pie Charts

A **circle graph**, also called a **pie chart**, shows categorical data with each category representing a percentage of the whole data set. To make a circle graph, the percent of the data set for each category must be determined. To do so, the frequency of the category is divided by the total number of data points and converted to a percent. For example, if 80 people were asked what their favorite sport is and 20 responded basketball, basketball makes up 25% of the data ($\frac{20}{80} = 0.25 = 25\%$). Each category in a data set is represented by a slice of the circle proportionate to its percentage of the whole.

Favorite Sport

Stem-and-Leaf Plots

A **stem-and-leaf plot** is a method of displaying sets of data by organizing numbers by their stems (usually the tens digit) and different leaf values (usually the ones digit).

For example, to organize a number of movie critic's ratings, as listed below, a stem-and-leaf plot could be utilized to display the information in a more condensed manner.

Movie critic scores: 47, 52, 56, 59, 61, 64, 66, 68, 68, 70, 73, 75, 79, 81, 83, 85, 86, 88, 88, 89, 90, 90, 91, 93, 94, 96, 96, 99.

	Movie Ratings
4	7
5	2 6 9
6	1 4 6 8 8
7	0 3 5 9
8	1 3 5 6 8 8 9
9	0 0 1 3 4 6 6 9
Key	6	1 represents 61

Looking at this stem and leaf plot, it is easy to ascertain key features of the data set. For example, what is the range of the data in the stem-and-leaf plot?

Using this method, it is easier to visualize the distribution of the scores and answer the question pertaining to the range of scores, which is $99 - 47 = 52$.

Tally Charts

A **tally chart** is a diagram in which tally marks are utilized to represent data. Tally marks are a means of showing a quantity of objects within a specific classification. Here is an example of a tally chart:

Number of days with rain	Number of weeks
0	$\|\|$
1	ЖНТ
2	ЖНТ
3	ЖНТ
4	ЖНТ ЖНТ ЖНТ $\|\|\|\|$
5	ЖНТ $\|$
6	ЖНТ $\|$
7	$\|\|\|\|$

Data is often recorded using fractions, such as half a mile, and understanding fractions is critical because of their popular use in real-world applications. Also, it is extremely important to label values with their units when using data. For example, regarding length, the number 2 is meaningless unless it is attached to a unit. Writing 2 cm shows that the number refers to the length of an object.

Frequency Distributions

A **frequency distribution** communicates the number of outcomes within a partial range of the data set. When displayed as a bar graph or histogram, a frequency distribution frequency distribution can visually indicate the spread and distribution of the data. A histogram resembling a bell curve approximates a normal distribution. A frequency distribution can also be displayed as a stem-and-leaf plot, which arranges data in numerical order and displays values similar to a tally chart with the stem being a range within the set and the leaf indicating the exact value (i.e., stems are whole numbers and leaves are tenths).

The plot provides more detail about individual data points and allows for easy identification of the median, as well as any repeated values in the set.

Investigating Key Features of a Graph

When a linear equation is written in standard form, $Ax + By = C$, it is easy to identify the x- and y-intercepts for the graph of the line. Just as the y-intercept is the point at which the line intercepts the y-axis, the x-intercept is the point at which the line intercepts the x-axis. At the y-intercept, $x = 0$, and at the x-intercept, $y = 0$. Given an equation in standard form, substitute $x = 0$ to find the y-intercept, and substitute $y = 0$ to find the x-intercept. For example, to graph $3x + 2y = 6$, substituting 0 for y results in $3x + 2(0) = 6$. Solving for x yields $x = 2$; therefore, an ordered pair for the line is $(2, 0)$. Substituting

0 for x results in $3(0) + 2y = 6$. Solving for y yields $y = 3$; therefore, an ordered pair for the line is $(0, 3)$. Plot the two ordered pairs (the x- and y-intercepts), and construct a straight line through them.

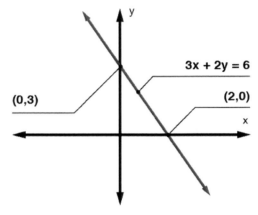

T - chart

x	y
0	3
2	0

Intercepts

x - intercept : (2,0)

y - intercept : (0,3)

(0,3)   3x + 2y = 6   (2,0)

The standard form of a quadratic function is $y = ax^2 + bx + c$. The graph of a quadratic function is a U-shaped (or upside-down U) curve, called a **parabola**, which is symmetric about a vertical line (axis of symmetry). To graph a parabola, determine its vertex (high or low point for the curve) and at least two points on each side of the axis of symmetry.

Given a quadratic function in standard form, the axis of symmetry for its graph is the line $x = -\frac{b}{2a}$. The vertex for the parabola has an x-coordinate of $-\frac{b}{2a}$. To find the y-coordinate for the vertex, substitute the calculated x-coordinate. To complete the graph, select two different x-values, and substitute them into the quadratic function to obtain the corresponding y-values. This will give two points on the parabola. Use these two points and the axis of symmetry to determine the two points corresponding to these. The corresponding points are the same distance from the axis of symmetry (on the other side) and contain the same y-coordinate.

Plotting the vertex and four other points on the parabola allows for construction of the curve.

Quadratic Function

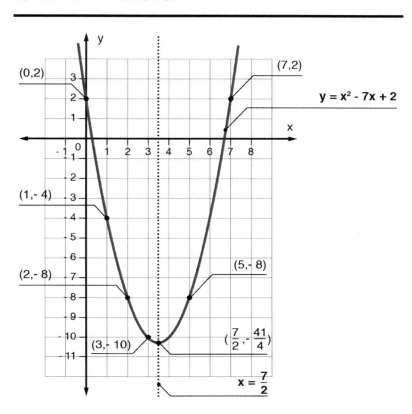

Exponential functions have a general form of $y = (a)(b^x)$. The graph of an exponential function is a curve that slopes upward or downward from left to right. The graph approaches a line, called an **asymptote**, as x or y increases or decreases. To graph the curve for an exponential function, select x-values, and substitute them into the function to obtain the corresponding y-values. A general rule of thumb is to select three negative values, zero, and three positive values.

Plotting the seven points on the graph for an exponential function should allow for the construction of a smooth curve through them.

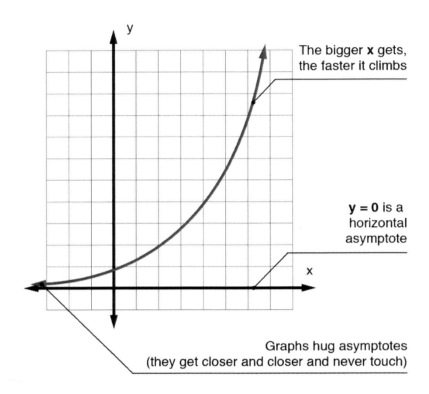

The bigger **x** gets, the faster it climbs

y = 0 is a horizontal asymptote

Graphs hug asymptotes (they get closer and closer and never touch)

Comparing Linear and Exponential Growth

Linear functions are simpler than exponential functions, and the independent variable x has an exponent of 1. Written in the most common form, $y = mx + b$, the coefficient of x indicates how fast the function grows at a constant rate, and the b-value denotes the starting point. An exponential function has independent variable in the exponent $y = ab^x$. The graph of these types of functions is described as **growth** or **decay**, based on whether the base, b, is greater than or less than 1. These functions are different from quadratic functions because the base stays constant. A common base is base e.

The following two functions model a linear and exponential function respectively: $y = 2x$ and $y = 2^x$. Their graphs are shown below. The first graph, modeling the linear function, shows that the growth is constant over each interval. With a horizontal change of 1, the vertical change is 2. It models constant positive growth. The second graph models the exponential function, where the horizontal change of 1 yields a vertical change that increases more and more with each iteration of horizontal change. The exponential graph gets very close to the x-axis, but never touches it, meaning there is an asymptote there. The y-value can never be zero because the base of 2 can never be raised to an input value that yields an output of zero.

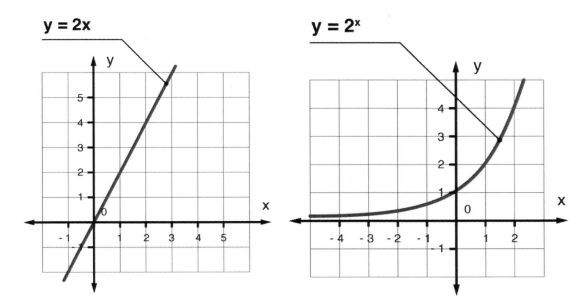

Given a table of values, the type of function can be determined by observing the change in y over equal intervals. For example, the tables below model two functions. The changes in interval for the x-values is 1 for both tables. For the first table, the y-values increase by 5 for each interval. Since the change is constant, the situation can be described as a linear function. The equation would be:

$$y = 5x + 3$$

For the second table, the change for y is 20, 100, and 500, respectively. The increases are multiples of 5, meaning the situation can be modeled by an exponential function. The equation below models this situation:

$$y = 5^x + 3$$

$y = 5x + 3$	
x	y
1	8
2	13
3	18
4	23

$y = 5^x + 3$	
x	y
1	8
2	28
3	128
4	628

Two-Way Tables

Data that isn't described using numbers is known as **categorical data.** For example, age is numerical data, but hair color is categorical data. Categorical data is summarized using two-way frequency tables.

A **two-way frequency table** counts the relationship between two sets of categorical data. There are rows and columns for each category, and each cell represents frequency information that shows the actual data count between each combination.

For example, the graphic on the left-side below is a two-way frequency table showing the number of girls and boys taking language classes in school. Entries in the middle of the table are known as the **joint frequencies**. For example, the number of girls taking French class is 12, which is a joint frequency. The totals are the **marginal frequencies**. For example, the total number of boys is 20, which is a marginal frequency. If the frequencies are changed into percentages based on totals, the table is known as a **two-way relative frequency table**. Percentages can be calculated using the table total, the row totals, or the column totals.

Here's the process of obtaining the two-way relative frequency table using the table total:

Two-Way Frequency Table

	Spanish	French	German	Total
Boys	10	2	8	20
Girls	15	12	3	30
Total	25	14	11	50

Joint frequencies
Marginal frequencies

Divide all tables entries by the table total (50) →

Two-Way Relative Frequency Table (with respect to table total)

	Spanish	French	German	Total
Boys	0.2	0.04	0.16	0.40
Girls	0.3	0.24	0.06	0.60
Total	0.5	0.28	0.22	1.00

The middle entries are known as **joint probabilities** and the totals are **marginal probabilities.** In this data set, it appears that more girls than boys take Spanish class. However, that might not be the case because more girls than boys were surveyed, and the results might be misleading. To avoid such errors, **conditional relative frequencies** are used. The relative frequencies are calculated based on a row or column.

Here are the conditional relative frequencies using column totals:

Two-Way Frequency Table

	Spanish	French	German	Total
Boys	10	2	8	20
Girls	15	12	3	30
Total	25	14	11	50

Divide each column entry by that column's total →

Two-Way Relative Frequency Table (with respect to table total)

	Spanish	French	German	Total
Boys	0.4	0.14	0.73	0.4
Girls	0.6	0.86	0.27	0.6
Total	1.00	1.00	1.00	1.00

Two-way frequency tables can help in making many conclusions about the data. If either the row or column of conditional relative frequencies differs between each row or column of the table, then an association exists between the two categories. For example, in the above tables, the majority of boys are taking German while the majority of girls are taking French. If the frequencies are equal across the rows, there is no association, and the variables are labelled as independent. It's important to note that the association does exist in the above scenario, though these results may not occur the next semester when students are surveyed.

When measuring event probabilities, two-way frequency tables can be used to report the raw data and then used to calculate probabilities. If the frequency tables are translated into relative frequency tables, the probabilities presented in the table can be plugged directly into the formulas for conditional probabilities. By plugging in the correct frequencies, the data from the table can be used to determine if events are independent or dependent.

Conditional probability is the probability that event A will happen given that event B has already occurred. An example of this is calculating the probability that a person will eat dessert once they have eaten dinner. This is different than calculating the probability of a person just eating dessert.

The formula for the conditional probability of event A occurring given B is:

$$P(A|B) = \frac{P(A \text{ and } B)}{P(B)}$$

It's defined as the probability of both A and B occurring divided by the probability of event B occurring. If A and B are independent, then the probability of both A and B occurring is equal to $P(A)P(B)$, so $P(A|B)$ reduces to just $P(A)$. This means that A and B have no relationship, and the probability of A occurring is the same as the conditional probability of A occurring given B. Similarly:

$$P(B|A) = \frac{P(B \text{ and } A)}{P(A)} = P(B)$$

(if A and B are independent)

Two events aren't always independent. For example, having glasses and having brown hair aren't independent characteristics. There definitely can be overlap because people with brown hair can wear glasses. Also, two events that exist at the same time don't have to have a relationship. For example, even if everyone in a given sample is wearing glasses, the characteristics aren't related. In this case, the probability of a brunette wearing glasses is equal to the probability of a person being a brunette multiplied by the probability of a person wearing glasses. This mathematical test of $P(A \cap B) = P(A)P(B)$ verifies that two events are independent.

Conditional probability is the probability that an event occurs given that another event has happened. If the two events are related, the probability that the second event will occur changes if the other event has happened. However, if the two events aren't related and are therefore independent, the first event to occur won't impact the probability of the second event occurring.

Making Inferences About Population Parameters

Inferential statistics attempts to use data about a subset of some population to make inferences about the rest of the population. An example of this would be taking a collection of students who received tutoring and comparing their results to a collection of students who did not receive tutoring, then using that comparison to try to predict whether the tutoring program in question is beneficial.

To be sure that inferences have a high probability of being true for the whole population, the subset that is analyzed needs to resemble a miniature version of the population as closely as possible. For this reason, statisticians like to choose random samples from the population to study, rather than picking a specific group of people based on some similarity. For example, studying the incomes of people who live in Portland does not reveal anything useful about the incomes of people who live in Tallahassee.

A **population** is the entire set of people or things of interest. Suppose a study is intended to determine the number of hours of sleep per night for college females in the United States. The population would consist of EVERY college female in the country. A **sample** is a subset of the population that may be used for the study. It would not be practical to survey every female college student, so a sample might consist of one hundred students per school from twenty different colleges in the country. From the results of the survey, a sample statistic can be calculated. A sample statistic is a numerical characteristic of the sample data, including mean and variance. A sample statistic can be used to estimate a corresponding population parameter. A **population parameter** is a numerical characteristic of the entire population. Suppose our sample data had a mean (average) of 5.5. This sample statistic can be used as an estimate of the population parameter (average hours of sleep for every college female in the United States).

A population parameter is usually unknown and therefore estimated using a sample statistic. This estimate may be very accurate or relatively inaccurate based on errors in sampling. A **confidence interval** indicates a range of values likely to include the true population parameter. These are constructed at a given confidence level, such as 95 percent. This means that if the same population is sampled repeatedly, the true population parameter would occur within the interval for 95 percent of the samples.

The accuracy of a population parameter based on a sample statistic may also be affected by **measurement error**. Measurement error is the difference between a quantity's true value and its measured value. Measurement error can be divided into random error and systematic error. An example of random error for the previous scenario would be a student reporting 8 hours of sleep when she sleeps 7 hours per night. Systematic errors are those attributed to the measurement system. Suppose the sleep survey gave response options of 2, 4, 6, 8, or 10 hours. This would lead to systematic measurement error.

Statistics

The field of **statistics** describes relationships between quantities that are related, but not necessarily in a deterministic manner. For example, a graduating student's salary will often be higher when the student graduates with a higher GPA, but this is not always the case. Likewise, people who smoke tobacco are more likely to develop lung cancer, but, in fact, it is possible for non-smokers to develop the disease as well. Statistics describes these kinds of situations, where the likelihood of some outcome depends on the starting data.

Measures of Central Tendency

Comparing data sets within statistics can mean many things. The first way to compare data sets is by looking at the center and spread of each set. The center of a data set is measured by mean, median, and mode.

Suppose that X is a set of data points $(x_1, x_2, x_3, \ldots x_n)$, and some description of the general properties of this data need to be found.

The first property that can be defined for this set of data is the **mean**. To find the mean, add up all the data points, then divide by the total number of data points. This can be expressed using **summation notation** as:

$$\overline{X} = \frac{x_1 + x_2 + x_3 + \cdots + x_n}{n} = \frac{1}{n}\sum_{i=1}^{n} x_i$$

For example, suppose that in a class of 10 students, the scores on a test were 50, 60, 65, 65, 75, 80, 85, 85, 90, 100. Therefore, the average test score will be:

$$\frac{1}{10}(50 + 60 + 65 + 65 + 75 + 80 + 85 + 85 + 90 + 100) = 75.5$$

The mean is a useful number if the distribution of data is normal (more on this later), which roughly means that the frequency of different outcomes has a single peak and is roughly equally distributed on both sides of that peak. However, it is less useful in some cases where the data might be split or where there are some **outliers**. Outliers are data points that are far from the rest of the data. For example, suppose there are 90 employees and 10 executives at a company. The executives make $1000 per hour, and the employees make $10 per hour. Therefore, the average pay rate will be $\frac{1000 \times 10 + 10 \times 90}{100} = 109$, or $109 per hour. In this case, this average is not very descriptive.

Another useful measurement is the **median**. In a data set X consisting of data points $x_1, x_2, x_3, \ldots x_n$, the median is the point in the middle. The middle refers to the point where half the data comes before it and half comes after, when the data is recorded in numerical order. If n is odd, then the median is $x_{\frac{n+1}{2}}$. If n is even, it is defined as $\frac{1}{2}\left(x_{\frac{n}{2}} + x_{\frac{n}{2}+1}\right)$, the mean of the two data points closest to the middle of the data points. In the previous example of test scores, the two middle points are 75 and 80. Since there is no single point, the average of these two scores needs to be found. The average is $\frac{75+80}{2} = 77.5$. The median is generally a good value to use if there are a few outliers in the data. It prevents those outliers from affecting the "middle" value as much as when using the mean.

Since an outlier is a data point that is far from most of the other data points in a data set, this means an outlier also is any point that is far from the median of the data set. The outliers can have a substantial effect on the mean of a data set, but they usually do not change the median or mode, or do not change them by a large quantity. For example, consider the data set (3, 5, 6, 6, 6, 8). This has a median of 6 and a mode of 6, with a mean of $\frac{34}{6} \approx 5.67$. Now, suppose a new data point of 1000 is added so that the data set is now (3, 5, 6, 6, 6, 8, 1000). The median and mode, which are both still 6, remain unchanged. However, the average is now $\frac{1034}{7}$, which is approximately 147.7. In this case, the median and mode will be better descriptions for most of the data points.

Outliers in a given data set are sometimes the result of an error by the experimenter, but oftentimes, they are perfectly valid data points that must be taken into consideration.

One additional measure to define for X is the **mode**. This is the data point that appears more frequently. If two or more data points all tie for the most frequent appearance, then each of them is considered a mode. In the case of the test scores, where the numbers were 50, 60, 65, 65, 75, 80, 85, 85, 90, 100, there are two modes: 65 and 85.

Measures of Position and Dispersion

The spread of a data set refers to how far the data points are from the center (mean or median). The spread can be measured by the range or by the quartiles and interquartile range. A data set with all its data points clustered around the center will have a small spread. A data set covering a wide range of values will have a large spread. There are multiple ways to refer to and separate data in a set to better analyze the spread. The most basic method splits a data set into fourths by number of data points, called **quartiles**. The median of a data set is the **second quartile** (written as Q_2). The data point between Q_2 and the lowest value is the **first quartile** (Q_1).

Similarly, the point between Q_2 and the highest value is the **third quartile** (Q_3). The **interquartile range** (IQR) is the range of data from the first quartile to the third quartile in a data set (IQR $= Q3 - Q1$). This range can be seen in the large rectangle on a box plot. The highest and lowest numbers in a data set that aren't outliers are called the **upper extreme** and **lower extreme**, respectively. Outliers are values that don't fall within the upper or lower extreme. The upper extreme is calculated by adding one and a half times the interquartile range to Q_3 (upper extreme $= Q_3 + 1.5 \times$ IQR). Similarly, the lower extreme extends to $Q_1 - 1.5 \times$ IQR.

With large data sets it may be helpful to split them into even smaller subsections. A similar method can be used to split a data set up into hundredths, known as **percentiles**. A percentile refers to one of the 99 points which separate a data set into 100 approximately equal portions. For example, the 50th percentile of a data set is equivalent to the median, or the point where 50% of the data is less than it.

Box-and-Whisker Plots

A **box plot**, also called a **box-and-whisker plot**, divides the data points into four groups and displays the five-number summary for the set as well as any outliers. The five-number summary consists of:

- The lower extreme: the lowest value that is not an outlier
- The upper extreme: the highest value that is not an outlier
- The median of the set: also referred to as the second quartile or Q_2
- The first quartile or Q_1: the median of values below Q_2
- The third quartile or Q_3: the median of values above Q_2

The following image is an example of this:

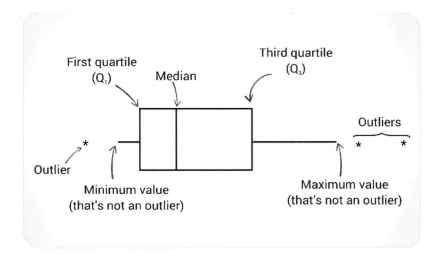

Suppose the box plot displays IQ scores for 12th grade students at a given school. The five-number summary of the data consists of: lower extreme (67); upper extreme (127); Q_2 or median (100); Q_1 (91); Q_3 (108); and outliers (135 and 140). Although all data points are not known from the plot, the points are divided into four quartiles each, including 25% of the data points. Therefore, 25% of students scored between 67 and 91, 25% scored between 91 and 100, 25% scored between 100 and 108, and 25% scored between 108 and 127. These percentages include the normal values for the set and exclude the outliers. This information is useful when comparing a given score with the rest of the scores in the set.

Standard Deviations

The **standard deviation (σ)** quantifies the amount of variation with respect to the mean. A lower standard deviation shows that the data set doesn't differ greatly from the mean. A larger standard deviation shows that the data set is spread out farther from the mean. The formula used for standard deviation depends on whether it's being used for a population or a sample (a subset of a population). The formula for sample standard deviation is:

$$s = \sqrt{\frac{\sum(x - \bar{x})^2}{n - 1}}$$

In this formula, s represents the standard deviation value, x is each value in the data set, $\bar{x}$ is the sample mean, and n is the total number of data points in the set. Note that sample standard deviations use *one less than the total* in the denominator. The population standard deviation formula is similar:

$$\sigma = \sqrt{\frac{\sum(x - \mu)^2}{N}}$$

For population standard deviations, sigma (σ) represents the standard deviation, x represents each value in the data set, mu (μ) is the population mean, and N is the total number of data points for the population.

Set Notation

Sometimes a group of data is so large that it's beneficial to refer to it collectively, or as a **set**. In mathematics, a set is a collection of distinct elements. This means that the items in a set are not mathematically equivalent to each other; there are no duplicates or repetition. A set may be ordered, but ordering is not required to meet the definition of a set. **Set notation** provides a standard way to create new sets from existing data. A set is typically denoted by an italicized uppercase letter. Each item, or **element**, in a finite set can be listed in brackets to indicate that it is part of the set.

For example, $\{3, 1, 5, 9\}$ is a set of four elements; it is also an example of a **finite** set, which means that it has a finite, or countable, number of elements. Sets may also be **infinite**, such as the set of all even numbers. The number of items in a set is known as its **cardinality**. The cardinality of the set $A = \{3, 1, 5, 9\}$ is 4, which can be expressed in set notation as $|A| = 4$. The collection of all elements not in a given set is called its **complement**. The concept of a set of all elements is called the **universal set**. Conversely, a set with no elements is called an **empty set**, represented as $\emptyset$.

Parts of a set may be thought of as **subsets** of the original. The set $\{9\}$ is both a subset of $A = \{4, 7, 9\}$ and $B = \{9, 10, 13\}$, since it is found in both sets. The notation for indicating one set is a subset of another is $\subset$, and is similar to less than and greater than symbols (< and >) because the direction matters in the same way. Similarly, a set with the elements $\{1, 2, 3\}$ is a **superset** of $\{1, 2\}$ because it contains all the elements of the other set; in set notation, this is $\{1, 2, 3\} \supset \{1, 2\}$. A line under the subset symbol means "subset of or equal to", so $A \subseteq A$ is true. The expression $\{12, 14\} \subset A$ states that the left side is a subset of set A.

Often, data sets need to be compared. When wanting to find the similarities or overlap of two sets of data, such as $A = \{7, 12, 14\}$ and $B = \{12, 15, 19\}$, the overlap is called the **intersection**. The intersection of two data sets is represented by the symbol $\cap$. Consequently, the intersection of A and B is twelve: $A \cap B = \{12\}$. The combination of two sets is called a **union**, represented by the symbol $\cup$, which can be remembered as union because it looks like an uppercase letter "U". The union of the previous two sets would be $A \cup B = \{7, 12, 14, 15, 19\}$. Note that the number 12 does not repeat in the union of these sets.

Subtraction can also be performed on sets to find the difference between them. The operator for set subtraction may be represented by either a minus symbol, $-$, or a set minus which resembles a backslash, $\backslash$. The subtraction of two sets, $A = \{2, 3\}$ and $B = \{3, 4, 5\}$, will leave the elements from one set not found in the other. For example, consider the subtraction of B from A:

$$A \backslash B = \{2, 3\} \backslash \{3, 4, 5\} = \{2\}$$

Similarly, the subtraction of set A from set B is $\{4, 5\}$.

One more tool for analyzing sets involves the **inclusion-exclusion principle**. This states that the total number of items between any two given sets is equal to the sum of their cardinalities minus the cardinality of their intersection:

$$|A \cup B| = |A| + |B| - |A \cap B|$$

Venn diagrams can be used to graphically represent sets. They provide a tool to help visualize the intersection and union of the sets. The following graphic shows examples of sets using Venn diagrams:

Set Theory Venn Diagrams

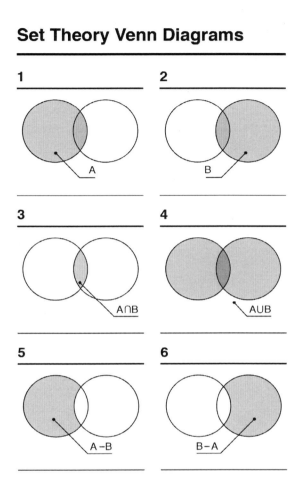

Factorials

Factorials are a way of expressing the number of ways objects can be arranged. Factorial notation uses an exclamation mark after an expression to indicate that it is the product of that number and all positive integers less than it. For example, the expression 3! is equal to $3 \times 2 \times 1 = 6$, which corresponds with the number of ways 3 unique objects can be arranged or ordered. For example, if there are three blocks the letters A, B, and C, they can be arranged in the following six ways:

1	2	3	4	5	6
ABC	ACB	BAC	BCA	CAB	CBA

This is used frequently in statistics to find and express the number of ways multiple elements can be arranged. The general form for factorials is given as:

$$n! = n \times (n-1) \times (n-2) \dots 1$$

Counting Techniques

There are many counting techniques that can help solve problems involving counting possibilities. For example, the **Addition Principle** states that if there are m choices from Group 1 and n choices from Group 2, then $n + m$ is the total number of choices possible from Groups 1 and 2. For this to be true, the groups can't have any choices in common. The **Multiplication Principle** states that if Process 1 can be completed n ways and Process 2 can be completed m ways, the total number of ways to complete both Process 1 and Process 2 is $n \times m$. For this rule to be used, both processes must be independent of each other. Counting techniques also involve permutations. A **permutation** is an arrangement of elements in a set for which order must be considered. For example, if three letters from the alphabet are chosen, ABC and BAC are two different permutations. The multiplication rule can be used to determine the total number of possibilities. If each letter can't be selected twice, the total number of possibilities is:

$$26 \times 25 \times 24 = 15{,}600$$

A formula can also be used to calculate this total. In general, the notation $P(n, r)$ represents the number of ways to arrange r objects from a set of n and, the formula is:

$$P(n, r) = \frac{n!}{(n - r)!}$$

In the previous example:

$$P(26, 3) = \frac{26!}{23!} = 15{,}600$$

Contrasting permutations, a **combination** is an arrangement of elements in which order doesn't matter. In this case, ABC and BAC are the same combination. In the previous scenario, there are six permutations that represent each single combination. Therefore, the total number of possible combinations is:

$$15{,}600 \div 6 = 2{,}600$$

In general, $C(n, r)$ represents the total number of combinations of n items selected r at a time where order doesn't matter. Another way to represent the combinations of r items selected out of a set of n items is $\binom{n}{r}$. The formula for select combinations of items is:

$$\binom{n}{r} = C(n, r) = \frac{n!}{(n - r)! \; r!}$$

Therefore, the following relationship exists between permutations and combinations:

$$C(n, r) = \frac{P(n, r)}{n!} = \frac{P(n, r)}{P(r, r)}$$

Probability

Given a set of possible outcomes X, a **probability distribution** on X is a function that assigns a probability to each possible outcome. If the outcomes are $(x_1, x_2, x_3, \dots x_n)$, and the probability distribution is p, then the following rules are applied.

- $0 \leq p(x_i) \leq 1$, for any i.

- $\sum_{i=1}^{n} p(x_i) = 1$.

In other words, the probability of a given outcome must be between zero and 1, while the total probability must be 1.

If $p(x_i)$ is constant, then this is called a **uniform probability distribution**, and $p(x_i) = \frac{1}{n}$. For example, on a six-sided die, the probability of each of the six outcomes will be $\frac{1}{6}$.

If seeking the probability of an outcome occurring in some specific range A of possible outcomes, written $P(A)$, add up the probabilities for each outcome in that range. For example, consider a six-sided die, and figure the probability of getting a 3 or lower when it is rolled. The possible rolls are 1, 2, 3, 4, 5, and 6. So, to get a 3 or lower, a roll of 1, 2, or 3 must be completed. The probabilities of each of these is $\frac{1}{6}$, so add these to get:

$$p(1) + p(2) + p(3) = \frac{1}{6} + \frac{1}{6} + \frac{1}{6} = \frac{1}{2}$$

Describing a Set of Data

A set of data can be described in terms of its center, spread, shape and any unusual features. The center of a data set can be measured by its mean, median, or mode. The spread of a data set refers to how far the data points are from the center (mean or median). A data set with all its data points clustered around the center will have a small spread. A data set covering a wide range of values will have a large spread.

When a data set is displayed as a graph like the one below, the shape indicates if a sample is normally distributed, symmetrical, or has measures of skewness. When graphed, a data set with a normal distribution will resemble a bell curve.

If the data set is symmetrical, each half of the graph when divided at the center is a mirror image of the other. If the graph has fewer data points to the right, the data is skewed right. If it has fewer data points to the left, the data is skewed left.

Right-Skewed   Symmetric   Left-Skewed

A description of a data set should include any unusual features such as gaps or outliers. A gap is a span within the range of the data set containing no data points. An outlier is a data point with a value either extremely large or extremely small when compared to the other values in the set.

The graphs above can be referred to as **unimodal** since they all have a single peak. This is in contrast to **multimodal** graphs that have multiple peaks.

Normal Distribution

A **normal distribution** of data follows the shape of a bell curve and the data set's median, mean, and mode are equal. Therefore, 50 percent of its values are less than the mean and 50 percent are greater than the mean. Data sets that follow this shape can be generalized using normal distributions. Normal distributions are described as **frequency distributions** in which the data set is plotted as percentages rather than true data points. A **relative frequency distribution** is one where the y-axis is between zero and 1, which is the same as 0% to 100%.

Within a standard deviation, 68 percent of the values are within 1 standard deviation of the mean, 95 percent of the values are within 2 standard deviations of the mean, and 99.7 percent of the values are within 3 standard deviations of the mean. The number of standard deviations that a data point falls from the mean is called the **z-score.** The formula for the z-score is $Z = \frac{x-\mu}{\sigma}$, where μ is the mean, σ is the standard deviation, and x is the data point. This formula is used to fit any data set that resembles a normal distribution to a standard normal distribution in a process known as **standardizing**.

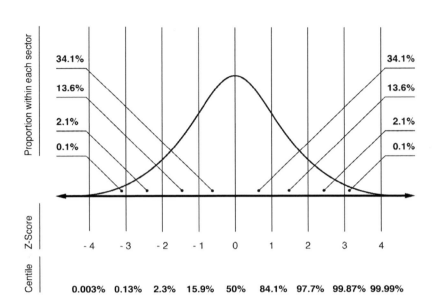

Here is a normal distribution with labeled z-scores:

Normal Distribution with Labelled Z-Scores

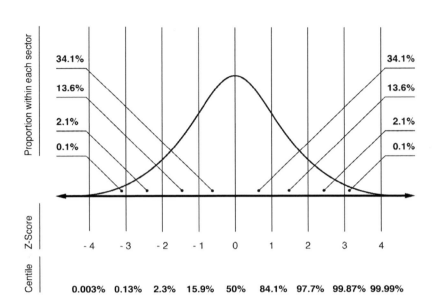

Population percentages can be estimated using normal distributions. For example, the probability that a data point will be less than the mean, or that the z-score will be less than 0, is 50%. Similarly, the probability that a data point will be within 1 standard deviation of the mean, or that the z-score will be between -1 and 1, is about 68.2%. When using a z-table, the left column states how many standard deviations (to one decimal place) away from the mean the point is, and the row heading states the second decimal place. The entries in the table corresponding to each column and row give the probability, which is equal to the area.

Areas Under the Curve

The area under the curve of a standard normal distribution is equal to 1. Areas under the curve can be estimated using the z-score and a table. The area is equal to the probability that a data point lies in that region in decimal form. For example, the area under the curve from $z = -1$ to $z = 1$ is 0.682.

Discrete and Continuous Random Variables

A **discrete random variable** consists of a collection of values that is either finite or countable. If there are infinitely many values, being countable means that each individual value can be counted. For example, the number of coin tosses before getting heads could potentially be infinite, but the total number of tosses is countable. A **continuous random variable** has infinitely many values and is not countable. The individual items cannot be counted, and an example is a measurement. Because of the use of decimals, there are infinitely many heights of human beings. Each type of variable has its own **probability distribution**, which is a description that shows the probability for each potential value of the random variable. They are usually seen in tables, formulas, or graphs. The **expected value** of a random variable represents what the mean value should be in either a large sample size or after many trials. According to the Law of Large Numbers, after many trials, the actual mean and that of the probability distribution should be approximately equal to the expected value. The expected value is a weighted average that is calculated as:

$$E(X) = \sum x_i p_i$$

where x_i represents the value of each outcome and p_i represents the probability of each outcome. The expected value if all probabilities are equal is:

$$E(X) = \frac{x_1 + x_2 + \cdots + x_n}{n}$$

Expected value is often called the **mean of the random variable** and is also a measure of central tendency. A **binomial probability distribution** is a probability distribution in which there is a fixed number of trials, all trials are independent, each trial has an outcome classified as either a success or a failure, and the probability of a success is the same in each trial. Within any binomial experiment, x is the number of resulting successes, n is the number of trials, P is the probability of success within each trial, and $Q = 1 - P$ is the probability of failure within each trial. The probability of obtaining x successes within n trials is:

$$\binom{n}{x} P^x (1 - P)^{n-x}$$

The combination $\binom{n}{x} = \frac{n!}{x!(n-x)!}$ is called the **binomial coefficient** and represents the number of possible outcomes where exactly x many successes occur out of n trials.

A **geometric probability distribution** is a binomial probability distribution where the number of trials is not fixed. A **uniform probability distribution** exists when there is constant probability. Each random variable has equal probability and its graph is a rectangle. Finally, a **uniform probability distribution** has a graph that is symmetric and bell-shaped.

Population percentages can be estimated using normal distributions. For example, the probability that a data point will be less than the mean is 50%. Similarly, the probability that a data point will be within one standard deviation of the mean, or that the z-score will be between -1 and 1, is about 68.2%. When using a z-table, the left column states how many standard deviations (to one decimal place) away from the mean the point lies, and the row heading states the second decimal place. The entries in the table corresponding to each column and each row gives the probability, which is equal to the area under the curve. The area under the entire curve of a standard normal distribution is equal to 1.

Evaluating Reports

The presentation of statistics can be manipulated to produce a desired outcome. Consider the statement, "Four out of five dentists recommend our toothpaste." This is a vague statement that is obviously biased. (Who are the five dentists this statement references?) This statement is quite different from the statement, "Four out of every five dentists recommend our toothpaste." Whether intentional or unintentional, statistics can be misleading. Statistical reports should be examined to verify the validity and significance of the results. The context of the numerical values allows for deciphering the meaning, intent, and significance of the survey or study. Questions on this material will require students to use critical-thinking skills to justify or reject results and conclusions.

When analyzing a report, consider who conducted the study and their intent. Was it performed by a neutral party or by a person or group with a vested interest? A study on health risks of smoking performed by a health insurance company would have a much different intent than one performed by a cigarette company. Consider the sampling method and the data collection method. Was it a true random sample of the population, or was one subgroup overrepresented or underrepresented?

The three most common types of data gathering techniques are sample surveys, experiments, and observational studies. **Sample surveys** involve collecting data from a random sample of people from a desired population. The measurement of the variable is only performed on this set of people. To have accurate data, the sampling must be unbiased and random. For example, surveying students in an advanced calculus class on how much they enjoy math classes is not a useful sample if the population should be all college students based on the research question. An **experiment** is the method by which a hypothesis is tested using a controlled process called the scientific method.

A cause and the effect of that cause are measured, and the hypothesis is accepted or rejected. Experiments are usually completed in a controlled environment where the results of a control population are compared to the results of a test population. The groups are selected using a randomization process in which each group has a representative mix of the population being tested. Finally, an **observational study** is similar to an experiment. However, this design is used when circumstances prevent or do not allow for a designated control group and experimental group (e.g., lack of funding or unrealistic expectations). Instead, existing control and test populations must be used, so this method has a lack of randomization.

Consider the sleep study scenario from the previous section. If all twenty schools included in the study were state colleges, the results may be biased due to a lack of private-school participants. Consider the measurement system used to obtain the data. Was the system accurate and precise, or was it a flawed system? If, for the sleep study, the possible responses were limited to 2, 4, 6, 8, or 10 hours, it could be argued that the measurement system was flawed. Would odd numbers be rounded up or down? Without clarifying the system, the results could vary greatly. What about students who sleep 12 hours per night? The closest option for them would be 10 hours, which is significantly less.

Every scenario involving statistical reports will be different. The key is to examine all aspects of the study before determining whether to accept or reject the results and corresponding conclusions.

Quantitative Reasoning Practice Quiz

Quantitative Comparison

Compare Quantity A to Quantity B, using additional information presented above the two quantities.

1. h is an integer in the following mathematical series: 4, h, 19, 39, 79

Quantity A	Quantity B
The value of h	9

a. Quantity A is greater.
b. Quantity B is greater.
c. The two quantities are equal.
d. The relationship cannot be determined from the information given.

Numeric Entry

Enter your answer in the box(es) below the question.

- Your answer may be an integer, a decimal, a fraction, and it may be negative.

- If a question asks for a fraction, there will be two boxes. One is for the numerator and one is for the denominator.

- Equivalent forms of the value, such as 1.5 and 1.50, are all correct. Fractions do not need to be reduced to lowest terms.

- Enter the exact answer unless your question asks you to round your answer.

2. Alan currently weighs 200 pounds, but he wants to lose weight to get down to 175 pounds. What is this difference in kilograms? (1 pound is approximately equal to 0.45 kilograms.)

[ ] kg

3. Johnny earns $2,334.50 from his job each month. He pays $1,437 for monthly expenses. Johnny is planning a vacation in 3 months that he estimates will cost $1,750 total. How much will Johnny have left over from three months of saving once he pays for his vacation?

$ [ ]

Multiple Choice

4. Five students took a test. Jenny scored the highest with a 94. James scored the lowest with a 79. Hector scored lower than Jenny, but higher than Sam. Sam scored lower than Mary who scored an 84. Which of the following statements must be true?

    a. There were 3 people who scored higher than Sam.
    b. The median test score was an 84.
    c. The average test score must be higher than 82.
    d. Jenny is the only student who scored above 90.
    e. Hector scored lower than Mary.

5. The following graph compares the various test scores of the top three students in each of these teacher's classes. Based on the graph, which teacher's students had the smallest range of test scores?

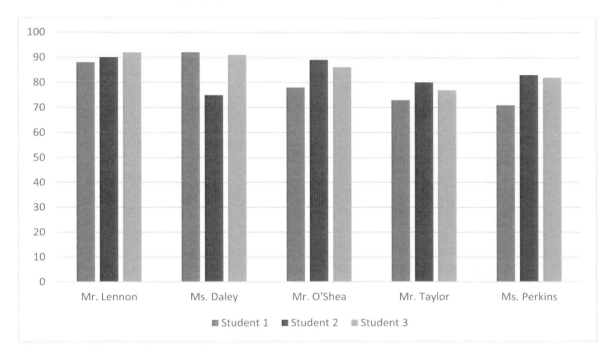

    a. Mr. Lennon
    b. Mr. O'Shea
    c. Mr. Taylor
    d. Ms. Daley
    e. Ms. Perkins

Answer Explanations

Quantitative Comparison

1. C: The equation that produces this series is $2x + 1$. This gives $2(4) + 1 = 9$, $2(9) + 1 = 19$, and so on. This means that the value of h in the series is 9, so Quantity A and Quantity B are equal.

Numeric Entry

2. 11.25: Using the conversion rate, multiply the projected weight loss of 25 lb by $0.45 \frac{kg}{lb}$ to get the amount in kilograms (11.25 kg).

3. 942.50: First, subtract $1,437 from $2,334.50 to find Johnny's monthly savings; this equals $897.50. Then, multiply this amount by 3 to find out how much he will have (in three months) before he pays for his vacation: this equals $2,692.50. Finally, subtract the cost of the vacation ($1,750) from this amount to find how much Johnny will have left: $942.50.

Multiple Choice

4. A & C: It can be determined from reading the information given that Jenny, Hector, and Mary scored higher than Sam, so Choice A is correct. There is no relation provided between Hector and Mary's scores. Given that Mary could have scored higher or lower than Hector, it cannot be determined if her score is the median, so Choice B is incorrect. Three of the test scores are given and since James has to be the lowest at 79, the lowest two missing scores possible are 80 and 81. This means that the lowest that the average could be is 83.6. So, Choice C is correct. With the information given, it is possible that Hector scored above 90, so Choice D is incorrect. There is no relation given between Hector and Mary's scores. This means that Hector could have scored higher or lower than Mary. So, Choice E is incorrect.

5. A: To calculate the range in a set of data, subtract the lowest value from the highest value. In this graph, the range of Mr. Lennon's students is 5, which can be seen physically in the graph as having the smallest difference between the highest value and the lowest value compared with the other teachers.

Analytical Writing

The GRE **Analytical Writing** Questions contain two analytical writing tasks: the **Analyze an Issue Task** and the **Analyze an Argument Task**.

Each of these responses will be separately timed. The writing prompt content is divided into the two separate tasks. The first task will be analyzing a general issue written as a prompt. This will allow you to make your own claim and provide different perspectives regarding that claim. The prompt may ask you to agree or disagree with the issue.

The second task will be analyzing an argument. It's necessary for you to test the logical soundness of the prompt's passage and evaluate the evidence given. You may also be asked to provide evidence that could strengthen or weaken the argument given.

The first two sections presented below are called "Writing the Essay" and "Conventions of Standard English." The first section is designed to help you structure your essay and employ prewriting strategies that will help you brainstorm and begin writing the essay. The second section is common mistakes used in the English language. The next sections are dedicated to giving an example Issue and Argument Task and explaining how to respond to those tasks.

Writing the Essay

Brainstorming
One of the most important steps in writing an essay is prewriting. Before drafting an essay, it's helpful to think about the topic for a moment or two to gain a more solid understanding of the task. Then, spending about five minutes jotting down the immediate ideas that could work for the essay is recommended. This serves as a way to get some words on the page and offer a reference for ideas when drafting. Scratch paper is provided for writers to use any prewriting techniques such as webbing, free writing, or listing. The goal is to get ideas out of the mind and onto the page.

Considering Opposing Viewpoints
In the planning stage, it's important to consider all aspects of the topic, including different viewpoints on the subject. There are more than two ways to look at a topic, and a strong argument considers those opposing viewpoints. Considering opposing viewpoints can help writers present a fair, balanced, and informed essay that shows consideration for all readers. This approach can also strengthen an argument by recognizing and potentially refuting opposing viewpoint(s).

Drawing from personal experience may help to support ideas. For example, if the goal for writing is a personal narrative, then the story should come from the writer's own life. Many writers find it helpful to draw from personal experience, even in an essay that is not strictly narrative. Personal anecdotes or short stories can help to illustrate a point in other types of essays as well.

Moving from Brainstorming to Planning
Once the ideas are on the page, it's time to turn them into a solid plan for the essay. The best ideas from the brainstorming results can then be developed into a more formal outline. An outline typically has one main point (the thesis) and at least three sub-points that support the main point.

Here's an example:

Main Idea

- Point #1
- Point #2
- Point #3

Of course, there will be details under each point, but this approach is the best for dealing with timed writing.

Time Management

It is important to manage your time effectively. It is recommended that you allocate time at the beginning of your writing to review the prompt and instructions multiple times and then outline your basic thoughts, either on paper or in your head. This initial thinking process will give you a clear plan of action before you put pen to paper and will result in a more concise and effective argument.

Similarly, it is recommended that you leave a few minutes at the end of your writing to review your piece and ensure it is coherent, includes examples that support each of your key argument points, and specifically addresses the instructions that were provided. Clarity of thought and staying focused on the assigned topic are more important than citing every example that supports your argument in excruciating detail.

Parts of the Essay

The **introduction** has to do a few important things:

- Establish the **topic** of the essay in original wording (i.e., not just repeating the prompt)

- Clarify the significance/importance of the topic or purpose for writing (not too many details, a brief overview)

- Offer a **thesis statement** that identifies the writer's own viewpoint on the topic (typically one or two brief sentences as a clear, concise explanation of the main point on the topic)

Body paragraphs reflect the ideas developed in the outline. Three or four points is probably sufficient for a short essay, and they should include the following:

- A **topic sentence** that identifies the sub-point (e.g., a reason why, a way how, a cause or effect)

- A detailed **explanation** of the point, explaining why the writer thinks this point is valid

- Illustrative **examples**, such as personal examples or real-world examples that support and validate the point

- A **concluding sentence** that connects the examples, reasoning, and analysis to the point being made

The **conclusion**, or final paragraph, should be brief and should reiterate the focus, clarifying why the discussion is significant or important. It is important to avoid adding specific details or new ideas to this paragraph. The purpose of the conclusion is to sum up what has been said to bring the discussion to a close.

Don't Panic!

Writing an essay can be overwhelming, and performance panic is a natural response. The outline serves as a basis for the writing and helps writers stay focused. Getting stuck can also happen, and it's helpful to remember that brainstorming can be done at any time during the writing process. Following the steps of the writing process is the best defense against writer's block.

Timed essays can be particularly stressful, but assessors are trained to recognize the necessary planning and thinking for these timed efforts. Using the plan above, and sticking to it, helps with time management. Timing each part of the process helps writers stay on track. Sometimes writers try to cover too much in their essays. If time seems to be running out, writers should take the opportunity to determine whether all of the ideas in the outline are necessary. Three body paragraphs are sufficient, and more than that is probably too much to cover in a short essay.

More isn't always *better* in writing. A strong essay will be clear and concise. It will avoid unnecessary or repetitive details. It is better to have a concise, five-paragraph essay that makes a clear point, than a ten-paragraph essay that doesn't. The goal is to write one to two pages of quality writing. Paragraphs should also reflect balance; if the introduction goes to the bottom of the first page, the writing may be going off-track or be repetitive. It's best to fall into the one-to-two-page range, but a complete, well-developed essay is the ultimate goal.

The Final Steps

Leaving a few minutes at the end to revise and proofread offers an opportunity for writers to polish things up. Putting oneself in the reader's shoes and focusing on what the essay actually says helps writers identify problems—it's a movement from the mindset of the writer to the mindset of the editor. The goal is to have a clean, clear copy of the essay. The following areas should be considered when proofreading:

- Sentence fragments
- Awkward sentence structure
- Run-on sentences
- Incorrect word choice
- Grammatical agreement errors
- Spelling errors
- Punctuation errors
- Capitalization errors

The Short Overview

The essay may seem challenging, but following these steps can help writers focus:

- Take one-two minutes to think about the topic.
- Generate some ideas through brainstorming (three-four minutes).
- Organize ideas into a brief outline, selecting just three-four main points to cover in the essay
- Develop essay in parts:
    - Introduction paragraph, with intro to topic and main points
    - Viewpoint on the subject at the end of the introduction
    - Body paragraphs, based on outline

- o Each paragraph: makes a main point, explains the viewpoint, uses examples to support the point
- o Brief conclusion highlighting the main points and closing
- Read over the essay (last five minutes).
- Look for any obvious errors, making sure that the writing makes sense.

Conventions of Standard English

Errors in Standard English Grammar, Usage, Syntax, and Mechanics

Sentence Fragments

A **complete sentence** requires a verb and a subject that expresses a complete thought. Sometimes, the subject is omitted in the case of the implied *you*, used in sentences that are the command or imperative form—e.g., "Look!" or "Give me that." It is understood that the subject of the command is *you*, the listener or reader, so it is possible to have a structure without an explicit subject. Without these elements, though, the sentence is incomplete—it is a **sentence fragment**. While sentence fragments often occur in conversational English or creative writing, they are generally not appropriate in academic writing. Sentence fragments often occur when dependent clauses are not joined to an independent clause:

Sentence fragment: Because the airline overbooked the flight.

The sentence above is a dependent clause that does not express a complete thought. What happened as a result of this cause? With the addition of an independent clause, this now becomes a complete sentence:

Complete sentence: Because the airline overbooked the flight, several passengers were unable to board.

Sentences fragments may also occur through improper use of conjunctions:

I'm going to the Bahamas for spring break. And to New York City for New Year's Eve.

While the first sentence above is a complete sentence, the second one is not because it is a prepositional phrase that lacks a subject [I] and a verb [am going]. Joining the two together with the coordinating conjunction forms one grammatically-correct sentence:

I'm going to the Bahamas for spring break and to New York City for New Year's Eve.

Run-Ons

A **run-on** is a sentence with too many independent clauses that are improperly connected to each other:

This winter has been very cold some farmers have suffered damage to their crops.

The sentence above has two subject-verb combinations. The first is "this winter has been"; the second is "some farmers have suffered." However, they are simply stuck next to each other without any punctuation or conjunction. Therefore, the sentence is a run-on.

Another type of run-on occurs when writers use inappropriate punctuation:

This winter has been very cold, some farmers have suffered damage to their crops.

Although a comma has been added, this sentence is still not correct. When a comma alone is used to join two independent clauses, it is known as a **comma splice**. Without an appropriate conjunction, a comma cannot join two independent clauses by itself.

Run-on sentences can be corrected by either dividing the independent clauses into two or more separate sentences or inserting appropriate conjunctions and/or punctuation. The run-on sentence can be amended by separating each subject-verb pair into its own sentence:

> This winter has been very cold. Some farmers have suffered damage to their crops.

The run-on can also be fixed by adding a comma and conjunction to join the two independent clauses with each other:

> This winter has been very cold, so some farmers have suffered damage to their crops.

Parallelism
Parallel structure occurs when phrases or clauses within a sentence contain the same structure. Parallelism increases readability and comprehensibility because it is easy to tell which sentence elements are paired with each other in meaning.

> Jennifer enjoys cooking, knitting, and to spend time with her cat.

This sentence is not parallel because the items in the list appear in two different forms. Some are **gerunds**, which is the verb + ing: *cooking, knitting*. The other item uses the **infinitive** form, which is to + verb: *to spend*. To create parallelism, all items in the list may reflect the same form:

> Jennifer enjoys cooking, knitting, and spending time with her cat.

All of the items in the list are now in gerund forms, so this sentence exhibits parallel structure. Here's another example:

> The company is looking for employees who are responsible and with a lot of experience.

Again, the items that are listed in this sentence are not parallel. "Responsible" is an adjective, yet "with a lot of experience" is a prepositional phrase. The sentence elements do not utilize parallel parts of speech.

> The company is looking for employees who are responsible and experienced.

"Responsible" and "experienced" are both adjectives, so this sentence now has parallel structure.

Dangling and Misplaced Modifiers
Modifiers enhance meaning by clarifying or giving greater detail about another part of a sentence. However, incorrectly-placed modifiers have the opposite effect and can cause confusion. A **misplaced modifier** is a modifier that is not located appropriately in relation to the word or phrase that it modifies:

> Because he was one of the greatest thinkers of Renaissance Italy, John idolized Leonardo da Vinci.

In this sentence, the modifier is "because he was one of the greatest thinkers of Renaissance Italy," and the noun it is intended to modify is "Leonardo da Vinci." However, due to the placement of the modifier next to the subject, John, it seems as if the sentence is stating that John was a Renaissance genius, not Da Vinci.

> John idolized Leonard da Vinci because he was one of the greatest thinkers of Renaissance Italy.

The modifier is now adjacent to the appropriate noun, clarifying which of the two men in this sentence is the greatest thinker.

Dangling modifiers modify a word or phrase that is not readily apparent in the sentence. That is, they "dangle" because they are not clearly attached to anything:

> After getting accepted to college, Amir's parents were proud.

The modifier here, "after getting accepted to college," should modify who got accepted. The noun immediately following the modifier is "Amir's parents"—but they are probably not the ones who are going to college.

> After getting accepted to college, Amir made his parents proud.

The subject of the sentence has been changed to Amir himself, and now the subject and its modifier are appropriately matched.

Inconsistent Verb Tense

Verb tense reflects when an action occurred or a state existed. For example, the tense known as **simple present** expresses something that is happening right now or that happens regularly:

> She *works* in a hospital.

Present continuous tense expresses something in progress. It is formed by to be + verb + -ing.

> Sorry, I can't go out right now. I *am doing* my homework.

Past tense is used to describe events that previously occurred. However, in conversational English, speakers often use present tense or a mix of past and present tense when relating past events because it gives the narrative a sense of immediacy. In formal written English, though, consistency in verb tense is necessary to avoid reader confusion.

> I traveled to Europe last summer. As soon as I stepped off the plane, I feel like I'm in a movie! I'm surrounded by quaint cafes and impressive architecture.

The passage above abruptly switches from past tense—*traveled, stepped*—to present tense—*feel, am surrounded*.

> I *traveled* to Europe last summer. As soon as I *stepped* off the plane, I *felt* like I was in a movie! I *was surrounded* by quaint cafes and impressive architecture.

All verbs are in past tense, so this passage now has consistent verb tense.

Split Infinitives

The **infinitive form** of a verb consists of "to + base verb"—e.g., to walk, to sleep, to approve. A **split infinitive** occurs when another word, usually an adverb, is placed between *to* and the verb:

I decided *to simply walk* to work to get more exercise every day.

The infinitive *to walk* is split by the adverb *simply*.

It was a mistake *to hastily approve* the project before conducting further preliminary research.

The infinitive *to approve* is split by *hastily*.

Although some grammarians still advise against split infinitives, this syntactic structure is common in both spoken and written English and is widely accepted in standard usage.

Subject-Verb Agreement

In English, verbs must agree with the subject. The form of a verb may change depending on whether the subject is singular or plural, or whether it is first, second, or third person. For example, the verb *to be* has various forms:

I <u>am</u> a student.

You <u>are</u> a student.

She <u>is</u> a student.

We <u>are</u> students.

They <u>are</u> students.

Errors occur when a verb does not agree with its subject. Sometimes, the error is readily apparent:

We is hungry.

Is is not the appropriate form of *to be* when used with the third person plural *we*.

We are hungry.

This sentence now has correct subject-verb agreement.

However, some cases are trickier, particularly when the subject consists of a lengthy noun phrase with many modifiers:

Students who are hoping to accompany the anthropology department on its annual summer trip to Ecuador needs to sign up by March 31st.

The verb in this sentence is *needs*. However, its subject is not the noun adjacent to it—Ecuador. The subject is the noun at the beginning of the sentence—students. Because *students* is plural, *needs* is the incorrect verb form.

Students who are hoping to accompany the anthropology department on its annual summer trip to Ecuador *need* to sign up by March 31st.

This sentence now uses correct agreement between *students* and *need*.

Another case to be aware of is a **collective noun**. A collective noun refers to a group of many things or people but can be singular in itself—e.g., family, committee, army, pair team, council, jury. Whether or not a collective noun uses a singular or plural verb depends on how the noun is being used. If the noun refers to the group performing a collective action as one unit, it should use a singular verb conjugation:

> The family is moving to a new neighborhood.

The whole family is moving together in unison, so the singular verb form *is* is appropriate here.

> The committee has made its decision.

The verb *has* and the possessive pronoun *its* both reflect the word *committee* as a singular noun in the sentence above; however, when a collective noun refers to the group as individuals, it can take a plural verb:

> The newlywed pair spend every moment together.

This sentence emphasizes the love between two people in a pair, so it can use the plural verb *spend*.

> The council are all newly elected members.

The sentence refers to the council in terms of its individual members and uses the plural verb *are*.

Overall, though, American English is more likely to pair a collective noun with a singular verb, while British English is more likely to pair a collective noun with a plural verb.

Analyze an Issue Task

The following section is designed to help you analyze an issue given by the GRE **Analytical Writing Section**. When given an issue, you will want to respond with support or nonsupport of the statement. To support your stance, you should evaluate how your position may or may not be true to the argument. You should also explain how you've come to your position and provide examples in support.

Let's look at the following sample issue and analyze the strategies for this topic:

Undocumented migrant farm workers are essential to our country, as they provide life-sustaining resources to society.

Strategies for Solving the Issue Task

In this task, you are asked to discuss the extent to which you agree or disagree with the statement. Responses may range from strong agreement or strong disagreement to qualified agreement or qualified disagreement. You are also instructed to explain your reasoning and consider ways in which the statement might or might not hold true. A successful response does not have to include all or any of the points listed below. You may discuss other reasons or examples not mentioned here in support of your position.

This section tests various levels of ability. Successful responses require that you focus on the task and provide clear examples relevant to support your view. Less successful responses lack clarity. They may provide examples of types of farm work but not explain the relationship between undocumented workers and their impact on society. For example, a response indicating strong agreement with the statement may simply reiterate that undocumented workers are essential to our society. That statement alone does not provide examples to support that view. The best response would be to explain how undocumented migrant farm workers are essential to our country. A successful response would also address the reasons why there are not proper and effective alternatives to employing undocumented farm workers. If alternatives existed, they would necessarily challenge or weaken the argument, so a good response should spend time discussing them.

There are various approaches to this topic, especially because there are political implications that may influence your response. It is essential that your response reflect the reasoning behind your agreement or disagreement. The focus should be supporting your stance on undocumented migrant farm workers. For example, their work provides most of our food supply. They also do work that most people refuse.

Agreeing with the Statement

Undocumented migrant workers are essential because their work supports America's food supply chain. Although there is technology that assists with aspects of farming, there are jobs that need to be done by hand.

Because these workers are not documented, their vulnerability leads them to take jobs that others refuse due to the hard work, low wages, and poor working conditions they entail. This results in lower retail pricing.

In many cases, children of undocumented workers become acclimated to U.S. culture, and their future generations may become U.S. citizens and contribute legally to the economy. A young, growing population is crucial to a healthy economy. Japan has shown that an aging population and low birth rate can cause 20 years of deflation and a stagnant economy.

Political Reasons

As the Latino community rises in number, this topic becomes increasingly pivotal in political elections. Politicians seek to sway the Latino vote because they rely on the community for a large majority of votes, and most Latino voters want to be assured that they and their peers are treated fairly. Since many undocumented migrant workers arrive from Latin American countries, it would be in a politician's best interest to include these workers in their vision of society, with fair and impartial treatment.

Social Reasons

A hot-button topic in the media for years, there are many sociological implications to consider. Closely tied with political effects, the United States would benefit socially from including undocumented migrant workers. Considering that the agricultural industry has greatly waned in recent years, it is not a coveted career path. Migrant work is even less coveted due to the difficult working conditions and, often, inhumane treatment. You could extrapolate that people who are willing to endure such conditions, while maintaining that work ethic, could also contribute socially in other ways.

Historical Reasons

America's acceptance of immigrants moving here in pursuit of the American dream helped to create the melting pot that the nation has since become. Generations of immigrants have built their lives, dreams, and families in the United States. In analyzing the historical aspect of the topic, you could consider that the country was founded on immigration and expand on that argument.

Economic Reason

Perhaps the most critical consideration for undocumented migrant farm workers is economic. Those who find benefit in migrant workers argue that they are essential to the economy and our quality of life. Agriculture is a multi-billion-dollar industry. Farmers and retailers utilize cheap labor, in turn giving consumers more economical choices. Also, migrant laborers tend to have higher production turnover than U.S. citizens. Simply put, they produce more for less.

For example, typically, corn detasseling is a youth-oriented job, as most adults shun such work. A farmer employs high school students to detassel corn. The students, due to child labor laws, are only available to work limited hours. In those hours, production is lacking. Migrant workers can work twice as many hours, yielding more results and cheaper wages. A lower expense for farmers translates to lower prices for consumers.

In support of this stance, there are many examples from which to draw upon. An anecdotal example could be provided from your own family background or that of someone you know. That background would enhance your argument supporting immigration and why it is important. Also, using influential or famous immigrants as examples is a great way to express how their acceptance has greatly benefited the country.

Disagreeing with the Statement

Farmers could hire documented farm workers and pay higher wages. Hiring U.S. citizens to do the farm work or using more technology will either create more jobs or more demand for agricultural equipment and technology, some of which are made or assembled by American workers.

Underprivileged Americans, who may not have access to other work, could benefit from those jobs.

Reducing the reliance on migrant farm workers may boost tax revenue and employment, contributing positively to the overall economy.

Explore different approaches in support of your stance. Political, sociological, historical, and economic factors may impact your response. Anecdotal examples are another option to include in your response.

It is important to be as specific and concise as possible. When you are providing examples, do not generalize your points in support of the examples.

Political Reasons

The American electorate is made up of many backgrounds, races, religions, ages, and affiliations. Some American citizens are supportive of undocumented migrant workers, while others believe that American jobs should only be reserved for its citizens. Again, politicians find themselves treading the delicate balance of addressing the concerns of citizens that hold the latter view, without alienating those who oppose it.

Social Reasons

Conversely, the analysis could be offered that the inhumane treatment of undocumented migrants is reason enough to oppose. Citizens, who care about their fellow civilians—legally documented or not—strongly oppose the state of undocumented workers and work on behalf of that cause. One could also argue that social policies, particularly immigration, are failing to bring undocumented workers into the fold with partial American citizenship or at least residency, thus losing out on a tax base, a more representative voting base, and a population growth driver.

Migrant worker camps often operate well below the basic level for human occupancy. Many workers share sparse accommodations with other workers, even sharing a bed with total strangers. The restroom facilities may be unsanitary, and the units may be unkempt with poor infrastructure.

Historical Reasons

Immigration questions have been a frequently highlighted issue in recent political history. Unprecedentedly high immigration has an impact on the workplace and quality of life for many communities. While many Americans want to adhere to the tradition of openness and acceptance for all, immigration has increased and changed within the last four decades, presenting new challenges. One could argue that other civil rights causes have fallen to the wayside. A potential strategy would be to highlight a social cause that has historically been prominent and argue that it has been overshadowed by immigration in some specific way. However, be careful to avoid false equivalencies, red herrings, or other common logical fallacies with this kind of argument.

Economic Reasons

Some may counter, reasoning that the economic benefits do not outweigh the inhumane treatment of workers, especially child laborers who can be even more efficient but are often exploited. Many would rather pay higher prices, with a good conscience.

Farmers and camps with a reputation for the mistreatment of their workers can suffer greatly if exposed. The farmer could be charged by OSHA or sued. Consumers could boycott items from that particular farm, and workers could simply avoid that employer.

Another consideration is the argument that undocumented workers have a negative impact on unskilled workers. Unskilled workers who pay taxes and contribute to and will benefit from social programs may lose out on possible job opportunities that are given to migrant workers. A lower tax base hurts the economy because the government—including federal, state, and all the municipalities—is directly responsible for 40 percent of GDP (gross domestic product) and indirectly responsible for more.

Analyze an Argument Task

The GRE **Analyze an Argument Task** presents a passage that argues a claim backed by reason and evidence. Your job in this section is to test the logical soundness of the author's claim. The instructions may ask you about how the evidence strengthens or weakens the argument, the assumptions of the argument, the reasonableness of the proposal, any questions concerning the argument that need to be answered, or how an alternative explanation might be given. Let's look at an example of an argument:

> Bullying has been an issue that has been in existence since the beginning of time. It is defined as long-term physical or mental violence aimed at specific targets. The devastation of peer abuse can have extreme emotional, psychological, spiritual, and physical effects on its victims years into adulthood, if not indefinitely.

> With the insurgence of cyberbullying in recent years, the abuse extends beyond school walls. Schools have been hesitant to step in and regulate bullying incidents, especially ones that occur outside of school hours. Parents and students have complained to schools for stricter punishment of bullies.

> Some schools argue that it is not their responsibility to police students and teach them right from wrong. Those principles should be taught at home. Specifically, they will not monitor after-

school or cyberbullying. Some victims of bullying experience anxiety, depression, and low self-esteem, which result in lower grades, antisocial behavior, hostile retaliation, and increased dropout rates.

To ensure a safer, more successful school environment, schools need to establish an anti-bully protocol, to include faculty training, student workshops, therapy, upstander (students who are allies for the bullied) programs, and stricter punishment of bullies.

Write a response in which you discuss what specific evidence is needed to evaluate the argument and explain how the evidence would weaken or strengthen the argument.

Strategies for Solving the Argument Task

This argument was included in a bill presented to the House of Representatives to establish an anti-bullying law. If the bill becomes a law, schools will be forced to establish the protocol stated above.

You are asked to discuss what specific evidence is needed to evaluate the argument and explain how the evidence would weaken or strengthen the argument. To ensure the highest score possible, you must provide how the evidence would weaken AND strengthen the argument. A response that is not fully completed will not receive top scores.

Some examples include:

- To strengthen the argument, the evidence supports that victims of bullying suffer from many effects. Psychological, emotional, and physical issues manifest from peer abuse. Schools need to address both the bully and the bullied to lessen these effects.

- The anxiety, depression, and hostile school environment result in higher dropout rates and lower grades. The school protocol would help to alleviate that.

- Cyberbullying extends bullying outside of school.

- Schools have been hesitant to step in to alleviate bullying.

- To ensure a safer, more successful school environment, schools need to establish an anti-bully protocol. Faculty training, student workshops, therapy, upstander (students who are allies for the bullied) programs, and stricter punishment of bullies are effective resolutions.

Evidence for Strengthening and Weakening the Argument

Psychological Effects

When most people think of bullying, they often only consider the physical aspects of the issue. However, the most damaging outcomes from peer abuse are mental and emotional.

Psychologically, the damage from bully abuse is extremely traumatic. Studies show that victims suffer from increased risk of psychological effects. Depression is most prevalent, and perhaps, the most critical element—for both the victim and the aggressor. Both groups have increased risk of suicidal thoughts and behaviors. Their depression manifests other issues, such as social anxiety, low self-esteem, and alienation.

Emotional Effects

Relationships, including romantic and friends, are affected, as victims can have issues with trust and vulnerability. Again, low self-esteem is a factor.

At the opposite end of the spectrum, bullies can have PTSD. Some may regret their past choices and experience depression and anxiety.

If aggression is someone's true nature, that character trait can follow them into adulthood. They may find it difficult to assimilate in the workplace, not to mention that their relationships and friendships are deeply affected by their antagonism. Most people have encountered or witnessed such people.

Other psychological effects include hyperawareness, hypervigilance, memory loss, panic attacks, fear, detachment, and the inability to concentrate.

Physical Effects

Studies have long shown a correlation between bullying and poor physical health. Sleep problems are a common issue. Nightmares and lack of and/or disruptive sleep occur in some situations. Lack of sleep creates a host of issues on its own, including loss of concentration, and increased fatigue, mental exhaustion, and irritability.

Other Effects

According to psychologists, students who are bullied perform worse academically. A study conducted by researchers monitored students by the level of bullying that they endured. The students rated their experiences on a scale and identified the type of bullying they experienced—physical, verbal, or reputational.

Students who experienced the highest level of bullying consistently scored lowest academically in comparison to their peers. Their grade average was lowered by as much as 1 to 1.5 points, on a 4-point scale.

Researchers also found that teachers noted a difference in how bullied students engage in class. They were less engaged, showed no interest in class, rarely participated in class discussions, and were less likely to complete their homework.

Cyberbullying

In recent years, bullying has become an even more complex issue with the advent of technology. In the past, students only had to be concerned with bullying during school hours, on school property. Social media has revolutionized the way in which we communicate and connect. There are many benefits that come with social media. People have a way to reach and reconnect with people like never before. However, this medium can also be used for very destructive purposes.

Since this type of bullying is done outside of school hours and venue, administrators have difficulty knowing how to approach the issue.

Some don't want to deal with it at all. Their argument is that what occurs during a student's personal time is not their responsibility. They have no way to monitor the student, much less discipline him or her. Also, due to the anonymity provided by online spaces, it is almost impossible, in most cases, to identify the bully.

On the other hand, the argument could be made that schools are still responsible for off-campus bullying of another student because the consequences of it affect the school environment as well as students' ability to learn.

With the escalating viciousness in cyberspace, parents are looking for protection for their children. There is little protocol in place to prepare educators for off-campus speech. Furthermore, educators are unwilling to police such behavior. Many feel that at that point, it is the sole responsibility of the parent and/or family of the bully to monitor the child. Parents may perceive educators to be indifferent to their child's plight.

Analysis of Administration's Role in the Problem of Bullying

Almost every state has anti-bully legislation to regulate how schools handle bullies. Some states' laws are stronger and more comprehensive than others. Scores of parents, students, and concerned community members have fought to change legislation for those states whose laws are weak. That is considered the ultimate step to helping eliminate the problem. It also makes schools, administrators, and teachers more accountable to address a student's complaint.

Even with the influx of media exposure shedding light on the dangers and effects of bullying and cautionary tales to support the coverage, schools have been hesitant to address this epidemic. Schools should work cohesively with parents to address bullying both at school and at home so that one of the places is not a safe zone and the other open to bullying of all types.

School administrations have several arguments for their lack of involvement in bullying incidences. Bullying has a long history, dating back to the one-room schoolhouses of centuries past. Because that has long been ingrained as simply a "rite of passage" for youth, most have dismissed it as just that. Schools are reluctant to take an active role because of staffing limitations, a lack of a historical precedent to be so involved outside of school hours, and funding limitations that cause schools to focus on the quality of their education and meeting test score goals to keep their funding flowing.

Possible Resolution

In order to ensure a safer and more productive school environment, administrators must take a more proactive role by educating students on the emotional and social mechanisms and impacts of bullying, paying attention to aggressive behavior and power imbalances among students, responding to reports of bullying, and intervening when appropriate. Many schools across the United States have done just that. Other schools have had little say, as they must adhere to the anti-bully laws specific to their state.

Many legislators who prescribe to outdated views on peer abuse have not been on the anti-bully bandwagon. Oftentimes, they must be pushed by civilians to establish stronger and more practical laws to protect students. As anti-bully advocates, groups, students, and individuals rally to push bills through the Senate, lawmakers are becoming increasingly aware of the significance of bullying. These laws can be one of the greatest resources in holding schools accountable to address and help resolve peer abuse.

Analytical Writing Example Prompts

Issue Task

> For-profit institutions of learning should be illegal because they suffer from a conflict of interest between the student receiving the best education and the institution minimizing costs in providing instruction and other services to remain profitable.

Write a response in support or nonsupport of the statement in regard to the position that is taken. To support your stance, evaluate how your position may or may not be true to the argument. Explain how you've come to your position and provide examples in support.

Argument Task

> Bob's lawnmower shop has an excess supply of lawnmowers at the end of the summer season for the first time in years. Bob's son reasons that this excess supply should be heavily discounted and sold as quickly as possible to make room for winter equipment such as snowblowers and snowmobiles to maximize profits and revenue. Bob wants to keep the unsold lawnmowers and attempt to sell them again next year when demand returns.

Write a response in which you discuss what questions should be asked and resolved in order to validate Bob's strategy as a valid one versus his son's idea. Be sure to explain how easy those answers are to obtain, what assumptions they involve, and how the answers to the questions support Bob's strategy and confirm that it has a high probability of success.

Practice Test #1

Section 1: Analytical Writing

Issue Task:

> The criminal justice system's primary purpose should be rehabilitation rather than retribution. Regardless of the crime committed, the goal should always be to release prisoners as soon as they are reformed and capable of assimilating back into society.

Write a response to this statement. Your response should include the extent to which you agree or disagree. Explain your reasoning, provide illustrative examples, and address relevant counter-arguments or exceptions.

Argument Task:

> A family-owned cinema is currently in financial distress. Movie studios are demanding an increased percentage of revenue from ticket sales, and the cinema can't reject this demand without losing access to the most popular movies. The cinema's two co-owners, Alexandra and Walter, have different strategies for recouping the loss in revenue. Alexandra wants to have special pricing for all matinees and all Tuesday showings. She believes this will not only lead to more ticket sales for those showings, but it will also increase customer loyalty. Walter proposes cutting prices at the concession stands to increase ticket sales. In addition, he argues that people will buy more food if it costs less.

Write a response in which you evaluate both co-owners' arguments. Your response should include what questions need to be answered before a reasonable conclusion can be drawn. When discussing potential sources of evidence, make sure to address how each would be obtained and any assumptions it relies upon.

Section 2: Verbal Reasoning

For questions 1-6, select the best word from the corresponding column of choices that most clearly completes the passage:

1. The term *introvert* was made popular by the theories of Carl Jung. An introverted personality displays (i) _____ *a* _____ personality traits. Usually, an introvert will not be the first volunteer to host a (ii) _____ *d* _____ event.

Blank (i)	Blank (ii)
a. Loquacious	d. Grandiose
b. Taciturn	e. Decorous
c. Verbose	f. Punctilious

2. The tadpole's (i) _____b_____ outer covering prevented the biologist from determining the stage of development of the internal organs.

Blank (i)
a. Luminous
b. Opaque
c. Sheer
d. Clear
e. Scaly

3. The members' (i) _____a_____ conversations gave way to one praiseworthy speech that (ii) _____f_____ the reputation of the new president.

Blank (i)	Blank (ii)
a. Garrulous	d. Lauded
b. Reserved	e. Diminished
c. Inhibited	f. Occluded

4. The chemist was disappointed when the solid structures began to (i) _____d_____, making his scientific expected outcome the opposite of what he had hoped.

Blank (i)
a. Petrify
b. Congeal
c. Stiffen
d. Liquefy
e. Fossilize

5. The search for the great (i) _____b_____ made all other adventures seem (ii) _____f_____ for the seasoned sailors.

Blank (i)	Blank (ii)
a. Achillobator	d. Pedestrian
b. Titanis	e. Erudite
c. Leviathan	f. Imperious

6. Much to the defense attorney's delight, the detectives were able to (i) _____a_____ that the prisoner on death row was actually innocent, by using DNA testing.

Blank (i)
a. Occlude
b. Infer
c. Prevaricate
d. Deny
e. Celebrate

Questions 7–11 are based on the following passage:

Becoming a successful leader in today's industry, government, and nonprofit sectors requires more than a high intelligence quotient (IQ). Emotional Intelligence (EI) includes developing the ability to know one's own emotions, to regulate impulses and emotions, and to use interpersonal communication skills with ease while dealing with other people. A combination of knowledge, skills, abilities, and mature emotional intelligence (EI) reflects the most effective leadership recipe. Successful leaders sharpen more than their talents and IQ levels; they practice the basic features of emotional intelligence. Some of the hallmark traits of a competent, emotionally intelligent leader include self-efficacy, drive, determination, collaboration, vision, humility, and openness to change. An unsuccessful leader exhibits opposite leadership traits: unclear directives, inconsistent vision and planning strategies, disrespect for followers, incompetence, and an uncompromising transactional leadership style. There are ways to develop emotional intelligence for the person who wants to improve their leadership style. For example, an emotionally intelligent leader creates an affirmative environment by incorporating collaborative activities, using professional development training for employee self-awareness, communicating clearly about the organization's vision, and developing a variety of resources for working with emotions. Building relationships outside the institution with leadership coaches and with professional development trainers can also help leaders who want to grow their leadership success. Leaders in today's work environment need to strive for a combination of skill, knowledge, and mature emotional intelligence to lead followers to success and to promote the vision and mission of their respective institutions.

Select only one answer choice:

7. The passage suggests that the term *emotional intelligence (EI)* can be defined as which of the following?
   a. A combination of knowledge, skills, abilities, and mature emotional intelligence reflects the most effective EI leadership recipe.
   b. An emotionally intelligent leader creates an affirmative environment by incorporating collaborative activities, using professional development training for employee self-awareness, communicating clearly about the organization's vision, and developing a variety of resources for working with emotions.
   c. EI includes developing the ability to know one's own emotions, to regulate impulses and emotions, and to use interpersonal communication skills with ease while dealing with other people.
   d. Becoming a successful leader in today's industry, government, and nonprofit sectors requires more than a high IQ.
   e. An EI leader exhibits the following leadership traits: unclear directives, inconsistent vision and planning strategies, disrespect for followers, incompetence, and uncompromising transactional leadership style.

114

Select only one answer choice:

8. Based on the information in the passage, a successful leader must have a high EI quotient.
   a. The above statement can be supported by the fact that Daniel Goldman conducted a scientific study.
   b. The above statement can be supported by the example that emotionally intelligent people are highly successful leaders.
   c. The above statement is not supported by the passage.
   d. The above statement is supported by the illustration that claims, "Leaders in today's work environment need to strive for a combination of skill, knowledge, and mature emotional intelligence to lead followers to success and to promote the vision and mission of their respective institutions."
   e. The above statement can be inferred because emotionally intelligent people obviously make successful leaders.

Select only one answer choice:

9. According to the passage, some of the characteristics of an unsuccessful leader include which of the following?
   a. Talent, IQ level, and abilities
   b. Humility, knowledge, and skills
   c. Loud, demeaning actions toward female employees
   d. Outdated technological resources and strategies
   e. Transactional leadership style

Select only one answer choice:

10. According to the passage, which of the following must be true?
   a. The leader exhibits a healthy work/life balance lifestyle.
   b. The leader is uncompromising in transactional directives for all employees, regardless of status.
   c. The leader learns to strategize using future trends analysis to create a five-year plan.
   d. The leader uses a combination of skill, knowledge, and mature reasoning to make decisions.
   e. The leader continually tries to improve their EI test quotient by studying the intelligence quotient of other successful leaders.

Consider each of the choices separately and select all that apply:

11. According to the passage, which of the following choices are true?
   a. To be successful, leaders in the nonprofit sector need to develop emotional intelligence.
   b. It is not necessary for military leaders to develop emotional intelligence, because they prefer a transactional leadership style.
   c. Leadership coaches can add value to someone who is developing their emotional intelligence.
   d. Humility is a valued character value; however, it is not necessarily a trademark of an emotionally intelligent leader.
   e. If a leader does not have the level of emotional intelligence required for a certain job, they are capable of increasing emotional intelligence.

For questions 12-15, select the two answer choices that can complete the sentence and create sentences that have complementary meaning.

12. Normally, I enjoy hearing new music that has an edgy sound; however, the music tonight sounded like a _____ of tones and beats that made me want to cover my ears.
    a. Accord
    b. Harmony
    c. Concordance
    d. Cacophony
    e. Composition
    f. Dissonance

13. The thief _____ with the purse before the geriatric patient knew someone was in the room.
    a. Yielded
    b. Absconded
    c. Appeared
    d. Erupted
    e. Bolted

14. The teacher recognized the immature writing style of the freshman because his essays used _____ language.
    a. Astute
    b. Apt
    c. Banal
    d. Trite
    e. Mediocre
    f. Middling

15. Unlike journalists, who avoid unsubstantiated narratives, politicians have a habit of _____ issues they find dubious.
    a. Pontificating
    b. Obscuring
    c. Explicating
    d. Obfuscating
    e. Discussing
    f. Confabulating

Questions 16–20 are based on the following passage:

Learning how to write a ten-minute play may seem like a monumental task at first; but, if you follow a simple creative writing strategy, similar to writing a narrative story, you will be able to write a successful drama. The first step is to open your story as if it is a puzzle to be solved. This will allow the reader a moment to engage with the story and to mentally solve the story with you, the author. Immediately provide descriptive details that steer the main idea, the tone, and the mood according to the overarching theme you have in mind. For example, if the play is about something ominous, you may open Scene One with a thunderclap. Next, use dialogue to reveal the attitudes and personalities of each of the characters who have a key part in the unfolding story. Keep the characters off balance in some way to create interest and dramatic effect. Maybe what the characters say does not match what they do. Show images on stage to speed up the narrative; remember, one picture speaks a thousand words. As the play progresses, the protagonist must cross the point of no return in some way; this is the climax of the story. Then, as in a written story, you create a resolution to the life-changing event of the protagonist. Let the characters experience some kind of self-discovery that can be understood and appreciated by the patient audience. Finally, make sure all things come together in the end so that every detail in the play makes sense right before the curtain falls.

Select only one answer choice:

16. Based on the passage above, which of the following statements is FALSE?
    a. Writing a ten-minute play may seem like an insurmountable task.
    b. Providing descriptive details is not necessary until after the climax of the story line.
    c. Engaging the audience by jumping into the story line immediately helps them solve the story's developing ideas with you, the writer.
    d. Descriptive details give clues to the play's intended mood and tone.
    e. The introduction of a ten-minute play does not need to open with a lot of coffee pouring or cigarette smoking to introduce the scenes. The action can get started right away.

Select only one answer choice:

17. Based on the passage above, which of the following is true?
    a. The class of eighth graders quickly learned that it is not that difficult to write a ten-minute play.
    b. The playwrights of the twenty-first century all use the narrative writing basic feature guide to outline their initial scripts.
    c. In order to follow a simple structure, a person can write a ten-minute play based on some narrative writing features.
    d. Women find playwriting easier than men because they are used to communicating in writing.
    e. The structure of writing a poem is similar to that of play writing and of narrative writing.

Consider each of the choices separately and select all that apply:

18. Based on your understanding of the passage, it can be assumed that which of the following statements are true?
    a. One way to reveal the identities and nuances of the characters in a play is to use dialogue.
    b. Characters should follow predictable routes in the challenge presented in the unfolding narrative, so the audience may easily follow the sequence of events.
    c. Using images in the stage design is an important element of creating atmosphere and meaning for the drama.
    d. There is no need for the protagonist to come to terms with a self-discovery; they simply need to follow the prescription for life lived as usual.
    e. It is perfectly fine to avoid serious consequences for the actors of a ten-minute play because there is not enough time to unravel perils.

Select only one answer choice:

19. In the passage, why does the writer suggest that writing a ten-minute play is accessible for a novice playwright?
    a. It took the author of the passage only one week to write his first play.
    b. The format follows similar strategies of writing a narrative story.
    c. There are no particular themes or points to unravel; a playwright can use a stream of consciousness style to write a play.
    d. Dialogue that reveals the characters' particularities is uncommonly simple to write.
    e. The characters of a ten-minute play wrap up the action simply by revealing their ideas in a monologue.

Select only one answer choice:

20. Based on the passage, which basic feature of narrative writing is not mentioned with respect to writing a ten-minute play?
    a. Character development
    b. Descriptive details
    c. Dialogue
    d. Mood and tone
    e. Style

Section 3: Quantitative Reasoning

For questions 1-8, compare Quantity A to Quantity B, using additional information presented above the two quantities.

1.

g inches

| |
| Area = 56 square inches   **4 inches** |

Quantity A	Quantity B
The value of g	13

a. Quantity A is greater.
b. Quantity B is greater.
c. The two quantities are equal.
d. The relationship cannot be determined from the information given.

2. $4x - 12 = -2x$

Quantity A	Quantity B
The value of x	3

a. Quantity A is greater.
b. Quantity B is greater.
c. The two quantities are equal.
d. The relationship cannot be determined from the information given.

3. Jimmy and Steve each have some colored marbles.

Jimmy	Steve
7 red marbles	6 green marbles
8 blue marbles	4 blue marbles

Quantity A	Quantity B
All of Jimmy's marbles divided by all of Steve's marbles	Jimmy's blue marbles divided by Steve's green marbles

a. Quantity A is greater.
b. Quantity B is greater.
c. The two quantities are equal.
d. The relationship cannot be determined from the information given.

4.

x inches

7 inches

x inches

13 inches

Quantity A	Quantity B
7 times the area of the triangle	2 times the area of the rectangle

a. Quantity A is greater.
b. Quantity B is greater.
c. The two quantities are equal.
d. The relationship cannot be determined from the information given.

5. Truck A drives 1236 yards and truck B drives 3680 feet.

Quantity A

The distance that truck *A* drove

Quantity B

The distance that truck *B* drove

(a.) Quantity A is greater.
b. Quantity B is greater.
c. The two quantities are equal.
d. The relationship cannot be determined from the information given.

6. $x > 6 > z$

$100 + 5 = 105$ $100 - 6 = 94$

Quantity A

$x + z$ 12

Quantity B

$x - 6$

(a.) Quantity A is greater.
b. Quantity B is greater.
c. The two quantities are equal.
d. The relationship cannot be determined from the information given.

7. There are 16 rocks in a bag. 12 of them are smooth and 4 of them are rough.

Quantity A

The probability of choosing a rough rock $\frac{4}{16} = \frac{2}{8}$

Quantity B

$\frac{2}{8}$

a. Quantity A is greater.
b. Quantity B is greater.
(c.) The two quantities are equal.
d. The relationship cannot be determined from the information given.

8. Bill is four years older than Jim.

Quantity A

Twice Jim's age

Quantity B

Bill's age

a. Quantity A is greater.
b. Quantity B is greater.
c. The two quantities are equal.
(d.) The relationship cannot be determined from the information given.

9. The width of a rectangular house is 22 feet. What is the perimeter of this house if it has the same area as a house that is 33 feet wide and 50 feet long?
a. 184 feet
b. 200 feet
c. 192 feet
d. 206 feet
(e.) 194 feet

$A = 33 \cdot 50$

10. Using the following diagram, what is the total circumference, rounding to the nearest decimal place?

5 cm

a. 25.0 cm
b. 15.7 cm
c. 78.5 cm
d. 31.4 cm
e. 75.6 cm

[handwritten work: $2\pi r$ $2\pi 5$; $3.14 \times 2 = 6.27$; $\times 5 = 31.40$]

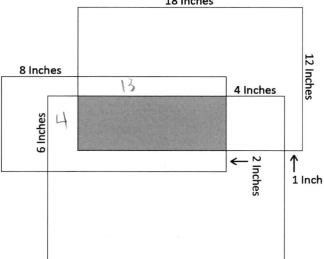

18 Inches

8 Inches

13

4 Inches

12 Inches

6 Inches

4

2 Inches

1 Inch

11. In the figure above, what is the area of the shaded region?
a. 48 sq. inches
b. 52 sq. inches
c. 44 sq. inches
d. 56 sq. inches
e. 46 sq. inches

12. What is $\frac{420}{98}$ rounded to the nearest integer?

4

13. If $3x = 6y = -2z = 24$, then what does $4xy + z$ equal?
a. 116
b. 130
c. 84
d. 108
e. 98

[handwritten: $3x = 6y = -2z = 24$; $x = 8$; $y = 4$; $z = -12$; $4(8)(4) + -12$]

14. A local candy store reports that of the 100 customers that bought suckers, 35 of them bought cherry. What is the probability of selecting 2 customers simultaneously at random that both purchased a cherry sucker?

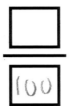

$2\sqrt{85}$

15. If $n = 2^2$, and $m = n^2$, then m^n equals?

   a. 2^{12}
   b. 2^{10}
   c. 2^{18}
   d. 2^{16}
   e. 2^{20}

$n = 4$ $m = 4^2$

16

16^4 $\begin{array}{r} 3 \\ 16 \\ \times 16 \\ \hline 182 \\ + 160 \\ \hline \end{array}$

4

16. The graph of the function $f(x) = |x + 3| - 4$ is graphed on the coordinate plane below.

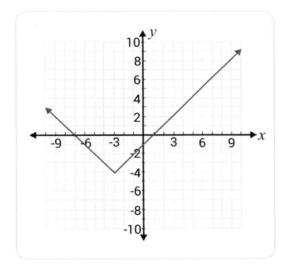

For which of the following functions does the graph of $g(x)$ intersect the function $f(x)$ exactly two times?

   a. $g(x) = x - 4$
   b. $g(x) = -x$
   c. $g(x) = x + 2$
   d. $g(x) = \frac{x}{2}$
   e. $g(x) = \frac{3}{2}x + 3$

17. A figure skater is facing north when she begins to spin to her right. She spins 2250 degrees. Which direction is she facing when she finishes her spin?

a. North
b. Southwest
c. East
d. West
e. Northeast

18. Simplify the following expression:

$$4\frac{2}{3} - 3\frac{4}{9}$$

19. Because of an increase in demand, the price of a designer purse has increased 25% from the original price of $128. What is the new price of the purse?

a. $32
b. $102
c. $192
d. $96
e. $160

20. What is the measure of angle P?

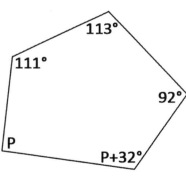

a. 84 degrees
b. 92 degrees
c. 96 degrees
d. 113 degrees
e. 124 degrees

Section 4: Verbal Reasoning

For questions 1-7, select the best word from the corresponding column of choices that most clearly completes the passage:

1. The famous paintings of Caspar David Friedrich, appreciated by patrons of Expressionism, do not convey the same (i) _____ emotion as the more (ii) _____ landscapes of the earlier Expressionist masters.

Blank (i)	Blank (ii)
a. Aesthetic	d. Classical
b. Maudlin	e. Spiritual
c. Effusive	f. Abstract

2. The obvious (i) _____ of the conquerors made the humiliated tribe dubious about promises of fair or humane treatment in the future.

Blank (i)
a. Depredation
b. Retrieval
c. Convalescence
d. Boon
e. Restoration

3. The renowned Pharaoh Ahmose I, who was not (i) _____ by the complexity of a construction plan, was remembered for his ability to cultivate an (ii) _____ building plan. Ahmose I oversaw the construction of the last native-built Egyptian pyramid.

Blank (i)	Blank (ii)
a. Inhibited	d. Ingenious
b. Mitigated	e. Indigenous
c. Placated	f. Insular

4. The representatives of the administration selected new interns, hoping that the important and applicable principles taught to them in college had a chance to (i) _____ over the summer.

Blank (i)
a. Soften
b. Ossify
c. Dissipate
d. Multiply
e. Disintegrate

5. The frightened coyote, trying to escape from the (i) _____ cougar, shifted his weight in the nick of time to avoid the edge of the (ii) _____, and the (iii) _____ intentions of the approaching cougar.

Blank (i)	Blank (ii)	Blank (iii)
a. Irascible	d. Precipice	g. Ponderous
b. Magnanimous	e. Buttress	h. Malevolent
c. Phlegmatic	f. Encomium	i. Sanguine

6. Even after eating three full meals and several snacks, the athlete was not (i) _____ to his appetite's satisfaction.

Blank (i)
a. Sated
b. Deprived
c. Lavished
d. Recompensed
e. Immured

7. Alison Creek, a waterway located in California that winds from the mountains to the Pacific Ocean, could not be used as a viable source of drinking water because of its unpredictable and (i) _____ quality. The concerns of the municipality were (ii) _____ by the suggested alternate use of the coastal area for recreational purposes.

Blank (i)	Blank (ii)
a. Erratic	d. Intensified
b. Invariable	e. Assuaged
c. Consistent	f. Exacerbated

Questions 8–11 are based on the following passage:

The town of Alexandria, Virginia was founded in 1749. Between the years 1810 and 1861, this thriving seaport was the ideal location for slave owners such as Joseph Bruin, Henry Hill, Isaac Franklin, and John Armfield to build several slave trade office structures, including slave holding areas. After 1830, when the manufacturing-based economy slowed down in Virginia, slaves were traded to plantations in the Deep South, in Alabama, Mississippi, and Louisiana. Joseph

Bruin, one of the most notorious of the slave traders operating in Alexandria, alone purchased hundreds of slaves from 1844 to 1861. Harriet Beecher Stowe claimed that the horrible slave traders mentioned in her novel, *Uncle Tom's Cabin*, are reminiscent of the coldhearted Joseph Bruin. The Franklin and Armfield Office was known as one of the largest slave trading companies in the country up to the end of the Civil War period. Slaves, waiting to be traded, were held in a two-story slave pen built behind the Franklin and Armfield Office structure on Duke Street in Alexandria. Yet, many people fought to thwart these traders and did everything they could to rescue and free slaves. Two Christian African American slave sisters, with the help of northern abolitionists who bought their freedom, escaped Bruin's plan to sell them into southern prostitution. In 1861, Joseph Bruin was captured and imprisoned and his property confiscated. The Bruin Slave Jail became the Fairfax County courthouse until 1865. The original Franklin and Armfield Office building still stands in Virginia and is registered in the National Register of Historic Places. The Bruin Slave Jail is still standing on Duke Street in Alexandria, but is not open to the public. The history of the slave trading enterprise is preserved and presented to the public by the Northern Virginia Urban League.

Consider each of the choices separately and select all that apply:

8. Based on the above passage, which of the following statements about the town of Alexandria are true?

a. Alexandria was a seaport town, which could not prosper, even with the advent of a slave trade business, because the manufacturing industry was not enough to stabilize the economy.

b. Slave traders such as Joseph Bruin, Henry Hill, Isaac Franklin, and John Armfield rented both slave trade office buildings and slave holding buildings from landlords of Old Town, Alexandria.

c. For over fifteen years, Joseph Bruin, a notorious slave trader, probably the one characterized in *Uncle Tom's Cabin*, bought hundreds of slaves with the intention of sending the purchased slaves to southern states such as Alabama, Mississippi, and Louisiana.

d. The Bruin Slave Jail is open to the public; the building is located in downtown Alexandria, and still stands in Virginia. The jail is registered in the National Register of Historic Places. The history of the slave trading enterprise is preserved and presented to the public by the Northern Virginia Urban League.

e. Isaac Franklin and John Armfield's slave-trade office structures, including slave holding areas in downtown Alexandria, remained open for their slave trade business until the end of the Civil War.

Consider each of the choices separately and select all that apply:

9. The passage about the Alexandria slave trade business suggests that which of the following statements can be regarded as true?
    a. The lucrative seaport town of Alexandria was supported by successful slave trade businesses of men like Joseph Bruin, Henry Hill, Isaac Franklin, and John Armfield, who bought slaves and sold them to the plantations in the Deep South.
    b. Joseph Bruin, a highly respected Alexandrian businessman, ran a slave trade business in downtown Alexandria until the business closed its doors at the end of the Civil War.
    c. The Franklin and Armfield Office was built by Isaac Franklin and John Armfield. Slaves, waiting to be traded, were held in a four-story slave pen built behind the Franklin and Armfield Office structure on Duke Street in Alexandria.
    d. When the Confederate Army positioned its command in Alexandria and closed slave traders' businesses, the Franklin and Armfield slave pen became the Fairfax County courthouse and was used to hold Union soldiers.
    e. The literature of the slave trading enterprise, like *Uncle Tom's Cabin*, is being preserved and presented to the public by the Northern Virginia Urban League.

Consider each of the choices separately and select all that apply:

10. Which of the following statements can be inferred to be accurate, based on the information provided in the passage?
    a. The town of Alexandria, founded in 1810, became one of the most infamous slave trading markets in the country.
    b. Harriet Beecher Stowe was an escaped slave who was held in the Franklin and Armfield slave pen, located on Duke Street in Alexandria. To avoid a life as a prostitute, Miss Stowe tried to escape from the control of Joseph Bruin, whose surly characteristics surfaced in her classic book, *Uncle Tom's Cabin*.
    c. Northern abolitionists were known to help runaway slaves escape the hands of their notorious owners.
    d. The Bruin Slave Jail, located in downtown Alexandria, still stands today, although it is not open for public viewing.
    e. For convenience, the slave traders took their slaves to nearby Annapolis, Maryland, because the cost of shipping them from there was less than the cost of shipping them from Alexandria.

Select only one answer choice:

11. Which of the following statements best illustrates the author's intended main point or thesis?
    a. Two Christian African American slave sisters, with the help of northern abolitionists who bought their freedom, escaped Bruin's plan to sell them into southern prostitution.
    b. The town of Alexandria, a thriving seaport founded in 1749, was the location for several lucrative slave trading companies from 1810 to 1861.
    c. After the start of the Civil War, Joseph Bruin was captured and his jail was no longer used for his slave trade business.
    d. The Bruin Slave Jail is still standing on Duke Street in Alexandria, but is not open to the public.
    e. In 1861, the Bruin Slave Jail in Alexandria became the Fairfax County courthouse.

For questions 12-16, select the <u>two</u> answer choices that can complete the sentence and create sentences that have complementary meaning.

12. The model was asked to _____ the demands of her coach to eat salad and protein twice a day, because walking down the runway gave her such pleasure.
   a. Dissent to
   b. Accede to
   c. Disparage
   d. Acquiesce to
   e. Object to
   f. Castigate

13. Much to the _____ of the unprepared students, the new professor called on students randomly to deliver impromptu speeches to the class.
   a. Feint
   b. Chagrin
   c. Mortification
   d. Diatribe
   e. Enmity
   f. Exuberance

14. The debate team was poised and ready for a persuasive topic to be announced; they were hoping for opponents who were _____.
   a. Vacuous
   b. Fervid
   c. Flamboyant
   d. Fatuous
   e. Heinous
   f. Ineluctable

15. The two friends who attended the party quietly slipped downstairs where they could watch sports and avoid the _____ holiday movies that the couples insisted on watching.
   a. Maudlin
   b. Requisite
   c. Valorous
   d. Moribund
   e. Nefarious
   f. Quixotic

16. During the ancient ceremony of death, the African tribe built several _____, lined up together, in order to burn their fallen warriors after battle.
   a. Pyres
   b. Bonfires
   c. Pariahs
   d. Juntas
   e. Liens
   f. Panoplies

Questions 17–20 are based on the following passage:

An Organization for Economic Cooperation and Development study of ten developing countries during the period from 1985 to 1992 found significant implementation of privatization in only three countries. The study concluded that "reductions in the central budget deficit can only be marginal" because the impact was not evaluated over several years to consider the effect of the revenues foregone from state-owned enterprises (SOEs). Several later studies measured the budgetary effects and reported significant increases in profitability and productivity as a result of privatization, but the methodological flaws related to the difficulty of isolating the performance of SOEs from other elements rendered the findings ambiguous. While the evidence on the performance of SOEs "shows that state ownership is often correlated with politicization, inefficiency, and waste of resources," the assumption that it is state ownership that creates an environment influencing the quality of performance is not proven, with the empirical research on this point having yielded conflicting results. Given the inconclusive evidence, many scholars did not concur on a World Bank statement in 1995 that SOEs "remain an important obstacle to better economic performance."

Reflecting a belief that the market is the best allocator of resources, experts have often recommended "unleashing" the private sector by removing regulations and privatizing SOEs. In 1995, to preclude hasty and simplistic privatization efforts, the World Bank recommended that SOEs be corporatized under commercial law and issued guidance on "[p]re-privatization interim measures and institutional arrangements for 'permanent SOEs.'" The bank also listed five preconditions for successful privatization: hard budget constraints; capital and labor market discipline; competition; corporate governance free of political interference; and commitment to privatization.

In view of the pervasive presence of SOEs in the global economy and their embodiment of political and economic considerations, SOEs are an entity to be considered and managed in the pursuit of stability.

"The State-Owned Enterprise as a Vehicle for Stability" by Neil Efird (2010), published by the Strategic Studies Institute (Department of Defense), pgs. 7–8

Consider each of the choices separately and select all that apply:

17. The World Bank issued which statement(s) in 1995?
    a. State-owned enterprises can impede economic performance.
    b. State-owned enterprises play a critical role in developing countries.
    c. State-owned enterprises promote economic and political stability.
    d. State-owned enterprises should be corporatized under commercial law gradually.
    e. State-owned enterprises might be inefficient, but the evidence is inconclusive.

Select only one answer choice:

18. Based on the passage above, which statement(s) can be properly inferred?
    a. State-owned enterprises always cause economic stagnation.
    b. Privatization is controversial, even among economic experts.
    c. Economic studies are always subject to intense criticism and secondhand guessing.
    d. State-owned enterprises violate commercial law.
    e. The World Bank holds the power to directly intervene in economies.

Consider each of the choices separately and select all that apply:

19. Which statement(s) about state-owned enterprises is true based on the passage above?
    a. The empirical research demonstrates that state-owned enterprises are efficient and productive.
    b. Developing countries have little influence on the World Bank's policies.
    c. Privatization enjoys widespread popular support wherever it is implemented.
    d. State-owned enterprises have sizable effects on the global economy.
    e. Among other factors, successful privatization requires competition and corporate governance that is free of political interference.

Select only one answer choice:

20. Which statement(s) most accurately identifies the author's ultimate conclusion?
    a. The market is the best allocator of resources, so private enterprises will always outperform state-owned enterprises.
    b. The World Bank holds considerable expertise in matters related to state-owned enterprises and privatization.
    c. State-owned enterprises should be managed in a way that promotes economic stability, which might require a measured approach to privatization.
    d. Studies conducted with a flawed methodology should not be the basis for economic decisions.
    e. State-owned enterprises should be privatized under commercial law as long as the government adheres to the five preconditions for privatization.

Section 5: Quantitative Reasoning

For questions 1-8, compare Quantity A to Quantity B, using additional information presented above the two quantities.

1. Angie has more cats than Janet.

Quantity A	Quantity B
Angie's number of cats	4 more than Janet's number of cats

    a. Quantity A is greater.
    b. Quantity B is greater.
    c. The two quantities are equal.
    d. The relationship cannot be determined from the information given.

2. Gage is twice as old as Cam.

Quantity A	Quantity B
Cam's age	Half of Gage's age

    a. Quantity A is greater.
    b. Quantity B is greater.
    c. The two quantities are equal.
    d. The relationship cannot be determined from the information given.

3.

Quantity A	Quantity B
$x - 2$	$x^2 + 5$

    a. Quantity A is greater.
    b. Quantity B is greater.
    c. The two quantities are equal.
    d. The relationship cannot be determined from the information given.

4. $y = x^2 - 4x + 5$

Quantity A	Quantity B
x	y

    a. Quantity A is greater.
    b. Quantity B is greater.
    c. The two quantities are equal.
    d. The relationship cannot be determined from the information given.

5. $a < 0$

Quantity A	Quantity B
a^3	$a^4 - a$

    a. Quantity A is greater.
    b. Quantity B is greater.
    c. The two quantities are equal.
    d. The relationship cannot be determined from the information given.

6.

Quantity A	Quantity B
Largest prime number less than 35	Smallest prime number greater than 25

    a. Quantity A is greater.
    b. Quantity B is greater.
    c. The two quantities are equal.
    d. The relationship cannot be determined from the information given.

7.

Quantity A	Quantity B
$\dfrac{xy^{-2}}{z^{-3}}$	$\dfrac{xz^3}{y^2}$

  a. Quantity A is greater.
  b. Quantity B is greater.
  c. The two quantities are equal.
  d. The relationship cannot be determined from the information given.

8.

Quantity A	Quantity B
$3^2 + 3^2 + 3^2$ $9 + 9 + 9$	3^6

  a. Quantity A is greater.
  b. Quantity B is greater.
  c. The two quantities are equal.
  d. The relationship cannot be determined from the information given.

$3 \times 3 \times 3 \times 3 \times 3 \times 3$
$9 \times 3 = 21$
$\times \ 3$
63
3
189

9. The expression $\dfrac{x-4}{x^2-6x+8}$ is undefined for what value(s) of x? Select all that apply.
  a. 4
  b. 2
  c. 0
  d. -2
  d. -4

10. Nina has a jar where she puts her loose change at the end of each day. There are 13 quarters, 25 dimes, 18 nickels, and 30 pennies in the jar. If she chooses a coin at random, what is the probability that the coin will not be a penny or a dime?
  a. 0.36
  b. 0.64
  c. 0.56
  d. 0.34
  e. 0.43

11. The Cross family is planning a trip to Florida. They will be taking two cars for the trip. One car gets 18 miles to the gallon of gas. The other car gets 25 miles to the gallon. If the total trip to Florida is 450 miles, and the cost of gas is $2.49/gallon, how much will the gas cost for both cars to complete the trip?
  a. $43.00
  b. $44.82
  c. $107.07
  d. $32.33
  e. $52.12

12. A store is having a sale on jackets and boots. The jackets are on sale for $47 each, and the boots are on sale for $38 each. How much would it cost to buy 2 jackets and 3 pairs of boots?

$ _____

13. If $3x - 4 + 5x = 8 - 10x$, what is the value of x?
   a. 6
   b. -6
   c. 0.5
   d. 1.33
   e. 0.67

14. The soccer team is selling donuts to raise money to buy new uniforms. For every box of donuts they sell, the team receives $3 towards their new uniforms. There are 15 people on the team. How many boxes does each player need to sell in order to raise $270 for their new uniforms?

   _____ Boxes

15. When added to -7, which of the following numbers is the farthest from 5 on the number line?
   a. 6
   b. 24
   c. -6
   d. 1
   e. 10

16. Given the triangle below, find the value of x if $y = 21$.

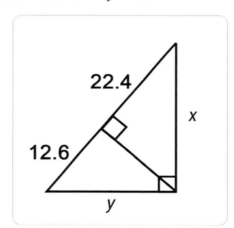

   a. 35
   b. 28
   c. 25
   d. 21
   e. 26

17. Which of the following lie between 1 and 3 on the number line? (Indicate all such numbers.)

   a. $\sqrt{5}$

   b. $4^{\frac{1}{2}}$

   c. $|-2.35|$

   d. 3^{-1}

   e. $\left(\frac{5}{2}\right)^2$

18. The ratio of boys to girls in Mrs. Lair's kindergarten class is 3 to 2. If there are 30 kids in the class, how many of them are boys?

   ☐ Boys

19. If h is a multiple of 5, which of the following must also be multiples of 5? (Indicate all such expressions.)

   a. $5h - 3$

   b. h^2

   c. $10h + 20$

   d. $h^3 + 6$

   e. $4h + 1$

20. Given $x > 0$ and $y < 0$, which expressions must always be true?

   a. $xy < 0$

   b. $x + y > 0$

   c. $y - x < 0$

   d. $2x + y^2 > 0$

   e. $\sqrt{x} \div y > 0$

Answer Explanations #1

Section 2: Verbal Reasoning

1. B, D: Introverted individuals are quieter than the more outspoken extroverts in a group. Knowing the characteristics of an introvert will help one select the correct answers. Both *verbose* and *loquacious* have to do with excessive speech, so *taciturn* is the answer for the first blank. *Grandiose* is the correct choice for the second blank, as an introvert probably does not like large, over-the-top events.

2. B: The key word in the sentence to signal an appropriate answer is "prevented." Therefore, the best answer cannot be *clear*, *sheer*, or *luminous*. The word *scaly* refers to the texture of the skin.

3. A, D: Readers should notice that the "praiseworthy speech" the members were giving sets the tone for their actions before and after. This will help one discern that a positive word, such as *lauded*, is necessary for the second blank. Therefore, the word *garrulous*, which means "excessive talking," would work for the intended meaning of the sentence with more clarity than either *reserved* or *inhibited*.

4. D: Many of the choices work grammatically with this sentence; however, the best option is the opposite of "solid" because that is the result that was unexpected in the scientist's mind. Therefore, the best possible answer based on the intended meaning of the sentence is *liquefy*.

5. C, D: Because the writer used *sailors*, the first blank must connect with a maritime adventure. Therefore, *leviathan* is the best choice for the first blank. A word that contrasts with an adventure is the word *pedestrian*, which signifies a more commonplace event.

6. B: In this case, the detectives are guessing or inferring that the original evidence was incorrect. *Deny* would not be the best answer because the defense attorney would not be happy if his client was found guilty. *Occlude* means to obstruct, which does not make sense in the sentence; *prevaricate* means to act evasively, which is another logical problem when placed in the blank, as the detectives wouldn't "act evasively that the prisoner on death row was actually innocent." Although the defense attorney expresses delight, the option *celebrate* contradicts the mood of the passage.

7. C: Because the details in Choice *A* and Choice *B* are examples of how an emotionally intelligent leader operates, they are not the best choice for the definition of the term *emotional intelligence*. They are qualities observed in an EI leader. Choice *C* is true as noted in the second sentence of the passage: Emotional Intelligence (EI) includes developing the ability to know one's own emotions, to regulate impulses and emotions, and to use interpersonal communication skills with ease while dealing with other people. It makes sense that someone with well-developed emotional intelligence will have a good handle on understanding their emotions, be able to regulate impulses and emotions, and use interpersonal communication skills. Choice *D* is not a definition of EI. Choice *E* is the opposite of the definition of EI, so both Choice *D* and Choice *E* are incorrect.

8. C: Choice *E* can be eliminated immediately because of the signal word "obviously." Choice *A* can be eliminated because it does not reflect an accurate fact. Choices *B* and *D* do not support claims about how to be a successful leader.

9. E: The qualities of an unsuccessful leader possessing a transactional leadership style are listed in the passage. Choices *A* and *B* are incorrect because these options reflect the qualities of a successful leader.

Choices *C* and *D* are definitely not characteristics of a successful leader; however, they are not presented in the passage and readers should do their best to ignore such options.

10. D: Even though some choices may be true of successful leaders, the best answer must be supported by sub-points in the passage. Therefore, Choices *A* and *C* are incorrect. Choice *B* is incorrect because uncompromising transactional leadership styles squelch success. Choice *E* is never mentioned in the passage.

11. A, C, E: After a careful reading of the passage about emotional intelligence, readers can select supporting points for the statements that are true in the selection. For example, the statement that supports Choice *A* says, "Becoming a successful leader in today's industry, government, and nonprofit sectors requires more than a high intelligence quotient (IQ)." Likewise, a supporting passage for Choice *C* is: "Building relationships outside the institution with leadership coaches and with professional development trainers can also help leaders who want to grow their leadership success." To support Choice *E*, the idea that a leader can develop emotional intelligence if desired, the passage says, "There are ways to develop emotional intelligence for the person who wants to improve their leadership style." Choices *B* and *D* do not have supporting evidence in the passage to make them true.

12. D, F: Even if readers don't know what *cacophony* means, they can tell that four of the words are closely related. Readers should try to eliminate what they know in order to focus on the remaining words. If two notes are not in perfect accord with each other, they are demonstrating *dissonance*. The words *accord*, *harmony*, *concordance*, and *composition* have a relationship with each other; therefore, the two words that mean the same and maintain the meaning of the sentence are *cacophony* and *dissonance*.

13. B, E: Knowing that a thief is part of the equation suggests that he would leave the scene of the crime; therefore, *absconded* and *bolted*, which mean "leave in a hurry," most accurately complete the meaning of the sentence. Readers may be able to find two other synonyms, however, that do not suggest leaving the scene of the crime.

14. C, D: Several of the choices fit nicely in the sentence; but, readers should complete the sentence with two synonyms that best fit the meaning the writer intended. *Astute* means "intelligent"; *apt* is close, but it means "relevant," which is not a synonym of intelligent. *Mediocre* and *middling* seem to mean the same thing, but they don't work with an immature writing style. Therefore, *banal* and *trite* are the best choices for this sentence.

15. B, D: If readers understand that "dubious" implies a challenge that the politicians would like to avoid, they will see that *obscuring* and *obfuscating* work the best to maintain the idea of the sentence. *Pontificating* suggests preaching. *Discussing* and *confabulating* could be synonyms; however, they do not fit with the negative word *dubious*. *Explicating* suggests a levelheaded explanation.

16. B: Readers should carefully focus their attention on the beginning of the passage to answer this series of questions. Even though the sentences may be worded a bit differently, all but one statement is true. It presents a false idea that descriptive details are not necessary until the climax of the story. Even if one does not read the passage, he or she probably knows that all good writing begins with descriptive details to develop the main theme the writer intends for the narrative.

17. C: This choice allows room for the fact that not all people who attempt to write a play will find it easy. If the writer follows the basic principles of narrative writing described in the passage, however, writing a play does not have to be an excruciating experience. None of the other options can be supported by points from the passage.

18. A, C: Choice *A* is true based on the sentence that reads, "Next, use dialogue to reveal the attitudes and personalities of each of the characters who have a key part in the unfolding story." Choice *C* is true based on the information that claims an image is like using a thousand words. Choice *B* is false because drama does not necessarily need to be predictable. Choice *D* contradicts the point that the protagonist should experience self-discovery. Finally, Choice *E* is incorrect because all drama suggests some challenge for the characters to experience.

19. B: To suggest that a ten-minute play is accessible does not imply any timeline, nor does the passage mention how long a playwright spends with revisions and rewrites. So, Choice *A* is incorrect. Choice *B* is correct because of the opening statement that reads, "Learning how to write a ten-minute play may seem like a monumental task at first; but, if you follow a simple creative writing strategy, similar to writing a narrative story, you will be able to write a successful drama." None of the remaining choices are supported by points in the passage.

20. E: Note that the only element not mentioned in the passage is the style feature that is part of a narrative writer's tool kit. It is not to say that ten-minute plays do not have style. The correct answer denotes only that the element of style was not illustrated in this particular passage.

Section 3: Quantitative Reasoning

1. A: The value of g can be found using the formula for area of a rectangle ($A = l \times w$). So, $56 = g \times 4$, and $g = 14$. This means that Quantity A is greater than Quantity B.

2. B: The first step is to solve for x. For this equation, that is:

$$4x - 12 = -2x$$

$$6x - 12 = 0$$

$$6x = 12$$

$$x = 2$$

Since the value of x is 2 and Quantity B is 3, it means that Quantity B is greater.

3. A: The first step here is to solve each of the ratios. The first ratio is all of Jimmy's marbles divided by all of Steve's marbles. This gives $\frac{15}{10} = \frac{3}{2}$. The second ratio is all of Jimmy's blue marbles divided by all of Steve's green marbles. This gives $\frac{8}{6} = \frac{4}{3}$. Since $\frac{3}{2}$ is greater than $\frac{4}{3}$, Quantity A is greater.

4. B: First, find the area of both figures in terms of x. The area of the triangle is $\frac{1}{2}(7) \times x = 3.5x$ square inches. The area of the rectangle is $13 \times x = 13x$ square inches. So, 7 times the area of the triangle would be $24.5x$ square inches, and 2 times the area of the rectangle would be $26x$ square inches. This means that Quantity B is greater.

5. A: First, convert the distance that truck *A* drove to feet. This is $1,236 \times 3 = 3,708$ feet. This means that truck *A* drove further than truck *B*. So, Quantity A is greater than Quantity B.

6. D: There is not enough information to determine which quantity is greater. Either quantity could be greater for given values of x and z. For example, if $x = 7$ and $z = 1$, then Quantity A is 8 and Quantity B is 1. If $x = 10$ and $z = -8$, then Quantity A is 2 and Quantity B is 4.

7. C: The probability of choosing a rough rock is $\frac{4}{16}$. This is equal to $\frac{2}{8}$, so both Quantity A and Quantity B are equal.

8. D: If Jim is 2 years old, then Bill is 6 years old. Twice Jim's age is 4, so Quantity B is greater. However, if Jim is 20 years old, then Bill is 24. Twice Jim's age is 40, so Quantity A is greater. Thus, the relationship cannot be determined from the given information.

9. E: First, find the area of the second house. The area is:

$$A = l \times w = 33 \times 50 = 1{,}650 \text{ square feet}$$

Then, use the area formula to determine what length gives the first house an area of 1,650 square feet.

$$1{,}650 = 22 \times l$$

$$l = \frac{1{,}650}{22} = 75 \text{ feet}$$

Then, use the formula for perimeter to get:

$$75 + 75 + 22 + 22 = 194 \text{ feet}$$

10. D: To calculate the circumference of a circle, use the formula $2\pi r$, where r equals the radius, or half of the diameter, of the circle and $\pi = 3.14$. Substitute the given information, $2\pi 5 = 31.4$, which is Choice D.

11. B: This can be determined by finding the length and width of the shaded region. The length can be found using the length of the top rectangle which is 18 inches, then subtracting the extra length of 4 inches and 1 inch. This means the length of the shaded region is 13 inches. Next, the width can be determined using the 6-inch measurement and subtracting the 2-inch measurement. This means that the width is 4 inches. Thus, the area is $13 \times 4 = 52$ sq. inches.

12. 4: Dividing by 98 can be approximated by dividing by 100, which would mean shifting the decimal point of the numerator to the left by 2. The result is 4.2, which rounds to 4.

13. A: First solve for x, y, and z. So, $3x = 24$, $x = 8$, $6y = 24$, $y = 4$, and $-2z = 24$, $z = -12$. This means the equation would be $4(8)(4) + (-12)$, which equals 116.

14. $\frac{119}{990}$: The probability of choosing two customers simultaneously is the same as choosing one and then choosing a second without putting the first back into the pool of customers. This means that the probability of choosing a customer who bought cherry is $\frac{35}{100}$. Then without placing them back in the pool, it would be $\frac{34}{99}$. So, the probability of choosing 2 customers simultaneously that both bought cherry would be:

$$\frac{35}{100} \times \frac{34}{99} = \frac{1{,}190}{9{,}900} = \frac{119}{990}$$

15. D: If $n = 2^2, n = 4$, and $m = 4^2 = 16$. This means that $m^n = 16^4$. This is the same as 2^{16}.

16. D: Each of the choices given is a linear function in the form of $y = mx + b$, where m is the slope, and b is the y-intercept. For the first function $g(x) = x - 4$, the slope is 1, and the y-intercept is -4. Placing this line on the graph would show that it does not intersect the absolute value function above. It crosses the y-axis at -4 with a slope equal to the right side of the absolute value graph, so the functions run parallel to one another. The second function will intersect the graph at 1 point because the y-intercept is 0.

The line will run parallel to the left side of the absolute value function, with a slope of -1. For the third function, the slope is 1, and the y-intercept is 2. It will cross the absolute value graph at 1 point because it runs parallel to the right side of the graph and runs through the y-axis at 2. The fourth function has a slope of ½ and a y-intercept of 0. This line will intersect the absolute value graph at exactly 2 points. One point is at (2, 1), and the other point will be between x-values of -4 and -5. This line is shown on the graph below.

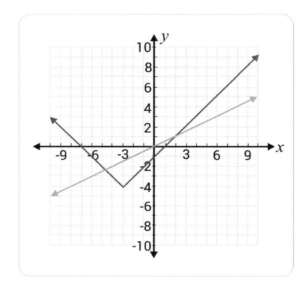

17. C: A full rotation is 360 degrees. Taking the total degrees that the figure skater spins and dividing by 360 yields 6.25. She spins 6 total times and then one quarter of a turn more. This quarter of a turn to her right means she ends up facing East.

18. $1\frac{2}{9}$: Simplify each mixed number of the problem into a fraction by multiplying the denominator by the whole number and adding the numerator:

$$\frac{14}{3} - \frac{31}{9}$$

Since the first denominator is a multiple of the second, simplify it further by multiplying both the numerator and denominator of the first expression by 3 so that the denominators of the fractions are equal.

$$\frac{42}{9} - \frac{31}{9} = \frac{11}{9}$$

Simplifying this further, divide the numerator 11 by the denominator 9; this leaves 1 with a remainder of 2. To write this as a mixed number, place the remainder over the denominator, resulting in $1\frac{2}{9}$.

19. E: The new price of the purse can be found by first multiplying the original price by 25%, or 0.25. This yields an increase of $32. Taking the original price of $128 and adding the increase in price of $32 yields a new price of $160.

20. C: The sum of all angles in a polygon with n sides is found by the expression $(n-2) \times 180$. Since this polygon has 5 sides, then the total degrees of the interior angles can be found using the equation $(5-2) \times 180 = 540$. The angles in the given pentagon can be set equal to the sum of the interior angles:

$$111° + 113° + 92° + (P + 32°) + P = 540°$$

Adding up each of the given angles yields a total of $111 + 113 + 92 + 32 = 348$ degrees. Taking the total of 540 degrees and subtracting the given sum of 348 degrees gives a missing value of 192 degrees for $2P$:

$$2P = 540° - (111° + 113° + 92° + 32°) = 192°$$

Dividing both sides by 2 gives the value of angle P:

$$P = \frac{192°}{2} = 96°$$

Therefore, the measure of angle P is 96 degrees, Choice C.

Section 4: Verbal Reasoning

1. A, D: If one is filling in the blanks individually, he or she may think of the term *aesthetic* because it captures the theme of the sentence. Similarly, the term *classical* is often used with master artists. In addition, the word *landscapes* helps to eliminate *spiritual* and *abstract* because they do not complete the idea of landscapes as well as the term *classical* does in this sentence.

2. A: There are several clues within the sentence to help readers select the choice with the best meaning that completes the sentence. For example, the word *humiliated* suggests that the conquerors were not only winning against the tribe, but that they also degraded them in the process. A *boon* is something that is good or an advantage for the recipient. Because an act of humiliation is not connected with the words *retrieval* or *convalescence*, the best choice is *depredation*.

3. A, D: The words *ability* and *cultivate* denote a certain confidence and forward-looking demeanor; thus, not being *inhibited* by a challenge makes the most sense. Challenges don't *placate* people; they often create anxiety. That Pharaoh Ahmose "oversaw" so much of the work also lets the reader know he was active and focused, so *ingenious* is the most logical choice. To be so involved would not make his ideas insular. *Indigenous* is more about staying with traditions or origins.

4. B: The representatives hoped that the principles the interns learned took hold or *ossified* over the summer break. The representatives wouldn't hope for the interns' principles to *soften, dissipate,* or *disintegrate*. The word *multiply* contradicts the logistics of the sentence, as pre-existing principles are incapable of *multiplying*.

5. A, D, H: The adverse words *irascible* and *malevolent* fit the first and last blanks best because the context implies an anxious, fearful atmosphere. The word *precipice* would fit best in the middle of the sentence because *buttresses* and *encomiums* don't have "edges" for coyotes to walk around on.

6. A: There is a clue to the answer of this question in the word "satisfaction." The root is similar to the choice, *sated*, which means "full to the brim." Some of the other choices are grammatically correct; however, they are not the best option to complete the meaning of the sentence.

7. A, E: If the water quality is "unpredictable," then it is *erratic*. *Invariable* and *consistent* mean "never changing," which is the opposite of "unpredictable." If the watershed can be used for tourists and residents as a recreational substitute, then the community members' concerns were alleviated, or *assuaged*.

8. C, E: Choice *A* is incorrect because the seaport is noted as "thriving"; also, the slave trading companies were noted as being "lucrative." Choice *B* is incorrect because the slave traders actually built both office structures and slave holding buildings in downtown Alexandria; there is no mention of renting, or of landlords. Choice *D* is incorrect because the Bruin Slave Jail is not open to the public. Choice *C* is correct because Joseph Bruin bought hundreds of slaves during the years 1844 to 1861. Choice *E* is correct because the passage notes that the offices and slave holding units were open until the end of the Civil War.

9. A: Choices *B*, *C*, *D*, and *E* can all be regarded as false based on the information provided in the passage. Choice *A* contains information provided in the passage; therefore, the statement is true. Choice *B* is false because the passage infers that Joseph Bruin was notorious as a slave trader; in fact, two sisters tried to run away from Joseph Bruin. Choice *C* is false because the slave pen was not four stories high; the passage specifically noted that the slave pen was two stories high. Choice *D* is false because the passage does not refer to Union or Confederate soldiers, and the Bruin Slave Jail was what became the Fairfax County courthouse. Choice *E* is false because there is no information in the passage that indicates that literature, like *Uncle Tom's Cabin*, was preserved by the Northern Virginia Urban League.

10. C, D: Choice *A* is false, based on the passage statement that Alexandria was founded in 1749. Choice *B* is false because the passage does not suggest that Harriet Beecher Stowe was a slave; rather, the passage states that Stowe was the author of *Uncle Tom's Cabin*. Choice *C* is true; the passage claims that northern abolitionists tried to save two Christian slave sisters from a fate of prostitution. Choice *D* is true based on the information found in the passage. Choice *E* is false; the town of Annapolis is not cited in the passage.

11. C: The purpose of the passage is to shed light on the history of Joseph Bruin's Slave Jail and what became of it. Choice *A* is incorrect because while the two sisters are mentioned in the story to provide details, they are not the main purpose of the story. Choice *B* is incorrect because while the beginning of the story contains the information about the town and its slave business, this answer option leaves out the fact that the passage is focused on one slave jail in particular and omits anything about the conclusion of the passage, which is actually key in the main focus of the passage—how Joseph Bruin's Slave Jail came about and what became of it. Choice *D* is incorrect because the point of the passage is not about where the historical Bruin Slave Jail currently stands but the history behind it.

12. B, D: The key word to understand how to fill in the blank in this sentence is "pleasure." Several of the choices take away the meaning when inserted. Therefore, the best phrases needed to complete the idea that modeling is pleasurable but requires sacrifices are *accede to* and *acquiesce to*.

13. B, C: Because the students were unprepared, two words that imply a negative emotion would be appropriate to complete the sentence. *Feint* suggests a sham or pretense, *diatribe* is a tirade, and *enmity* and *exuberance* do not complete the meaning of the sentence.

14. A, D: In order for the debate team to win, their opponents must not be as intelligent or quick-witted as their own team members. So *vacuous* and *fatuous* are the synonyms that work best. *Fatuous* means "dense" or "dim-witted," while *vacuous* means "lacking intelligence."

15. A, F: Without the word "holiday," several of the choices might work to complete the meaning of the sentence. However, the best two synonyms that mean "overly emotional" or "sentimental" are *maudlin* and *quixotic*. If readers are not sure which words to pick, they can use the process of elimination. A *nefarious* or *moribund* movie would not be uplifting. Even though a *valorous* movie could be a holiday movie theme, it does not have a matching synonym as a choice.

16. A, B: Readers may have to draw on their understanding of the Greek word "pur," which means "fire," to come up with the best choices for this sentence equivalence. *Bonfires* as a synonym choice then makes sense.

17. A, D: The passage references statements made by the World Bank in 1995 at the end of the first paragraph and in the middle of the second. The first reference says that state-owned enterprises "remain an important obstacle to better economic performance," and the second reference says the "World Bank recommended that SOEs be corporatized under commercial law and issued guidance." Thus, Choices A and D are the correct answers. Although the World Bank is probably discussing developing countries, they are not mentioned in the statements quoted in the passage, so Choice B is incorrect. Choice C is contradicted by the rest of the passage and never mentioned in connection with statements issued by the World Bank. While the passage discusses studies similar to what's described in Choice E, they are not included in the World Bank's statements.

18. B: The passage repeatedly mentions disputes over privatization, including inconclusive studies, scholars refuting the World Bank's statements about state-owned enterprises, and differences between free market advocates who want to "unleash" the private sector and the World Bank's more gradual approach. Thus, Choice B is the correct answer. Choice A is incorrect because "always" is too strong. The studies are inconclusive and have yielded conflicting results. Choice C is incorrect for similar reasons. Although the studies in this passage are criticized, it's too much to say economic studies in general are always subject to such criticism. The World Bank recommends that state-owned enterprises be privatized in accordance with commercial law, but that doesn't necessarily mean those enterprises violate commercial law, so Choice D is incorrect. Nowhere in the passage does it say the World Bank holds the power to intervene in economies; its statements are referred to as recommendations. Thus, Choice E is incorrect.

19. D, E: The passage states that state-owned enterprises have a "pervasive presence" in the global economy, and the World Bank includes competition and corporate governance free of political interference in its five preconditions for successful privatization. Therefore, Choices D and E are the correct answers. The empirical research is inconclusive but, if anything, it leans toward the opposite of what's described in Choice A. Influences on the World Bank's policies and popular support are never mentioned in the passage; therefore, Choices B and C are incorrect.

20. C: The author's conclusion is that "SOEs are an entity to be considered and managed in the pursuit of stability." As such, it can be inferred that the author supports the World Bank's measured approach of implementing privatization gradually to avoid the type of hasty action advocated by free market enthusiasts. Thus, Choice C is the correct answer. The author believes the market is the best allocator of resources, but it's unclear whether the author thinks private enterprises will always outperform state-owned enterprises, so this can't be the conclusion. Thus, Choice A is incorrect. The author would agree with Choices B, D, and E; however, all three are incorrect because they don't reflect the author's emphasis on stability.

Section 5: Quantitative Reasoning

1. D: If Angie has 5 cats, then Janet may have 4 cats. Four more than Janet is 8 cats, so Quantity B would be greater. If Angie has 10 cats and Janet has 2 cats, then four more cats than Janet is 6, and Quantity A is greater. Thus, there is not enough information to determine which quantity is greater.

2. C: If Cam is 10 years old, then Gage is 20 years old. Cam's age is 10, and half of Gage's age is 10, so the quantities are equal. If Gage is 50 years old, then Cam is 25. Cam's age is 25, and half of Gage's age is 25, so the quantities are equal. No matter what Cam's age is, it will always be equal to half of Gage's age. The correct answer is Choice C, the two quantities are equal.

3. B: The first step is to set up the comparison:

$$x - 2 \qquad ? \qquad x^2 + 5$$

The first thing to notice is that the first expression has a single x-value, and the second expression has a squared x-value. In the second expression, no matter what the value of x is, it becomes greater than or equal to 0 when squared. From there, the number is increased by 5. In the first expression, the value of x is only decreased by 2. Regardless of the value of x, the second expression increases it by at least 5, and the first expression decreases it by 2. Therefore, Quantity B is greater. The correct answer is B because no matter what value is chosen for x, Quantity B will always be greater.

4. D: When the value of x is 2, then the y-value can be found by substituting 2 for x. The equation becomes $y = 2^2 - 4(2) + 5$, where $y = 1$. In this case, the x-value of 2 is greater than y. The answer would be A because Quantity A is greater. However, if the value of x is 4, then the equation becomes:

$$y = 4^2 - 4(4) + 5$$

The value of y works out to be 5. In this case, the answer would be B, because the value of y is greater than x. Quantity B would be greater. Since there are two situations that have opposite answers, the relationship cannot be determined. More information is needed to determine which quantity is greater. The correct answer is D because the relationship cannot be determined from the information given.

5. B: Quantity A will always yield a negative answer because the exponent is odd, and the base is always less than 0, or negative. Anytime the exponent is odd and the base number is negative, then the answer will be negative. As for Quantity B, the base number is negative, but the exponent is even. Since this exponent is even, then the first part of the expression yields a positive number. Then the second part of the expression is the subtraction of a negative number. This operation will yield the addition of the number every time. No matter what negative number is substituted into the a-value, Quantity B will be greater. The correct answer is B because Quantity B will always be greater than Quantity A, no matter what negative value is given for Quantity A.

6. A: A prime number is a number that only has factors of 1 and itself. Quantity A is the largest prime number less than 35. 34 is even, or divisible by 2, so it is not prime. The number 33 is divisible by 3 and

11, and the number 32 is even, so neither of those is prime. The number 31 has factors of only 1 and itself, so it is the largest prime number less than 35. Quantity B is the smallest prime number greater than 25. The next number is 26, which is even. The number 27 has factors of 3 and 9, while the number 28 is even. The number 29 has factors of only 1 and itself; therefore, it is the smallest prime number greater than 25. Comparing these two numbers, 31 and 29, Quantity A is greater. The correct answer is A because Quantity A is greater.

7. C: The first step in comparing these two quantities is to simplify Quantity A. The negative in the exponent of y moves the y squared to the denominator, making the expression $\frac{x}{z^{-3}y^2}$. The negative in the exponent of z moves the variables to the top. Taking the reciprocal of the variable raised to a negative exponent makes the exponent positive. The new, simplified expression for Quantity A is $\frac{xz^3}{y^2}$. Once the expression is simplified to eliminate the negative exponents, both values are equal. Since both expressions can be written as x times z cubed divided by y squared, making Quantity A and Quantity B equal, the correct answer is C.

8. B: To compare these quantities, Quantity A can be rewritten. Three squared is added to itself three times. Since the definition of multiplication is repeated addition, then multiplication can be used to rewrite the expression as 3×3^2. Expanding these threes yields the expression $3 \times 3 \times 3$. Using exponents, the value can be turned into 3^3. Now that both Quantity A and Quantity B are written as exponents of 3, the values can be compared. The correct answer is B because Quantity B's value of 3^6 is greater than Quantity A's value of 3^3.

9. A and B: The expression in the denominator can be factored into the two binomials $(x-4)(x-2)$. Once the expression is rewritten as $\frac{x-4}{(x-4)(x-2)}$, the values of $x=4$ and $x=2$ result in a denominator with a value of 0. Since 0 cannot be in the denominator of a fraction, the expression is undefined at the values of $x=2, 4$.

10. A: The total number of coins in the jar is 86, which is the sum of all the coins. The probability of Nina choosing a coin other than a penny or a dime can be found by calculating the total of quarters and nickels. This total is 31. Taking 31 and dividing it by 86 gives the probability of choosing a coin that is not a penny or a dime. The decimal found from the fraction $\frac{31}{86}$ is 0.36.

11. C: For the first car, the trip will be 450 miles at 18 miles to the gallon. The total gallons needed for this car will be $450 \div 18 = 25$. For the second car, the trip will be 450 miles at 25 miles to the gallon, or $450 \div 25 = 18$, which will require 18 gallons of gas. Adding these two amounts of gas gives a total of 43 gallons of gas. If the gas costs $2.49 per gallon, the cost of the trip for both cars is $43 \times 2.49 = 107.07$ dollars.

12. 208: To find the cost of the jackets, 47 can be multiplied by 2. This yields a cost of $94. To find the cost of the boots, 38 can be multiplied by 3. This yields a cost of $114. Adding these two values gives a total cost of $208. This number can be typed directly into the box without the dollar sign, since the dollar sign is already given at the front of the box.

13. E: The first step in solving this equation is to collect like terms on the left side of the equation. This yields the new equation $-4 + 8x = 8 - 10x$. The next step is to move the x-terms to one side by adding 10 to both sides, making the equation $-4 + 18x = 8$. Then the -4 can be moved to the right side of the equation to form $18x = 12$. Dividing both sides of the equation by 18 gives a value of 0.67, or $\frac{2}{3}$.

14. 6: The team needs a total of $270, and each box earns them $3. Therefore, the total number of boxes needed to be sold is $270 \div 3$, which is 90. With 15 people on the team, the total of 90 can be divided by 15, which equals 6. This means that each member of the team needs to sell 6 boxes for the team to raise enough money to buy new uniforms. The answer entered in the box should be 6, because the label "boxes" is already placed outside the answer box.

15. C: The problem asks for the distance of the given numbers from 5, if the numbers are added to -7. Subtracting 7 from each of the choices gives -1, 17, -13, -6, and 3. The number line below can be labeled with all 5 numbers.

The number 5 is shown with the open dot. By observing the placement of the dots and their relation to the open dot at 5, the inner numbers can be eliminated because they are closer—one of the outermost numbers must be the answer. The distance to the outer dots can then be counted. The distance is shown below with the arcs.

As demonstrated from the arcs showing distance on the number line, the number -13 is furthest from 5 on the number line at a distance of 18.

The problem can also be solved numerically by using absolute value. The distance between any two numbers is equal to the absolute value of the difference between them, such that $|a - b|$ yields the absolute difference between the numbers a and b.

16. B: This triangle can be labeled as a right triangle because it has a right-angle measure in the corner. The Pythagorean Theorem can be used here to find the missing side lengths. The Pythagorean Theorem states that $a^2 + b^2 = c^2$, where a and b are side lengths and c is the hypotenuse. The hypotenuse, c, is equal to 35, and 1 side, a, is equal to 21. Plugging these values into the equation forms $21^2 + b^2 = 35^2$. Squaring both given numbers and subtracting them yields the equation $b^2 = 784$. Taking the square root of 784 gives a value of 28 for b. In the equation, b is the same as the missing side length x.

17. A, B, and C: For the value of A, the square root of 5 lies between the square roots of 4 and 9. Since $\sqrt{4} = 2$ and $\sqrt{9} = 3$, then the $\sqrt{5}$ lies somewhere between 2 and 3 on the number line. For the value of B, 4 raised to the ½ power is the same as the square root of 4. The square root of 4 is 2, so it lies between 1 and 3 on the number line. For the value of C, the absolute value of -2.35 is the distance from the number to 0, so it makes the number positive. When it is changed to a positive 2.35, it lies between 1 and 3 on the number line. For the value of D, 3 raised to a power of -1 means to take the reciprocal of 3, which is 1/3. This value does not lie between 1 and 3 on the number line, so it is not selected in the answer. For the value of E, $\left(\frac{5}{2}\right)^2$ is $\frac{5}{2} \times \frac{5}{2} = \frac{25}{4} = 6.25$, so it is also not selected.

18. 18: This situation can be modeled using equivalent ratios. Since the ratio of boys to girls is 3 to 2, then the total for that ratio is 5. The ratio of boys to total kids is 3 to 5. Using these numbers, the following equation can be written:

$$\frac{3}{5} = \frac{x}{30}$$

Since 30 is the given total number of kids in the class, the value of x represents the number of boys. To solve this equation, cross-multiplication can be used. This turns the equation into:

$$3 \times 30 = 5 \times x$$

Next, solve this equation in the following steps:

$$90 = 5x$$

$$18 = x$$

There are 18 boys in the kindergarten class. To check that the ratios are correct, subtraction can be used to find the number of girls in the class: $30 - 18 = 12$. The ratio of boys to girls is 18 to 12, which can be reduced to a ratio of 3 to 2.

19. B and C: The value of $5h - 3$ cannot be a multiple of 5 because of the minus 3 at the end of the expression. Multiplying h by 5 yields a multiple of 5, but subtracting 3 means the final answer will no longer be a multiple of 5. For h^2, the expression is $h \times h$. Since h is a multiple of 5, then multiplying by the same multiple of 5 will yield a result that is divisible by 5. For $10h + 20$, both the number multiplied by h and the number added to h are divisible by 5. The result will always be divisible by 5. For the final expression $h^3 + 6$, the value of h cubed yields an answer divisible by 5, but the addition of 6 means the answer is no longer divisible by 5.

20. A, C, and D: If x is a positive number, and y is a negative number, then their product is always negative. Therefore, the equation in Choice A is always true. For the value of B, if a positive value x is added to a negative value y, then the result may be positive or negative. For example, if $x = 4$ and $y = -6$, then their sum is -2. This proves the expression is not always true. For the value of C, a negative number y subtracting a positive number x will always result in a number less than 0. For the value of D, multiplying a positive number x by positive 2 does not change the sign of the number. Squaring the negative number y will always yield a positive number. Since both terms are positive, then their sum will always be greater than 0. For the value of E, dividing any positive number by a negative number will always yield a negative number, so it is false.

Practice Test #2

Section 1: Analytical Writing

Issue Task:

Teaching children to respect and obey authority could become detrimental to their safety. Even adults who can seemingly be trusted have turned out to be abusive or manipulative.

Explain your position on this statement. In your response, evaluate the positive and negative aspects of teaching children to respect authority figures. Describe how society might look differently if the general expectations on this matter changed.

Argument Task:

The following paragraph appeared in the editorial section of a business magazine concerning on-call hours in retail stores:

On-call hours in retail are when employees are scheduled to be "on-call" and are called into work at the last minute when the company needs them. All retail stores know that providing on-call hours helps the business save money by tailoring product sales to hours worked. Therefore, it is safe to say that implementing on-call hours is better for the business, which in turn is better for the workers.

In your essay response, evaluate the underlying logic of the given argument above. Analyze its use of evidence as well as its assumptions. You might also think about what kind of evidence might weaken or strengthen the argument.

Section 2: Verbal Reasoning

For questions 1-7, select the best word from the corresponding column of choices that most clearly completes the passage:

1. In the fifth century BC, Herodotus shared his interpretations of culture and politics as a great historian and scholar. Even though his stories may have (i) _____ reality, as he added excessive details, he was often referred to as "the father of history."

Blank (i)
a. Propitiated
b. Precipitated
c. Exacerbated
d. Aggrandized
e. Emulated

2. In the (i) _____ field of big data, a recent term used to identify very large collections of data and statistical analysis, many scholarly researchers are contributing significant findings to Fortune 500 research and development programs.

Blank (i)
a. Diminishing
b. Burgeoning
c. Ambiguous
d. Disparaging
e. Floundering

3. The challenge the pollsters found in working with rural community populations was that the poll results were taken from a (i) _____ group. Therefore, the findings were often (ii) _____ because the participants were very similar in nature.

Blank (i)	Blank (ii)
a. Heterogeneous	d. Skewed
b. Disparate	e. Valid
c. Homogeneous	f. Accurate

4. The board members wrote in their public (i) _____ that Mr. Albert Stanley, the chairman of the UERL (Underground Electric Railways Company of London), would always be remembered for his outstanding innovations using public relations to increase the company's profit margins.

Blank (i)
a. Memoirs
b. Panegyric
c. Meditations
d. Reproofs
e. Obloquy

5. Artificial intelligence is on the brink of a major breakthrough in communication. As few as five years ago, artificial intelligence could not (i) _____ process verbal command. Now, artificial intelligence immediately recognizes the (ii) _____ of what someone is saying at a minimum. With time, it's expected that machines will equal and perhaps even (iii) _____ humanity's communication skills.

Blank (i)	Blank (ii)	Blank (iii)
a. Chronologically	d. Aesthetic	g. Aggregate
b. Effectively	e. Coda	h. Mollify
c. Zealously	f. Gist	i. Surpass

149

6. John was running out of time to study before his big test. To maximize his chances of passing, John began exclusively concentrating on the main topics instead of the (i) _____ material.

Blank (i)
a. fatuous
b. specious
c. tangential

7. Grassroots organizers have become increasingly (i) _____ by the electoral process. Despite raising money from more donors and doing exponentially more community outreach every election cycle, they've been repeatedly steamrolled by candidates funded by billionaires. Consequently, some of the organizers have started to consider (ii) _____ support for radical action to circumvent the electoral process.

Blank (i)	Blank (ii)
a. appeased	d. fluctuating
b. oscillated	e. fomenting
c. vexed	f. forestalling

Questions 8–11 are based on the following passage:

Scholars who have examined how national leaders historically craft public speeches in response to accusations of offensive words or deeds conclude that such officials generally rely upon one of two recurrent strategic approaches. The first of these is apologia, which William Benoit and Susan Brinson define as "a recurring type of discourse designed to restore face, image, or reputation after an alleged or suspected wrongdoing," which occurs during many apologies. The second is reconciliation, which John Hatch defines as "a dialogic rhetorical process of healing between the parties."

Speakers using apologia strive to restore their own credibility and remove any perception they might be guilty of involvement in the transgression. Speakers seeking reconciliation are interested in restoring dialogue instead of pursuing the purposes of shifting blame, denying charges, or some other form of blame avoidance or image repair.

Apologia focuses on short-term gains achievable by regaining favor with audiences already predisposed to the speaker's arguments. Reconciliation, by contrast, has a goal of understanding the long-term processes of image restoration and mutual respect between the aggrieved and the transgressor. Attempts at credible reconciliation utilize symbols of reunion to demonstrate that the aggrieved has *genuinely* granted the forgiveness sought by the offender. Visual images freeze the moment of genuine forgiveness and, when replayed in the online environment, carry forward the steps of reunification into perpetuity.

Not all offending images circulating in the online environment warrant a visual response or even an apology by national leaders. Nevertheless, failure to respond to the small number of potent images of transgressions that share characteristics qualifying them for continued recirculation in future propaganda efforts could be a costly mistake. Reconciliation provides a fruitful choice, as its long-term goals match the ongoing need to handle ever-circulating images that offend.

Visual Propaganda and Extremism the Online Environment, edited by Carol K. Winkler and Cori E. Dauber (2014), published by the Strategic Studies Institute (Department of Defense), "Visual Reconciliation as Strategy of Response to Offending Images" by Carol K. Winkler, excerpted from pages 63-64, 71-72, and 74

Consider each of the choices separately and select all that apply:

8. Which statement(s) accurately describes the difference between apologia and reconciliation based on the passage?
   a. Apologia is a dialogic rhetorical process that involves healing, while reconciliation seeks to restore the image of a party suspected of wrongdoing.
   b. Reconciliation utilizes symbols to demonstrate forgiveness, while apologia is always delivered in writing.
   c. Apologia is more effective in the short term, while reconciliation is more useful for improving relationships in the long term.
   d. Reconciliation seeks to open channels of communication, while apologia is more closely related to shifting blame and rehabilitating credibility.
   e. Apologia requires the aggrieved party's forgiveness, while reconciliation is a strategic approach to delivering visual responses.

Select only one answer choice:

9. Based on the passage, which statement(s) can be properly inferred?
   a. National leaders should never apologize because reconciliation is always the superior option.
   b. Reconciliation is more effective than apologia because it is not self-serving.
   c. Apologia and reconciliation are most effective when delivered together.
   d. Apologia and reconciliation only function properly in the online environment.
   e. Maintaining a positive national image is an important part of governance.

Consider each of the choices separately and select all that apply:

10. Which statement(s) describes a feature of reconciliation?
   a. Reconciliation involves restoring dialogue and repairing relationships in the long term.
   b. Reconciliation leverages symbols of reunion to demonstrate that the aggrieved has genuinely granted the forgiveness sought by the offender.
   c. Reconciliation focuses on shifting blame, denying charges, restoring credibility, or otherwise repairing the offender's image.
   d. Reconciliation should be used when the audience is already predisposed to the speaker's argument.
   e. Reconciliation prioritizes short-term gains over substantively altering the underlying relationship.

Select only one answer choice:

11. Which statement(s) describes how the author believes national leaders should respond to offending images circulating in the online environment?
   a. National leaders should censor all offending images and attack any group that disseminates propaganda.
   b. National leaders should conduct an anti-propaganda campaign to raise public awareness about the dangers of sensationalism.
   c. The circulation of offending images in online environments is inevitable but relatively harmless, so this phenomenon should be ignored.
   d. All offending images should be addressed with either apologia or reconciliation, depending on which is more appropriate based on context.
   e. Some offending images do not warrant any response, but for the ones that do, reconciliation is the more appealing option due to its long-term impact.

For questions 12 and 13, select the <u>two</u> answer choices that can complete the sentence and create sentences that have complementary meaning.

12. The technology seminar's keynote speaker started out with simple terms, which grew more and more _____ as he continued the lecture.
   a. Lucid
   b. Esoteric
   c. Abstruse
   d. Acerbic
   e. Caustic
   f. Perspicacious

13. Miles Davis, the famous jazz legend, made a/an _____ impact on the development of jazz music because of his ability to make the sounds mimic the sounds of human voices.
   a. Incorrigible
   b. Viscous
   c. Ineradicable
   d. Sedulous
   e. Palpable
   f. Indelible

Questions 14–20 are based on the following passages.

Passage I

Lethal force, or deadly force, is defined as the physical means to cause death or serious harm to another individual. The law holds that lethal force is only accepted when you or another person are in immediate and unavoidable danger of death or severe bodily harm. For example, a person could be beating a weaker person in such a way that they are suffering severe enough trauma that could result in death or serious harm. This would be an instance where lethal force would be acceptable and possibly the only way to save that person from irrevocable damage.

Another example of when to use lethal force would be when someone enters your home with a deadly weapon. The intruder's presence and possession of the weapon indicate mal-intent and the ability to inflict death or severe injury to you and your loved ones. Again, lethal force can be used in this situation. Lethal force can also be applied to prevent the harm of another individual. If a woman is being brutally assaulted and is unable to fend off an attacker, lethal force can be used to defend her as a last-ditch effort. If she is in immediate jeopardy of rape, harm, and/or death, lethal force could be the only response that could effectively deter the assailant.

The key to understanding the concept of lethal force is the term *last resort*. Deadly force cannot be taken back; it should be used only to prevent severe harm or death. The law does distinguish whether the means of one's self-defense is fully warranted, or if the individual goes out of control in the process. If you continually attack the assailant after they are rendered incapacitated, this would be causing unnecessary harm, and the law can bring charges against you. Likewise, if you kill an attacker unnecessarily after defending yourself, you can be charged with murder. This would move lethal force beyond necessary defense, making it no longer a last resort but rather a use of excessive force.

Passage II

Assault is the unlawful attempt of one person to apply apprehension on another individual by an imminent threat or by initiating offensive contact. Assaults can vary, encompassing physical strikes, threatening body language, and even provocative language. In the case of the latter, even if a hand has not been laid, it is still considered an assault because of its threatening nature.

Let's look at an example: A homeowner is angered because his neighbor blows fallen leaves into his freshly mowed lawn. Irate, the homeowner gestures a fist to his fellow neighbor and threatens to bash his head in for littering on his lawn. The homeowner's physical motions and verbal threat heralds a physical threat against the other neighbor. These factors classify the homeowner's reaction as an assault. If the angry neighbor hits the threatening homeowner in retaliation, that would constitute an assault as well because he physically hit the homeowner.

Assault also centers on the involvement of weapons in a conflict. If someone fires a gun at another person, it could be interpreted as an assault unless the shooter acted in self-defense. If an individual drew a gun or a knife on someone with the intent to harm them, it would be considered assault. However, it's also considered an assault if someone simply aimed a weapon, loaded or not, at another person in a threatening manner.

Select only one answer choice:

14. What is the purpose of the second passage?
    a. To inform the reader about what assault is and how it is committed
    b. To inform the reader about how assault is a minor example of lethal force
    c. To disprove the previous passage concerning lethal force
    d. To argue that the use of assault is more common than the use of lethal force
    e. To recount an incident in which the author was assaulted

Select only one answer choice:

15. Which of the following situations, according to the passages, would not constitute an illegal use of lethal force?

    a. A disgruntled cashier yells obscenities at a customer.

    b. A thief is seen running away with stolen cash.

    c. A man is attacked in an alley by another man with a knife.

    d. A woman punches another woman in a bar.

    e. A driver accidently slams into another person's car and injures them.

Select only one answer choice:

16. Given the information in the passages, which of the following must be true about assault?

    a. All assault is considered an expression of lethal force.

    b. There are various forms of assault.

    c. Smaller, weaker people cannot commit assault.

    d. Assault is justified only as a last resort.

    e. Assault charges are more severe than unnecessary use of force charges.

Select only one answer choice:

17. Which of the following, if true, would most seriously undermine the explanation proposed by the author in the third paragraph of Passage I?

    a. An instance of lethal force in self-defense is not absolutely absolved from blame. The law takes into account the necessary use of force at the time it is committed.

    b. An individual who uses necessary defense under lethal force is in direct compliance of the law under most circumstances.

    c. Lethal force in self-defense should be forgiven in all cases for the peace of mind of the primary victim.

    d. The use of lethal force is not evaluated on the intent of the user but rather the severity of the primary attack that warranted self-defense.

    e. It's important to note that once lethal force goes beyond the necessary attempt to protect oneself, there's a chance it could turn into a deadly assault of excessive force.

Select only one answer choice:

18. Based on the passages, what can we infer about the relationship between assault and lethal force?

    a. An act of lethal force always leads to a type of assault.

    b. An assault will result in someone using lethal force.

    c. An assault with deadly intent can lead to an individual using lethal force to preserve their well-being.

    d. If someone uses self-defense in a conflict, it is called deadly force; if actions or threats are intended, it is called assault.

    e. Assault and lethal force have no conceivable connection.

Select only one answer choice:

19. Which of the following best describes the way the passages are structured?
    a. Both passages open by defining a legal concept and then continue to describe situations in order to further explain the concept.
    b. Both passages begin with situations, introduce accepted definitions, and then cite legal ramifications.
    c. The first passage presents a long definition while the second passage begins by showing an example of assault.
    d. Both cite specific legal doctrines, then proceed to explain the rulings.
    e. The first passage explains both concepts and then focuses on lethal force. The second passage picks up with assault and explains the concept in depth.

Select only one answer choice:

20. What can we infer about the role of intent in lethal force and assault?
    a. Intent is irrelevant. The law does not take intent into account.
    b. Intent is vital for determining the lawfulness of using lethal force.
    c. Intent is only taken into account for assault charges.
    d. The intent of the assailant is the main focus for determining legal ramifications; it is used to determine if the defender was justified in using force to respond.
    e. Intent is very important for determining both lethal force and assault; intent is examined in both parties and helps determine the severity of the issue.

Section 3: Quantitative Reasoning

For questions 1-8, compare Quantity A to Quantity B, using additional information presented above the two quantities.

1.

Quantity A	Quantity B
28% of 345	$\frac{1}{5}$ of 300

a. Quantity A is greater.
b. Quantity B is greater.
c. The two quantities are equal.
d. The relationship cannot be determined from the information given.

2. A cone has a radius of 3 feet and a volume of 25 cubic feet.

Quantity A	Quantity B
3 feet	The height of the cone

a. Quantity A is greater.
b. Quantity B is greater.
c. The two quantities are equal.
d. The relationship cannot be determined from the information given.

3.

Quantity A	Quantity B
$-\sqrt{72}$	-8

a. Quantity A is greater.
b. Quantity B is greater.
c. The two quantities are equal.
d. The relationship cannot be determined from the information given.

4. x is a positive integer.

Quantity A	Quantity B
$\dfrac{x+3}{x}$	$\dfrac{3-x}{-(x^2)}$

a. Quantity A is greater.
b. Quantity B is greater.
c. The two quantities are equal.
d. The relationship cannot be determined from the information given.

5.

Quantity A	Quantity B
Sum of perfect squares between 101 and 200	Least perfect square greater than 600

a. Quantity A is greater.
b. Quantity B is greater.
c. The two quantities are equal.
d. The relationship cannot be determined from the information given.

6.

Quantity A	Quantity B
Circumference of a circle with radius x cm	Perimeter of a rectangle with sides 5 cm and x cm

a. Quantity A is greater.
b. Quantity B is greater.
c. The two quantities are equal.
d. The relationship cannot be determined from the information given.

7.

<u>Quantity A</u>	<u>Quantity B</u>
$x^2 + 8x$	$x^2 + 16$

    a. Quantity A is greater.
    b. Quantity B is greater.
    c. The two quantities are equal.
    d. The relationship cannot be determined from the information given.

8.

<u>Quantity A</u>	<u>Quantity B</u>
$\frac{1}{4} - \frac{1}{2} + \frac{1}{6} - \frac{1}{8}$	$-\frac{1}{6}$

    a. Quantity A is greater.
    b. Quantity B is greater.
    c. The two quantities are equal.
    d. The relationship cannot be determined from the information given.

9. Of the given sets of coordinates below, which ones lie on the line that is perpendicular to $y = 2x - 3$ and passes through the point $(0, 5)$?
    a. $(2, 4)$
    b. $(-2, 7)$
    c. $(2, 6)$
    d. $(4, 3)$
    e. $(-6, 10)$

10. The equation $|y| = x$ forms a graph on the coordinate plane. Choose all of the following points that could lie on the graph of the given equation.
    a. $(-2, 2)$
    b. $(3, 3)$
    c. $(4, -4)$
    d. $(-10, 10)$
    e. $(-7, -7)$

11. To achieve a final grade of B for an English class, the numerical grade must be between 80 and 89. Josh has 6 tests with an average grade of 85. His quiz average is 78, and his classwork average is 92. The grades are averaged by percentage as follows:

- Test: 40%
- Quiz: 30%
- Classwork: 20%
- Homework: 10%

Indicate all possible values for Josh's homework average that would still allow him to have a B in English on his report card.

a. 90
b. 50
c. 40
d. 35
e. 100

12. An accounting firm charted its income on the following pie graph. If the income received from Accounting Services for the year was $100,000, how much income was received from Audit and Taxation Services?

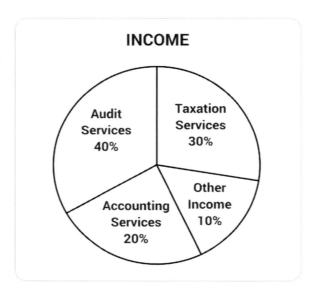

$ [   ]

13. The following graph shows the average snowfall for New York and Chicago for each month of the year. Indicate all months where the average snowfall was higher in New York than in Chicago.

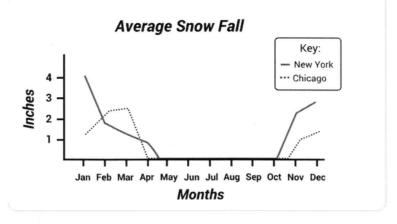

a. January
b. February
c. June
d. September
e. November

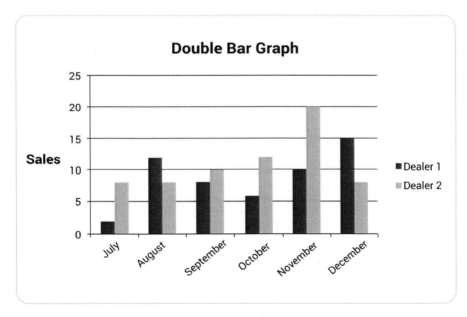

14. The chart above shows the average car sales for the months of July through December for two different car dealers. What is the average number of cars sold in the given time period for Dealer 1? Round your answer to the nearest whole number.

[ ] Cars

15. Circle A is tangent to circle B, and the radii of circles A and B are 5 and 7 inches, respectively. What is the circumference of the circle, in terms of pi, that circumscribes circles A and B?

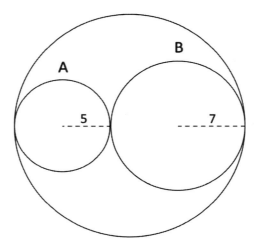

    a. 12π inches
    b. 24π inches
    c. 72π inches
    d. 144π inches
    e. 288π inches

16. If a is even, and b is odd, indicate which expressions below must result in an even number.
    a. ab
    b. $3a + 5b$
    c. $-5a + 7b^2$
    d. $a^3 + 2b^5$
    e. $b^{a+b} + a^2$

17. Choose all answers below that could possibly be side lengths for a right triangle.
    a. 7, 8, 12
    b. 3, 4, 5
    c. 4, 8, 13
    d. 6, 8, 10
    e. 5, 7, 11

18. Gary is driving home to see his parents for Christmas. He travels at a constant speed of 60 miles per hour for a total of 350 miles. How long will it take him to travel home if he takes a break for 10 minutes every 100 miles?

19. If $-\frac{x}{11}$ is even, then which of the following is true?
    a. x is even
    b. x is odd
    c. x is positive
    d. x is negative
    e. x is a perfect square

20. What is the average of the following: $x, x + 3, x + 5, x + 7,$ and $x + 15$?

    a. $x + 2$
    b. $x + 4$
    c. $x + 5$
    d. $x + 6$
    e. $x + 7$

Section 4: Verbal Reasoning

For questions 1-6, select the best word from the corresponding column of choices that most clearly completes the passage:

1. Juan is a talented painter best known for his use of (i) _____. His most famous painting depicts American colonialists huddled around a television watching cartoons as the Revolutionary War wages in a field visible through an open window. This work (ii) _____ confusion and horror in viewers who don't understand why the colonialists are watching television as their countrymen are fighting and dying for freedom.

Blank (i)	Blank (ii)
a. anachronism	d. abates
b. hyperbole	e. elicits
c. irony	f. obviates

2. Jacob is a terrific team leader. Even on short notice, Jacob is able to (i) _____ his team to produce rapid results. In contrast, Lisa is (ii) _____. Whenever confronted with a difficult situation, she becomes angry and unapproachable.

Blank (i)	Blank (ii)
a. enervate	d. irascible
b. galvanize	e. tortuous
c. venerate	f. zealous

3. There are several key differences between the United States and Scandinavia. First, the United States is a multicultural country of immigrants, while Scandinavia is mostly (i) _____.
Second, the mainstream political (ii) _____ leans farther to the right in the United States than in Scandinavia. Third, the United States carries out a more (iii) _____ and interventionist foreign policy than Scandinavia.

Blank (i)	Blank (ii)	Blank (iii)
a. ambiguous	d. cacophony	g. ambivalent
b. homogeneous	e. hegemony	h. bellicose
c. sedulous	f. ideology	i. timorous

4. Tensions were running high between two employees, so the employer pulled each employee aside separately in the hopes of (i) _____ them. The employer needed the pair to stop (ii) _____ each other before a workable solution could be (iii) _____.

Blank (i)	Blank (ii)	Blank (iii)
a. placating	d. denigrating	g. effectuated
b. prevaricating	e. disabusing	h. exculpated
c. refuting	f. venerating	i. extrapolated

5. We learned that, due to his uncertainty on the subject, the politician was (i) _____ about the president's role in (ii) _____ in the Yemen civil war. On the other hand, our state senator was shocked by the (iii) _____ decision to help Saudi Arabia.

Blank (i)	Blank (ii)	Blank (iii)
a. ebullient	d. refraining	g. impetuous
b. ambivalent	e. renouncing	h. temperate
c. hapless	f. engaging	i. impassive

6. The chief police of Hilltop, Indiana was (i) _____ to patrolman due to his inability to (ii) _____ the city's crime rates.

Blank (i)	Blank (ii)
a. relegated	d. escalate
b. endorsed	e. mitigate
c. promoted	f. transmit

Questions 7–12 are based on the following passage.

Dana Gioia argues in his article that poetry is dying, now little more than a limited art form confined to academic and college settings. Of course poetry remains healthy in the academic setting, but the idea of poetry being limited to this academic subculture is a stretch. New technology and social networking alone have contributed to poets and other writers' work being shared across the world. YouTube has emerged to be a major asset to poets, allowing live performances to be streamed to billions of users. Even now, poetry continues to grow and voice topics that are relevant to the culture of our time. Poetry is not in the spotlight as it may have been in earlier times, but it's still a relevant art form that continues to expand in scope and appeal.

Furthermore, Gioia's argument does not account for live performances of poetry. Not everyone has taken a poetry class or enrolled in university—but most everyone is online. The Internet is a perfect launching point to get all creative work out there. An example of this was the performance of Buddy Wakefield's *Hurling Crowbirds at Mockingbars*. Wakefield is a well-known poet who has published several collections of contemporary poetry. One of my favorite works by Wakefield is *Crowbirds*, specifically his performance at New York University in 2009. Although his reading was a campus event, views of his performance online number in the thousands. His poetry attracted people outside of the university setting.

Naturally, the poem's popularity can be attributed both to Wakefield's performance and the quality of his writing. *Crowbirds* touches on themes of core human concepts such as faith, personal loss, and growth. These are not ideas that only poets or students of literature understand, but all human beings: "You acted like I was hurling crowbirds at mockingbars / and abandoned me for not making sense. / Evidently, I don't experience things as rationally as you do" (Wakefield 15-17). Wakefield weaves together a complex description of the perplexed and hurt emotions of the speaker undergoing a separation from a romantic interest. The line "You acted like I was hurling crowbirds at mockingbars" conjures up an image of someone confused, seemingly out of their mind . . . or in the case of the speaker, passionately trying to grasp at a relationship that is fading. The speaker is looking back and finding the words that described how he wasn't making sense. This poem is particularly human and gripping in its message, but the entire effect of the poem is enhanced through the physical performance.

At its core, poetry is about addressing issues/ideas in the world. Part of this is also addressing the perspectives that are exiguously considered. Although the platform may look different, poetry continues to have a steady audience due to the emotional connection the poet shares with the audience.

Select only one answer choice:

7. Which one of the following best explains how the passage is organized?
   a. The author begins with a long definition of the main topic, and then proceeds to prove how that definition has changed over the course of modernity.
   b. The author presents a puzzling phenomenon and uses the rest of the passage to showcase personal experiences in order to explain it.
   c. The author contrasts two different viewpoints, then builds a case showing preference for one over the other.
   d. The passage is an analysis of another theory that the author has no stake in.
   e. The passage is a summary of a main topic from its historical beginnings to its contemplated end.

Select only one answer choice:

8. The author of the passage would likely agree most with which of the following?
   a. Buddy Wakefield is a genius and is considered at the forefront of modern poetry.
   b. Poetry is not irrelevant; it is an art form that adapts to the changing time while containing its core elements.
   c. Spoken word is the zenith of poetic forms and the premier style of poetry in this decade.
   d. Poetry is on the verge of vanishing from our cultural consciousness.
   e. Poetry is a writing art. While poetry performances are useful for introducing poems, the act of reading a poem does not contribute to the piece overall.

Select only one answer choice:

9. Which one of the following words, if substituted for the word *exiguously* in the last paragraph, would LEAST change the meaning of the sentence?
   a. Indolently
   b. Inaudibly
   c. Interminably
   d. Infrequently
   e. Impecunious

Select only one answer choice:

10. Which of the following is most closely analogous to the author's opinion of Buddy Wakefield's performance in relation to modern poetry?
   a. Someone's refusal to accept that the Higgs Boson will validate the Standard Model.
   b. An individual's belief that soccer will lose popularity within the next fifty years.
   c. A professor's opinion that poetry contains the language of the heart, while fiction contains the language of the mind.
   d. An individual's assertion that video game violence was the cause of the Columbine shootings.
   e. A student's insistence that psychoanalysis is a subset of modern psychology.

Select only one answer choice:

11. What is the primary purpose of the passage?
   a. To educate readers on the development of poetry and describe the historical implications of poetry in media.
   b. To disprove Dana Gioia's stance that poetry is becoming irrelevant and is only appreciated in academia.
   c. To inform readers of the brilliance of Buddy Wakefield and to introduce them to other poets that have influenced contemporary poetry.
   d. To prove that Gioia's article does have some truth to it and to shed light on its relevance to modern poetry.
   e. To recount the experience of watching a live poetry performance and to look forward to future performances.

Select only one answer choice:

12. What is the author's main reason for including the quote in the passage?
    a. To give an example of speaking meter, the writing style of spoken word poets.
    b. To demonstrate that people are still writing poetry even if the medium has changed in current times.
    c. To prove that poets still have an audience to write for even if the audience looks different than from centuries ago.
    d. To illustrate the complex themes poets continue to address, which still draw listeners and appreciation.
    e. To open up opportunity to disprove Gioia's views.

For questions 13-15, select the <u>two</u> answer choices that can complete the sentence and create sentences that have complementary meaning.

13. The summer interns looked forward to working with the congressman, not knowing that he was also a _____.
    a. Tyro
    b. Zealot
    c. Savant
    d. Philanthropist
    e. Misogynist
    f. Novice

14. Much to the surprise of the senator, the interview questions focused on forgotten _____ rather than on his impressive voting record.
    a. Peccadilloes
    b. Indiscretions
    c. Efficacies
    d. Anachronisms
    e. Diatribes
    f. Misnomers

15. The Prell shampoo commercials stayed in the minds of the viewers due to the _____ movement of the pearl dropped into the golden bottle of premium, thick shampoo. It became a classic advertisement in the 1970s.
    a. Viscous
    b. Ambrosial
    c. Caustic
    d. Ephemeral
    e. Insular
    f. Gradual

Questions 16–20 are based on the following passage.

In the quest to understand existence, modern philosophers must question if humans can fully comprehend the world. Classical western approaches to philosophy tend to hold that one can understand something, be it an event or object, by standing outside of the phenomena and observing it. It is then by unbiased observation that one can grasp the details of the world. This seems to hold true for many things. Scientists conduct experiments and record their findings, and thus many natural phenomena become comprehendible. However, several of these observations were possible because humans used tools in order to make these discoveries.

This may seem like an extraneous matter. After all, people invented things like microscopes and telescopes in order to enhance their capacity to view cells or the movement of stars. While humans are still capable of seeing things, the question remains if human beings have the capacity to fully observe and see the world in order to understand it. It would not be an impossible stretch to argue that what humans see through a microscope is not the exact thing itself, but a human interpretation of it.

This would seem to be the case in the "Business of the Holes" experiment conducted by Richard Feynman. To study the way electrons behave, Feynman set up a barrier with two holes and a plate. The plate was there to indicate how many times the electrons would pass through the hole(s). Rather than casually observe the electrons acting under normal circumstances, Feynman discovered that electrons behave in two totally different ways depending on whether or not they are observed. The electrons that were observed had passed through either one of the holes or were caught on the plate as particles. However, electrons that weren't observed acted as waves instead of particles and passed through both holes. This indicated that electrons have a dual nature. Electrons seen by the human eye act like particles, while unseen electrons act like waves of energy.

This dual nature of the electrons presents a conundrum. While humans now have a better understanding of electrons, the fact remains that people cannot entirely perceive how electrons behave without the use of instruments. We can only observe one of the mentioned behaviors, which only provides a partial understanding of the entire function of electrons. Therefore, we're forced to ask ourselves whether the world we observe is objective or if it is subjectively perceived by humans. Or, an alternative question: can man understand the world only through machines that will allow them to observe natural phenomena?

Both questions humble man's capacity to grasp the world. However, those ideas don't take into account that many phenomena have been proven by human beings without the use of machines, such as the discovery of gravity. Like all philosophical questions, whether man's reason and observation alone can understand the universe can be approached from many angles.

Select only one answer choice:

16. What is the author's motivation for writing the passage?
   a. To bring to light an alternative view on human perception by examining the role of technology in human understanding.
   b. To educate the reader on the latest astroparticle physics discovery and offer terms that may be unfamiliar to the reader.
   c. To argue that humans are totally blind to the realities of the world by presenting an experiment that proves that electrons are not what they seem on the surface.
   d. To reflect on opposing views of human understanding.
   e. To disprove classical philosophy by comparing more accurate technology to the speculations of the ancient philosophers.

Select only one answer choice:

17. Which of the following most closely resembles the way in which paragraph four is structured?
    a. It offers one solution, questions the solution, and then ends with an alternative solution.
    b. It presents an inquiry, explains the detail of that inquiry, and then offers a solution.
    c. It presents a problem, explains the details of that problem, and then ends with more inquiry.
    d. It gives a definition, offers an explanation, and then ends with an inquiry.
    e. It presents a problem, offers an example, and then ends with a solution.

Select only one answer choice:

18. Which best describes how the electrons in the experiment behaved like waves?
    a. The electrons moved up and down like actual waves.
    b. The electrons passed through both holes and then onto the plate.
    c. The electrons converted to photons upon touching the plate.
    d. The electrons were seen passing through one hole or the other.
    e. The electrons were glowing during the experiment, indicating light waves were moving them.

Select only one answer choice:

19. The author mentions "gravity" in the last paragraph in order to do what?
    a. In order to show that different natural phenomena test man's ability to grasp the world.
    b. To prove that since man has not measured it with the use of tools or machines, humans cannot know the true nature of gravity.
    c. To demonstrate an example of natural phenomena humans discovered and understood without the use of tools or machines.
    d. To show an alternative solution to the nature of electrons that humans have not thought of yet.
    e. To look toward the future of technology so that we may understand the dual nature of all phenomena, including gravity.

Select only one answer choice:

20. Which situation best parallels the revelation of the dual nature of electrons discovered in Feynman's experiment?
a. Ancient Greeks believed that Zeus hurled lightning down to Earth. In reality, lightning is caused by supercharged electrons, and happens either inside the clouds or between the cloud and the ground.
b. The coelacanth was thought to be extinct, but a live specimen was just recently discovered. There are now two living species of coelacanth known to man, and both are believed to be endangered.
c. In the Middle Ages, blacksmiths added carbon to iron, thus inventing steel. The consequences of this important discovery would have its biggest effects during the industrial revolution.
d. In order to better examine and treat broken bones, the x-ray machine was invented and put to use in hospitals and medical centers.
e. A man is born color-blind and grows up observing everything in lighter or darker shades. With the invention of special goggles he puts on, he discovers that there are other colors in addition to different shades.

Section 5: Quantitative Reasoning

For questions 1-9, compare Quantity A to Quantity B, using additional information presented above the two quantities.

1.

Quantity A	Quantity B
$4(x + 12)$	48

a. Quantity A is greater.
b. Quantity B is greater.
c. The two quantities are equal.
d. The relationship cannot be determined from the information given.

2.

Quantity A	Quantity B
4^{48}	8^{36}

a. Quantity A is greater.
b. Quantity B is greater.
c. The two quantities are equal.
d. The relationship cannot be determined from the information given.

3.

Quantity A	Quantity B
$12z$	$15z$

a. Quantity A is greater.
b. Quantity B is greater.
c. The two quantities are equal.
d. The relationship cannot be determined from the information given.

4.

Quantity A	Quantity B
$(-2)^x$	3^x

a. Quantity A is greater.
b. Quantity B is greater.
c. The two quantities are equal.
d. The relationship cannot be determined from the information given.

5.

Quantity A	Quantity B
$\frac{3}{16}$	$0.75 \times 25\%$

a. Quantity A is greater.
b. Quantity B is greater.
c. The two quantities are equal.
d. The relationship cannot be determined from the information given.

6.
$$x^2 < 100$$

Quantity A	Quantity B
11	x

a. Quantity A is greater.
b. Quantity B is greater.
c. The two quantities are equal.
d. The relationship cannot be determined from the information given.

7. A student paid $125 for a textbook. The sales tax on the book was more than 8%.

Quantity A	Quantity B
The total cost of the textbook	$133

a. Quantity A is greater.
b. Quantity B is greater.
c. The two quantities are equal.
d. The relationship cannot be determined from the information given.

8.

Quantity A	Quantity B
The products of the integers from 6 to 18, inclusive.	The products of the integers from 1 to 16, inclusive.

a. Quantity A is greater.
b. Quantity B is greater.
c. The two quantities are equal.
d. The relationship cannot be determined from the information given.

9. $$x < 0$$

Quantity A	Quantity B
x^5	x^7

a. Quantity A is greater.
b. Quantity B is greater.
c. The two quantities are equal.
d. The relationship cannot be determined from the information given.

10. If $5 + 8|x + 6| = 61$, then which of the following could x be equal to? Select all that apply.

a. 13
b. 1
c. -6
d. -13
e. 6

11. If $m + n = 8$, then $m^2 + 2mn + n^2 =$

a. 16
b. 4
c. 32
d. 64
e. 8

12. Ariana rents a studio for her yoga class. The rent she pays is $900 per month. Her income from her yoga classes is $3500. The heating and air conditioning bill averages $75 per month, and the water bill averages $10 per month. After paying her rent and bills, what percentage of the income from yoga classes does she receive as a profit? (Round the answer to the nearest whole percent.)

☐ percent

13. If $a - 9 = 18$, then which is the correct value of $(a + 5)^2$?

a. 32
b. 324
c. 1024
d. 25
e. 729

14. Brinley leaves her house at 7 a.m. and bikes at a constant speed of 12 miles per hour due east. Trey lives 85 miles due east of Brinley. He leaves his house at 8 a.m. and bikes at a constant speed of 10 miles per hour due west. At what time do they meet?

☐

15. Given that $7^x + 7^x + 7^x + 7^x + 7^x + 7^x = 7^{11}$, what is the value of x?

    a. 5

    b. $\frac{7}{6}$

    c. $\frac{11}{6}$

    d. 6

    e. 10

16. The ratio of fruit to vegetables at a grocery store is 5:3. If the total number of produce items (fruits and vegetables) is 120, how many vegetables are in the store?

    a. 45

    b. 75

    c. 100

    d. 50

    e. 30

17. Simplify the following expression: $\frac{(xy)^4 z}{x^2 y z^0}$, where $xyz \neq 0$.

    a. $x^2 y^3$

    b. $x^2 y^3 z$

    c. $\frac{1}{x^2 y^2 z}$

    d. $\frac{y^2 z}{x}$

    e. xyz

18. If a school has 550 boys and 635 girls, what is the percentage of the students that are girls? (Round the answer to the nearest tenth percent.)

    [   ] percent

19. If 40% of y is 24, then y is what percent of 120?

    a. 30%

    b. 40%

    c. 50%

    d. 60%

    e. 70%

20. Katie ran 18 miles in 4 hours. Her rate in miles per hour is equivalent to which of the following proportions? Select all that apply.

    a. 4 to 36

    b. 36 to 8

    c. 9 to 2

    d. 180 to 20

    e. 4 to 9

Answer Explanations #2

Section 2: Verbal Reasoning

1. D: *Aggrandize* is the correct answer because "adding excessive details" to reality would make reality greater than it really is. *Propitiate* is incorrect because one wouldn't try to "win the favor of" reality, nor is *precipitate* the correct answer, which means to instigate something. *Exacerbate* is more likely to fit, although the word implies a negative connotation rather than "adding excessive details." *Imitate* doesn't make sense within the context because "adding excessive details" would mean to go beyond reality, not to imitate it.

2. B: The answer *burgeoning* means to grow rapidly, which is an appropriate name for a field where "researchers are contributing significant findings to Fortune 500 research." The terms *diminishing*, *disparaging*, and *floundering* all indicate a lessening or a failing and thus do not fit into the sentence. *Ambiguous* means open to more than one meaning, which negates the context of surety and growth.

3. C, D: The key phrase for the first blank is "very similar." Go back to the first grouping of choices to find a word that has a relationship to the phrase "very similar." Readers will identify the word *homogeneous*, which means "the same." Then one can infer that the pollsters' results were not valid because of a grouping that did not have many variables. As readers look at the options for the second blank, they should think about the logical result of this poll. Being *accurate* is not an issue here. To be *valid* is also not quite the purpose of polling. The heavily biased results would be a problem for the pollsters.

4. B: One of the key words to help readers select the best choice in this sentence is "outstanding." There is a tone of praise and acclaim to the main idea promoted in the sentence. Readers can eliminate words that have a negative connotation, such as *reproofs* and *obloquy*. *Meditations* does not fit within the context of the passage. *Memoirs* might work; however, it does not complete the full meaning of providing public praise for Mr. Stanley.

5. B, F, I: *Effectively* (Choice B) means producing the desired result, and it's the best fit for Blank (i). The passage is describing a major breakthrough happening in the present day, and five years ago artificial intelligence was having a problem processing verbal commands. *Chronology* (Choice A) has to do with placing events in the correct order, and *zealously* (Choice C) means doing something with energy or enthusiasm. Thus, Choice B is the correct answer.

Gist (Choice F) is the main thrust of an idea without details, and that completes Blank (ii), which is describing a new development in artificial intelligence's ability to process verbal commands. *Aesthetic* (Choice D) is related to beauty, and *coda* (Choice E) is the concluding part of a musical piece or movement. Thus, Choice F is the correct answer.

Surpass (Choice I) fits Blank (iii) because the rest of the sentence is implying that artificial intelligence will at least equal humanity's communication skills, and *surpass* means to exceed. *Aggregate* (Choice G) is the combining of parts into a whole, and *mollify* (Choice H) means to soothe someone who is angry or anxious. Thus, Choice I is the correct answer.

6. C: John is running out of time and has chosen to concentrate on the main topics instead of some other material. So, Blank (i) should be something less important than those main topics. *Tangential* (Choice C) is something that's incidental or on the periphery, which fits this context. *Fatuous* (Choice A) is the second-best answer choice because it can mean inane or pointless; however, *fatuous* connotes foolishness, so *tangential* is the better match. *Specious* (Choice *B*) means deceptively attractive—something that looks right but is really wrong—so it doesn't make sense that John would study specious material even if he had more time. Thus, Choice *C* is the correct answer.

7. C, E: The second sentence describes how grassroots organizers keep losing elections despite their best efforts. *Vexed* (Choice *C*) means feeling irritated, annoyed, or distressed, which accurately expresses the organizers' attitude toward the electoral process. *Appeasing* (Choice *A*) someone or something involves making concessions. In this context, *oscillate* (Choice *B*) would mean the organizers are alternating between favoring and opposing the electoral process. Thus, Choice *C* is correct.

Since the electoral process has vexed the organizers, Blank (ii) will express their desire to move away from that process, like actively supporting radical action. To *foment* (Choice *E*) is to instigate or promote, and this matches the organizers' desire to circumvent the electoral process by supporting radical action. *Fluctuating* (Choice *D*) refers to shifting one's position because of uncertainty, and *forestalling* (Choice *F*) means preemptively taking action to prevent or obstruct something, which is the opposite of what's intended here. Thus, Choice *E* is the correct answer.

8. C, D: The author mentions in the third paragraph how apologia focuses on the short term and reconciliation has long-term goals. In addition, in the second paragraph it describes how reconciliation aims to restore dialogue and apologia seeks to shift blame. Thus, Choices *C* and *D* are the correct answers. The first clause in Choice *A* describes reconciliation rather than apologia, so it's incorrect. Choice *B* is incorrect because it's never stated or implied that apologia is always delivered in writing. The author doesn't claim that apologia requires actually receiving forgiveness to be effective, and reconciliation involves more than just delivering visual responses, so Choice *E* is incorrect.

9. E: The author states that national leaders use apologia and reconciliation to restore their image, so it can be inferred that a positive national image is an important part of governance. Thus, Choice *E* is the correct answer. The author clearly favors reconciliation, but it's unlikely they would agree that national leaders should never apologize. Thus, Choice *A* is incorrect. Similarly, the author implies that apologia is self-serving but, as described by the author, reconciliation also seems to be self-serving. In any event, the author thinks reconciliation is generally more effective because of its long-term effect, not because it's less self-serving. Thus, Choice *B* is incorrect. Choices *C* and *D* are never mentioned or alluded to in the passage, so they cannot be properly inferred.

10. A, B: Reconciliation's use of symbolic visual images and impact on the long-term relationship between the aggrieved and the transgressor is described in the third paragraph. Thus, Choices *A* and *B* are the correct answers. The other answer choices describe features of apologia, not reconciliation, so Choices *C*, *D*, and *E* are all incorrect.

11. E: The author states in the fourth paragraph that offending images don't always require a visual response, but when they do, reconciliation is the better choice due to its long-term goals. Thus, Choice *E* is the correct answer. Censorship and anti-propaganda campaigns are never mentioned in the passage, so Choices *A* and *B* are incorrect. Choices *C* and *D* are incorrect because they are directly contradicted in the fourth paragraph.

12. B, C: The clue in this sentence is the word "started," which implies that things will become increasingly one way or the other. Looking over the choices, none of the words are similar to "simple," so the best choice is to find synonyms that describe a more difficult or clouded meaning, such as *esoteric* and *abstruse*.

13. C, F: Because of the word "legend," the missing word should complete the meaning of the sentence by adding something that means "long lasting." Both the words *ineradicable* and *indelible* suggest leaving a mark forever.

14. A: The purpose is to inform the reader about what assault is and how it is committed. Choice *B* is incorrect because the passage does not state that assault is a lesser form of lethal force, only that an assault can use lethal force, or alternatively, lethal force can be utilized to counter a dangerous assault. Choices *C* and *D* are incorrect because the passage is informative and does not have a set agenda. Finally, Choice *E* is incorrect because although the author uses an example in order to explain assault, it is not indicated that this is the author's personal account.

15. C: The situation of the man who is attacked in an alley by another man with a knife would most merit the use of lethal force. If the man being attacked used self-defense by lethal force, it would not be considered illegal. The presence of a deadly weapon indicates mal-intent and because the individual is isolated in an alley, lethal force in self-defense may be the only way to preserve his life. Choices *A* and *B* can be ruled out because in these situations, no one is in danger of immediate death or bodily harm by someone else. Choice *D* is an assault that does exhibit intent to harm, but this situation isn't severe enough to merit lethal force; there is no intent to kill. Choice *E* is incorrect because this is a vehicular accident, and the driver did not intend to hit and injure the other driver.

16. B: As discussed in the second passage, there are several forms of assault, like assault with a deadly weapon, verbal assault, or threatening posture or language. Choice *A* is incorrect because lethal force and assault are separate as indicated by the passages. Choice *C* is incorrect because anyone is capable of assault; the author does not state that one group of people cannot commit assault. Choice *D* is incorrect because assault is never justified. Self-defense resulting in lethal force can be justified. Choice *E* is incorrect because the author does mention what the charges are on assaults; therefore, we cannot assume that they are more or less than unnecessary use of force charges.

17. D: The use of lethal force is not evaluated on the intent of the user but rather the severity of the primary attack that warranted self-defense. This statement most undermines the last part of the passage because it directly contradicts how the law evaluates the use of lethal force. Choices *A*, *B*, and *E* are stated in the paragraph, and therefore do not undermine the explanation from the author. Choice *C* does not necessarily undermine the passage, but it does not support the passage either. It is more of an opinion that does not strengthen or weaken the explanation.

18. C: An assault with deadly intent can lead to an individual using lethal force to preserve their well-being. Choice *C* is correct because it clearly establishes what both assault and lethal force are and gives the specific way in which the two concepts meet. Choice *A* is incorrect because lethal force doesn't necessarily result in assault. This is also why Choice *B* is incorrect. Not all assaults would necessarily be life-threatening to the point where lethal force is needed for self-defense. Choice *D* is compelling but ultimately too vague; the statement touches on aspects of the two ideas but fails to present the concrete way in which the two are connected to each other. Choice *E* is incorrect because it contradicts the information in the passage (that assault with deadly intent can lead to an individual using lethal force).

19. A: Both passages open by defining a legal concept and then describing situations in order to further explain the concept. Choice *D* is incorrect because while the passages utilize examples to help explain the concepts discussed, the author doesn't indicate that they are specific court cases. It's also clear that the passages don't open with examples, but instead, begin by defining the terms addressed in each passage. This eliminates Choice *B* and ultimately reveals Choice *A* to be the correct answer. Choice *A* accurately outlines the way both passages are structured. Because the passages follow a near identical structure, the rest of the choices can easily be ruled out.

20. E: Intent is very important for determining both lethal force and assault; intent is examined by both parties and helps determine the severity of the issue. Choices *A*, *B*, and *C* are incorrect because it is clear in both passages that intent is a prevailing theme in both lethal force and assault. Choice *D* is compelling, but if a person uses lethal force to defend themselves, the intent of the defender is also examined in order to help determine if there was excessive force used. Choice *E* is correct because it states that intent is important for determining both lethal force and assault, and that intent is used to gauge the severity of the issues. Remember, just as lethal force can escalate to excessive use of force, there are different kinds of assault. Intent dictates several different forms of assault.

Section 3: Quantitative Reasoning

1. A: The percent of a number can be found by using the equation $\frac{\%}{100} = \frac{is}{of}$. After filling in the values for Quantity A, this equation becomes:

$$\frac{28}{100} = \frac{x}{345}$$

Since the "is," or x-portion, of the equation is missing, it can be solved using cross multiplication. This yields the equation: $28 \times 345 = 100 \times x$. Multiplying 28 by 345 and then dividing by 100 gives an x-value of 96.6. Quantity B is 1/5 of 300. Splitting 300 into 5 equal parts of 60 means Quantity B is equal to 60. The value of 96.6 is greater than 60. Therefore, Quantity A is greater than Quantity B. The correct answer is *A*. Quantity A, with a value of 96.6, is greater than Quantity B, with a value of 60.

2. A: To find whether the radius or the height of the cone is greater, the equation for the volume of a cone, $V = \pi r^2 h / 3$, must first be rearranged to solve for height, h:

$$h = \frac{V \times 3}{\pi r^2}$$

Insert the known values and solve for h:

$$h = \frac{25 \text{ ft}^3 \times 3}{\pi \times 3^2 \text{ ft}^2} = \frac{75 \text{ ft}^3}{3.14 \times 9 \text{ ft}^2} = 2.65 \text{ ft}$$

The height of the cone is 2.65 feet. Thus, Quantity A is greater than Quantity B.

3. B: Quantity A has a value read as the negative square root of 72. Finding the square root of this number is finding a number that can be multiplied by itself to get a product of 72. Since 8 squared is 64, and 9 squared is 81, it can be determined that the square root of 72 is somewhere between 8 and 9. Taking the negative of this number means it is found between negative 8 and negative 9. If placed on a number line, Quantity A would lie between -8 and -9, while Quantity B would lie at -8. Because of this order, Quantity B is greater. The correct answer is *B* because Quantity B, with a value of -8, is greater than Quantity A, with a value between -8 and -9.

4. A: The way to compare these expressions is to consider their value when x is at and near zero, and as x becomes larger. When x approaches infinity, all constants are effectively zero. The value of Quantity A begins at $y = 2$ when $x = 1$ and approaches $y = 1$ as x goes to infinity, whereas Quantity B begins at $y = -2$ when $x = 1$ and approaches $y = 0$ as x goes to infinity. This can be also checked by testing a few small and large values of x for Quantities A and B—for any positive integer, Quantity A is greater than Quantity B.

5. A: A perfect square is a number that can be written as the square of an integer. For example, 4 is a perfect square because it can be written as 2^2, or 2×2. The perfect squares from 101 to 200 start with $11^2 = 121$. The next perfect squares are 144, 169, and 196. The sum of these perfect squares is found by adding $121 + 144 + 169 + 196 = 630$. Quantity B is the least perfect square greater than 600. A common perfect square close to 600 is 20 squared, which is 400. Increasing this number to 25 squared yields the product 625. To test that this is the least perfect square greater than 600, the square of 24 can be found as $24 \times 24 = 576$. Therefore, Quantity B is equal to 625. When comparing the sum of the perfect squares in Quantity A and the perfect square of 625 in Quantity B, the value in Quantity A is greater at 630. The correct answer is A because Quantity A is greater than Quantity B.

6. D: The circumference of a circle can be found by using the formula $C = 2\pi r$. Using this formula with the radius of x cm produces the circumference $C = 2(5) + 2(x) = 6.28x$ cm. The perimeter of a rectangle can be found by using the formula $P = 2l + 2w$. Plugging in the values for the sides given produces the equation $P = 2(5) + 2(x) = 10\ cm + 2x\ cm$. Because the linear equations for both quantities have different slopes, there must be a point where they are equal, which is found by setting both equations equal to each other and solving for x:

$$6.28x \text{ cm} = 10 \text{ cm} + 2x \text{ cm}$$

$$4.28x \text{ cm} = 10 \text{ cm}$$

$$x \text{ cm} = \frac{10}{4.28} \text{ cm} = 2.35 \text{ cm}$$

Therefore, at values of x less than 2.35, the perimeter of Quantity B is larger, while for values of x greater than 2.35, the circumference of Quantity A is larger. These two quantities can be compared because they both describe the distance around the outside of a 2-dimensional shape. The correct answer is Choice D because either quantity may be larger depending on the value of x.

7. D: If $x > 2$, then Quantity A is greater. For instance, if $x = 4$, Quantity A is equal to 48, and Quantity B is equal to 32. Therefore, Choices B and C are incorrect since Quantity B is not greater and the quantities are not equal. However, if we let $x = 1$ then Quantity A is equal to 9 and Quantity B is equal to 17. In this scenario, Quantity B is larger than Quantity A. Therefore, the relationship between the quantities depends on the value of x, and a relationship cannot be determined.

8. B: We can rewrite Quantity A as having a common denominator of 24: $\frac{6}{24} - \frac{12}{24} + \frac{4}{24} - \frac{3}{24}$, which is equal to $-\frac{5}{24}$. Quantity B can be rewritten as $-\frac{4}{24}$, and $-\frac{5}{24} < -\frac{4}{24}$. Therefore, Quantity B is greater than Quantity A.

9. A and D: The first step is to find the equation of the line that is perpendicular to $y = 2x - 3$ and passes through the point $(0, 5)$. The slope of a perpendicular line is found by the negative reciprocal of 2, which is $-\frac{1}{2}$. The y-intercept is the value of y when $x = 0$, so the y-intercept is 5. The new equation is $y = -\frac{1}{2}x + 5$. In order to find which points lie on the new line, the values of x and y can be substituted

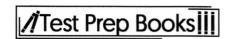

into the equation to determine if they form a true statement. For Choice A, the equation $4 = -\frac{1}{2}(2) + 5$ makes a true statement, so the point $(2, 4)$ lies on the lines. For B, the equation $7 = -\frac{1}{2}(-2) + 5$ makes the statement $7 = 6$, which is not a true statement. Therefore, Choice B is not a point that lies on the line. For Choice C, the equation $6 = -\frac{1}{2}(2) + 5$ is the same as $6 = 4$, so it is similarly false. For D, the equation $3 = -\frac{1}{2}(4) + 5$ makes a true statement, so the point $(4, 3)$ lies on the line. For the last point in E, the equation $10 = -\frac{1}{2}(-6) + 5$ makes the statement $10 = 8$. This is not a true statement, so the point $(-6, 10)$ does not lie on the line.

10. B and C: When graphed on the coordinate plane, this equation forms the line shown below.

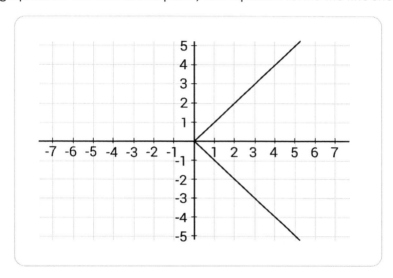

As seen in the graph, there cannot be any values of x that are negative. By looking at the equation, x is equal to the absolute value of y. When the absolute value of any number is taken, the number turns into a positive value. Since x is equal to the absolute value of y, then x can never be a negative number. This fact and the graph show that the points in Choices A, D, and E will not lie on the line and are not possible coordinates for the given equation. The points in Choices B and C are possible values because they will form true statements when plugged into the absolute value equation.

11. A, B, and E: To find the final grade based on the percentages given, an expression can be generated. The following expression takes each average and relates it to the percentage to calculate the final grade:

$$0.4(test) + 0.3(quiz) + 0.2(classwork) + 0.1(homework)$$

By plugging in the given averages for each type of assignment, the equation becomes:

$$0.4(85) + 0.3(78) + 0.2(92) + 0.1(homework)$$

Each of the 4 values above can be plugged into the equation to determine if the resulting grade lies between 80 and 89. For each of the values 90, 50, and 100, a final grade between 80 and 89 will be achieved. The homework averages of 35 and 40 are too low to give Josh a B average in English.

12. 350,000: Since Accounting Services have an income of $100,000, which is 20% of the total, a proportion can be set up to find the total income. Using the decimal form of 20% (0.2) gives:

$$\frac{0.2}{100000} = \frac{1}{x}$$

$$x = 100000 \times \frac{1}{0.2} = 100000 \times 5 = 500000$$

Since the total income is $500,000, then a percentage of that can be found by multiplying the percent of Audit Services as a decimal, or 0.40, by the total of 500,000. This answer is found from the equation:

$$500000 \times 0.4 = 200000$$

The total income from Audit Services is $200,000.

For the income received from Taxation Services, the following equation can be used:

$$500000 \times 0.3 = 150000$$

The total income from Audit Services and Taxation Services is $150,000 + 200,000 = 350,000$.

Another way of approaching the problem is to calculate the easy percentage of 10% then multiply it by 7 because the total percentage for Audit and Taxation Services was 70%. Half of 100,000 (20%) is 50,000 (10%). Then multiplying this number by 7 yields the same income of $350,000.

13. A and E: By looking at both lines on the graph, the solid line runs higher than the dotted line when New York has more snowfall than Chicago. In the month of February, Chicago had more snowfall because the dotted line runs above the solid line for the duration of the month. In the months of June and September, both cities had no snowfall. In January and November, New York had more snowfall than Chicago because the solid line runs higher than the dotted line during both months.

14. 9: The average is calculated by adding up each month's sales and dividing the sum by the total number of months in the time period. Dealer 1 sold 2 cars in July, 12 in August, 8 in September, 6 in October, 10 in November, and 15 in December. The sum of these sales is:

$$2 + 12 + 8 + 6 + 10 + 15 = 53 \text{ cars}$$

To find the average, this sum is divided by the total number of months, which is 6. When 53 is divided by 6, it yields 8.8333… Since cars are sold in whole numbers, the answer is rounded to 9 cars.

15. B: If two circles are tangent, they touch at exactly one point. A circle which circumscribes these two circles be tangent at opposite sides of both circles. Its radius will be equal to the sum of the smaller circles' radii, so 5 in + 7 in = 12 in. Using the formula for circumference, $C = 2\pi r$, the circumference of the larger circle is $2 \times \pi \times 12$ inches, or 24π inches.

16. A and D: If an even number is multiplied by an odd number, the result is always even. In Choice B, multiplying 3 by an even number still results in an even number. However, multiplying 5 by an odd number does not mean the result is even, so B is not included in the possible answers. Squaring an odd number results in an odd number, which means Choice C is not a possible answer. For the value of Choice D, raising an odd number to an odd power may still result in an odd number, such as $3^5 = 243$. However, when this number is multiplied by 2, it results in an even number. Adding this result to an even number that is cubed, which is also even, results in an even answer. In Choice *E*, the value of an odd number raised to any power is still an odd number, and adding an even number to it remains odd, so Choice *E* is not a possible answer.

17. B and D: For the side lengths of a triangle, the first rule is that the sum of any two sides must be greater than the third side. Using this rule, Choice *C* can be eliminated because $8 + 4$ is not greater than 13. In order for the lengths to be sides of a right triangle, they must satisfy the equation $a^2 + b^2 = c^2$. For the values in *A*, the equation becomes $7^2 + 8^2 = 12^2$. Because this does not form a true statement, $113 = 144$, then *A* is not a possible answer. For the values in Choice *E*, $5^2 + 7^2 = 11^2$ is false, so it is also eliminated. The lengths in Choice *B* form a true statement with $3^2 + 4^2 = 5^2$, so *B* is included in the possible answers. For Choice *D*, a true statement, $6^2 + 8^2 = 10^2$, is formed. The side lengths in Choices *B* and *D* contain values that satisfy the Pythagorean Theorem; therefore, they are possible side lengths for a right triangle.

18. 380 Minutes: To find the total driving time, the total distance of 350 miles can be divided by the constant speed of 60 miles per hour. This yields a time of 5.8333 hours, which is then rounded. Once the driving time is computed, the break times need to be found. If Gary takes a break for 10 minutes every 100 miles, he will take 3 breaks on his trip. This will yield a total of 30 minutes of break time. Since the answer is needed in minutes, 5.8333 can be converted to minutes by multiplying by 60, giving a driving time of 350 minutes. Adding the break time of 30 minutes to the driving time of 350 minutes gives a total travel time of 380 minutes.

19. A: If $x = 22$, then $-\frac{x}{11} = -\frac{22}{11} = 2$, which is even. Therefore, x is both even and positive. However, if $x = -22$, then $-\frac{x}{11} = \frac{22}{11} = -2$, which is even. In this case x is both even and negative. The sign of x does not matter, and x does not have to be a perfect square. Plugging in any odd value for x will not result in an even number. For example, if $x = 23$,

$$-\frac{x}{11} = -\frac{23}{11} \approx 2.09$$

Therefore, x must be even.

20. D: To find the average, sum the expressions and divide by 5. The sum is $x + (x + 3) + (x + 5) + (x + 7) + (x + 15) = 5x + 30$. Dividing by 5 results in the average: $x + 6$.

Section 4: Verbal Reasoning

1. A, E: The second sentence describes a panting depicting American colonialist watching television, which is a shocking image since television was invented more than a century after the American Revolution. Since this is Juan's most famous painting, it likely involves Juan's signature style, which is what's needed to complete Blank (i). *Anachronism* (Choice *A*) is something that stands out for being conspicuously placed in the wrong time period. *Hyperbole* (Choice *B*) is an exaggeration that serves some rhetorical or comedic purpose, and *irony* (Choice *C*) is using a word or phrase that expresses the literal opposite of its standard meaning, typically for comedic effect. Thus, Choice *A* is the correct answer.

Blank (ii) is a verb that describes how the work makes viewers feel confusion and horror. *Elicit* (Choice *E*) means to evoke an emotional reaction. *Abates* (Choice *D*) denotes a declining intensity, and *obviates* (Choice *F*) means to avoid or preempt something. Thus, Choice *E* is the correct answer.

2. B, D: Jacob is a terrific team leader, so Blank (i) will be a verb that supports his ability to produce rapid results. *Galvanize* (Choice *B*) denotes causing a person or group to take sudden action. *Enervate* (Choice *A*) means to drain someone's mental or physical energy. *Venerate* (Choice *C*) means to treat with respect. Thus, Choice *B* is the correct answer.

Blank (ii) will describe why Lisa is a poor team leader and possibly relate to how she becomes angry and unapproachable when confronted with a difficult situation. *Irascible* (Choice *D*) denotes being hotheaded or easily angered. *Tortuous* (Choice *E*) describes a series of twists and turns, and *zealous* (Choice *F*) relates to energetically supporting a cause or person. Thus, Choice *D* is the correct answer.

3. B, F, H: The first sentence states that the United States and Scandinavia are different. Blank (i) comes after a clause describing the United States as a multicultural country of immigrants, so the correct answer will be the opposite of multiculturalism. *Homogeneous* (Choice *B*) denotes something with a universal composition and, in this context, homogenous means monoculture. *Ambiguous* (Choice *A*) denotes an uncertain meaning, and *sedulous* (Choice *C*) describes a person who's dedicated or diligent. Thus, Choice *B* is the correct answer.

Blank (ii) will be a noun that can be attached to "political." *Ideology* (Choice *F*) is a set of ideas and values that influences one's beliefs. *Cacophony* (Choice *D*) is a harsh combination of sounds, and *hegemony* (Choice *E*) denotes dominance over all competitors. Thus, Choice *F* is the correct answer.

Blank (iii) will complement *interventionist* in describing a foreign policy. *Bellicose* (Choice *H*) denotes a willingness to enter conflicts. *Ambivalent* (Choice *G*) refers to having contradictory thoughts about something, and *timorous* (Choice *I*) means being timid, nervous, or scared. Thus, Choice *H* is the correct answer.

4. A, D, G: The employer pulled the employees aside to prevent a fight from breaking out, so Blank (i) will involve decreasing the tension. *Placating* (Choice *A*) means to lessen the tension, anger, or hostility. *Prevaricating* (Choice *B*) means to behave evasively or to hide the truth, and *refuting* (Choice *C*) denotes proving something is wrong. *Refuting* is close but *placating* relates more directly to dissolving tension and needing to find a workable solution. Thus, Choice *A* is the correct answer.

Blank (ii) is what the employer wants the employees to stop doing to each other. *Denigrating* (Choice *D*) means attacking someone unfairly or disparagingly. *Disabusing* (Choice *E*) refers to showing someone why they're wrong, and *venerating* (Choice *F*) denotes having respect for someone. Thus, Choice *D* is the correct answer.

Blank (iii) is what the employer hopes will happen with the solution. *Effectuated* (Choice *G*) would mean the solution went into effect. *Exculpated* (Choice *H*) means proving someone's innocence, and *extrapolated* (Choice *I*) involves projecting data into the future. Thus, Choice *G* is the correct answer.

5. B, F, G: For **i**, If someone has "uncertainty" pertaining to a subject, the idea is that they are *ambivalent* about the subject, which means they have conflicting emotions about it. Choice *A*, *ebullient*, means enthusiastic, and someone who is "uncertain" about a subject cannot also be *enthusiastic* about it. Choice *C*, *hapless*, means deserving pity, and being uncertain about a president's decision doesn't necessarily call for pity. For **ii**, the best word here is *engaging*, which means participating in something. A war is something that one *engages* in. Choice *D*, *refraining*, is incorrect, because we see that the president *did participate* in the civil war by the end of the sentence, and also one *refrains from* and does not *refrain in* something. Choice *E*, *renounce*, means to abandon or reject, which is the opposite of *engaging in*, and does not make sense by the end of the sentence. For **iii**, the best choice is *impetuous*, because it means acting without thinking. Usually an impetuous decision will cause a "shocked" reaction. Choices *H* and *I*, *temperate* and *impassive*, do not cause "shocked" reactions in people because they mean calm or aloof.

6. A, E: For **i**, *relegated* is the best answer choice because it means to demote to a lower position. The chief was demoted to patrolman. Choices *B* and *C*, *endorsed* and *promoted*, are incorrect, because these imply a raise or an honor of some kind, and we see that the chief was unable to lessen the city's crime rates. For **ii**, *mitigate* means to lessen. Choice *D*, *escalate*, is the opposite of *mitigate*, and the chief wouldn't be demoted because of his inability to *increase* the crime rates. Choice *F*, *transmit*, is also incorrect because this means to spread.

7. C: The author contrasts two different viewpoints, then builds a case showing preference for one over the other. Choice *A* is incorrect because the introduction does not contain an impartial definition, but rather another's opinion. Choice *B* is incorrect. There is no puzzling phenomenon given, as the author doesn't mention any peculiar cause or effect that is in question regarding poetry. Choice *D* does contain another's viewpoint at the beginning of the passage; however, to say that the author has no stake in this argument is incorrect; the author uses personal experiences to build their case. Finally, Choice *E* is incorrect because there is no description of the history of poetry offered within the passage.

8. B: Choice *B* accurately describes the author's argument in the text—that poetry is not irrelevant. While the author does praise—and even value—Buddy Wakefield as a poet, he or she never heralds Wakefield as a genius. Eliminate Choice *A*, as it is an exaggeration. Not only is Choice *C* an exaggerated statement, but the author never mentions spoken word poetry in the text. Choice *D* is incorrect because this statement contradicts the writer's argument. Choice *E* can also be eliminated, because the author mentions how performance actually *enhances* poetry and that modern technology is one way poetry remains vital.

9. D: *Exiguously* means not occurring often, or occurring rarely, so Choice *D* would LEAST change the meaning of the sentence. Choice *A*, *indolently*, means unhurriedly, or slow, and does not fit the context of the sentence. Choice *B*, *inaudibly*, means quietly or silently. Choice *C*, *interminably*, means endlessly, or all the time, and is the opposite of the word *exiguously*. Choice *E*, *impecunious*, means impoverished or destitute, and does not fit within the context of the sentence.

10. E: The author of the passage tries to insist that performance poetry is a subset of modern poetry, and therefore prove that modern poetry is not "dying," but thriving on social media for the masses. Choice *A* is incorrect, as the author is not refusing any kind of validation. Choice *B* is incorrect; the author's insistence is that poetry will *not* lose popularity. Choice *C* mimics the topic but compares two different genres, while the author makes no comparison in this passage. Choice *D* is incorrect as well; again, there is no cause or effect the author is trying to prove.

11. B: The author's purpose is to disprove Gioia's article claiming that poetry is a dying art form that only survives in academic settings. In order to prove his argument, the author educates the reader about new developments in poetry (Choice *A*) and describes the brilliance of a specific modern poet (Choice *C*), but these are used to serve as examples of a growing poetry trend that counters Gioia's argument. Choice *D* is incorrect because it contradicts the author's argument. Choice *E* is incorrect because the passage uses the performance as a way to convey the author's point; it's not the focus of the piece. It's also unclear if the author was actually present at the live performance.

12. D: This question is difficult because four out of the five choices offer real reasons as to why the author includes the quote. However, the question specifically asks for the *main reason* for including the quote. First off, eliminate Choice A. "Speaking meter" doesn't exist and isn't mentioned in the passage. The quote from a recently written poem shows that people are indeed writing, publishing, and performing poetry (Choice B). The quote also shows that people are still listening to poetry (Choice C). These things are true and, by their nature, serve to disprove Gioia's views (Choice E), which is the author's goal. However, Choice D is the most direct reason for including the quote, because the article analyzes the quote for its "complex themes" that "draws listeners and appreciation" right after it's given.

13. A, F: Initially, readers may select a choice that misses the clearest idea of the sentence, just because it works. But remember both synonyms must work to maintain the main idea of the sentence. Two words that do that in this case are *tyro* and *novice*, because they both mean someone who is new at their job.

14. A, B: Notice the signal words "rather than." Look for synonyms that mean something other than a stellar voting record. Note the logic for selecting the first two choices, which insinuate that the senator had past sins that were brought to light. The other choices not only do not have synonyms, but some of them do not complete the full meaning of the sentence.

15. A, F: The key word in the passage is "thick." Even if readers have not seen the commercial, they can visualize the slow motion of a pearl dropped into a bottle of thick shampoo. Choices B, C, D, and E do not suggest a relationship to slow movement. Although *viscous* and *gradual* are not synonyms, they both indicate properties that have a thick, or slow, movement.

16. A: This is a challenging question because the author's purpose is somewhat open-ended. The author concludes by stating that the questions regarding human perception and observation can be approached from many angles. Thus, the author does not seem to be attempting to prove one thing or another. Choice B is incorrect because we cannot know for certain whether the electron experiment is the latest discovery in astroparticle physics because no date is given. Choice C is a broad generalization that does not reflect accurately on the writer's views. While the author does appear to reflect on opposing views of human understanding (Choice D), the best answer is Choice A. Choice E is also wrong because the author never says that classical philosophy is wrong or directly attempts to debunk it.

17. C: It presents a problem, explains the details of that problem, and then ends with more inquiry. The beginning of this paragraph literally "presents a conundrum," explains the problem of partial understanding, and then ends with more questions, or inquiry. There is no solution offered in this paragraph, making Choices A, B, and E incorrect. Choice D is incorrect because the paragraph does not begin with a definition.

18. B: The electrons passed through both holes and then onto the plate. Choices A, C, and E are wrong because such movement is not mentioned at all in the text. In the passage, the author says that electrons that were physically observed appeared to pass through one hole or another. Remember, the electrons that were observed doing this were described as acting like particles. Therefore, Choice D is incorrect. Recall that the plate actually recorded electrons passing through both holes simultaneously and hitting the plate This behavior—the electron activity that wasn't seen by humans—was characteristic of waves. Thus, Choice B is the right answer.

19. C: The author uses "gravity" to demonstrate an example of natural phenomena humans discovered and understood without the use of tools or machines. Choice A mirrors the language in the beginning of the paragraph, but is incorrect in its intent. Choice B is incorrect; the paragraph mentions nothing of "not knowing the true nature of gravity." Choices *D* and *E* are both incorrect as well. There is no mention of an "alternative solution" or "looking forward" to new technology in this paragraph.

20. E: The important thing to keep in mind is that we must choose a scenario that best parallels, or is most similar to, the discovery of the experiment mentioned in the passage. The important aspects of the experiment can be summed up like so: humans directly observed one behavior of electrons and then through analyzing a tool (the plate that recorded electron hits), discovered that there was another electron behavior that could not be physically seen by human eyes. This best parallels the scenario in Choice *E*. Like Feynman, the colorblind person is able to observe one aspect of the world but through the special goggles (a tool) he is able to see a natural phenomenon that he could not physically see on his own. While Choice *D* is compelling because an x-ray helps humans see the broken bone, it is not necessarily revealing that the bone is broken in the first place. The other choices do not parallel the scenario in question. Therefore, Choice *E* is the best choice.

Section 5: Quantitative Reasoning

1. D: If you let $x = 2$, Quantity A is equal to 56, which is larger than Quantity B. Therefore, Choices *B* and *C* can be eliminated. However, if you let $x = 0$, Quantities A and B are both equal to 48, so the quantities are equal. Therefore, the relationship between the quantities depends on the value of x, and a relationship cannot be determined.

2. A: A calculation is not necessary to determine this answer; both expressions can be rewritten with a base of 2. Quantity A can be rewritten as $(2^2)^{48} = 2^{96}$. Quantity B can be rewritten as $(2^3)^{36} = 2^{72}$. Because they have the same base, the expression with the larger exponent is greater. Quantity A is larger than Quantity B.

3. D: If $z = 1$, Quantity A is equal to 12, which is less than Quantity B, which is equal to 15. Therefore, Choices *A* and *C* are incorrect since Quantity B is greater, and the quantities are not equal. However, if $z = 0$, Quantity A and Quantity B are both equal to 0, so the quantities are equal. Therefore, the relationship between the quantities depends on the value of z and a relationship cannot be determined.

4. D: If $x = 1$, Quantity A is equal to -2 and is less than Quantity B, which is equal to 3. Therefore, Choices *A* and *C* are incorrect. However, if $x = 0$, Quantity A and Quantity B are both equal to 0, so the quantities are equal. Therefore, the relationship between the quantities depends on the value of x, and a relationship cannot be determined.

5. C: Quantity A can be simplified into a decimal. Divide 3 by 16 to obtain 0.1875. Also, Quantity B can be simplified. Multiply 0.75×0.25 to obtain 0.1875. Therefore, the two quantities are always equal.

6. A: If $x = 11$ then $x^2 = 121$ which is greater than 100. Therefore, to satisfy the inequality $x^2 < 100$, x has to be less than 11. Another approach would be to take the square root of both sides of the inequality to show that $x < 10$. Therefore, Quantity A is greater than Quantity B.

7. A: Working backwards, the correct choice can be determined. If the total cost of the textbook, including tax, was $133, then the sales tax was $133-$125=$8. Taking this as a percentage of the cost, the tax was $\frac{8}{125} = 6.4\%$. Because this amount is less than 8%, the total cost of the textbook has to be greater than $133. Another approach would be to multiply $125 by 0.08 to obtain $10, which is the minimum amount of sales tax. $125 + $10 = 135, which is an amount larger than $133. Therefore, any sales tax greater than 8% would result in an amount larger than $133. Therefore, Quantity A is greater than Quantity B.

8. A: The quantitates in common can be divided out. Each quantity has the products from 6 to 16 in common. Quantity A is left with $17 \times 18 = 306$, and Quantity B is left with $1 \times 2 \times 3 \times 4 \times 5 = 120$. Therefore, Quantity A is greater than Quantity B.

9. D: If $x = -1$, Quantity A and Quantity B are both equal to -1. However, if $x = -3$, Quantity A is equal to -243, and Quantity B is equal to -2,187. In this case, Quantity A is greater than Quantity B. Therefore, the relationship between the quantities depends on the value of x, and a relationship cannot be determined.

10. B and D: Subtracting 5 from both sides of the equation results in $8|x + 6| = 56$. Then, dividing both sides by 8 obtains $|x + 6| = 7$. After using the property of absolute value, there are two equations to solve: $x + 6 = 7$ and $x + 6 = -7$. Therefore, $x = 1$ and -13.

11. D: Notice that $(m + n)^2 = m^2 + 2mn + n^2$. Therefore, we square $m + n = 8$ to obtain the result of:

$$(m + n)^2 = 8^2 = 64$$

12. 72: The total for Ariana's bills is $985. This total is found by adding the rent, heating and air conditioning, and water bills for the studio. The income from yoga classes is $3500. The money she profits after the bills is found by subtracting 985 from 3500, which equals 2515. This profit of $2515 divided by the money she receives from the yoga classes is $2515 \div 3500 = 0.71857$, which is rounded. To change this value into a percent, the decimal can be moved two places to the right. Rounding to a whole percent yields a value of 72%.

13. C: In order to solve for a, add 9 to both sides of the given equation. This results in $a = 27$. Then, plug this value in and square the result to obtain:

$$(a + 5)^2 = (27 + 5)^2 = 32^2 = 1024$$

14. 11:19 a.m.: The position of these bikers should be equal at the time that they meet. Brinley's position can be represented by the expression $12(t - 7)$, because she is traveling at a pace of 12 miles per hour and she leaves at 7 a.m. Trey leaves his house, which is 85 miles away, at 8 a.m. He then travels at a speed of 10 miles per hour. His position can be represented by the expression $85 - 10(t - 8)$. These two expressions are set equal to one another to represent a common position where the two meet, which yields the equation $12(t - 7) = 85 - 10(t - 8)$. Solving for the t-value gives a time of 11.317, rounded. Since time is not expressed using decimals, the decimal can be converted to minutes by multiplying 0.317 by 60. The time that they meet is 11:19 a.m.

To check your work, the total distance that Brinley traveled can be found by multiplying 12 by 4.317, which is speed times time. This position is 51.8 miles. The total distance that Trey traveled can be found by multiplying 10 by 3.317, since he left an hour later than Brinley. His distance is 33.17 miles. Combining these distances yields a total distance of 85 miles, which is how far Brinley's house is from Trey's house.

15. E: The equation can be rewritten as $7(7^x) = 7^{11}$, since there are 7 terms on the left-hand side. This is the same as $7^{x+1} = 7^{11}$. We can equate the exponents to obtain $x + 1 = 11$, or $x = 10$.

16. A: Because the ratio of fruit to vegetables is 5 to 3, that means that 3 out of every 8 produce items are vegetables. $\frac{3}{8} = 0.375$, or 37.5%. 37.5% of 120 is equal to $0.375 \times 120 = 45$. Therefore, 45 of the total 120 produce items are vegetables and $120 - 45 = 75$ are fruit.

17. B: First, distribute the exponent in the numerator to obtain $\frac{x^4 y^4 z}{x^2 y z^0}$. Also, note that $z^0 = 1$, so this expression is equivalent to $\frac{x^4 y^4 z}{x^2 y}$. Laws of exponents state that $\frac{a^b}{a^c} = a^{b-c}$, so the equivalent simplified expression is:

$$x^{4-2} y^{4-1} z = x^2 y^3 z$$

18. 53.6: The first step in solving this problem is finding the total number of students in the school. The sum of students is $550 + 635 = 1185$. Out of the 1185 total students, 635 of them are girls. To find the percentage of girls, the number 635 can be divided by 1185. This division yields a decimal of 0.5358. Multiplying this number by 100 turns it into a percentage of 53.6.

19. C: Because 40% of y is 24, then $0.4y = 24$. Dividing both sides of the equation by 0.4 results in $y = 60$. Also, it is true that $\frac{60}{120} = 0.5$, so 60 is 50% of 120. Therefore, the answer is 50.

20. B and C: The given rate is equal to $\frac{18}{4} = \frac{9}{2}$ miles per hour. Choice A is equal to $\frac{4}{36} = \frac{1}{9}$, so this is not a correct option. Choice B is equal to $\frac{36}{4} = \frac{9}{2}$, so this is a correct option. Choice C is equal to $\frac{9}{2}$, so this is correct as well. Choice D simplifies to $\frac{180}{20} = 9$, and this is not equal to the given rate. Finally, Choice E is equal to $\frac{4}{9}$, which is an incorrect option. The two equivalent proportions are Choices B and C.

Practice Test #3

Section 1: Analytical Writing

Issue Task:

Grades are a poor indicator of academic success. Schools should opt for success measurements that more closely resemble those in the workplace.

Write a response to this statement in which you explain the extent to which you agree or disagree. Provide examples of alternative performance measurements and how each of them might be better or worse than grades.

Argument Task:

The following is a persuasive paragraph written for the beginning of a history lecture:

"Evidently, our country has overlooked both the importance of learning history and the appreciation of it. But why is this a huge problem? Other than historians, who really cares how the War of 1812 began, or who Alexander the Great's tutor was? Well, not many, as it turns out. So, *is* history really that important? Yes! History is *critical* to help us understand the underlying forces that shape decisive events, to prevent us from making the same mistakes twice, and to give us context for current events."

In your essay response, evaluate the underlying logic of the given argument above. Analyze its use of evidence as well as its assumptions. You might also think about what kind of evidence might weaken or strengthen the argument.

Section 2: Verbal Reasoning

For questions 1-6, select the best word from the corresponding column of choices that most clearly completes the passage. Select only one answer choice for each question.

1. Because of her increase in sales, the writer was able to contribute to her two favorite charities, causing her to have a (i) _____ year.

Blank (i)
a. noxious
b. munificent
c. inveterate
d. inimical
e. fallacious

2. The team member (i) _____ to the suggestions of his coworker when he found out that she had singlehandedly (ii) _____ the Peterson account last year.

Blank (i)	Blank (ii)
a. admonished	d. procured
b. swooned	e. aggregated
c. acceded	f. precipitated

3. The island was (i) _____ with turmoil due to its recent hurricane destruction.

Blank (i)
a. sanguine
b. obdurate
c. mawkish
d. prudent
e. rife

4. While camping, we were (i) _____ of any sounds we heard during the night because of the recent bear attack. However, we knew that the night rangers were (ii) _____ of any threat to the campers while they were on night patrol.

Blank (i)	Blank (ii)
a. leery	d. cognizant
b. elated	e. oblivious
c. assuaged	f. quarantined

5. The captain's (i) _____ was that the storm would be much worse than the authorities predicted, so he turned the boat around and headed for shore.

Blank (i)
a. dialect
b. visage
c. premonition
d. psyche
e. prestige

6. The law student immediately recognized the (i) _____ argumentation on the exam and set the question right. Those (ii) _____ years in law school had finally paid off.

Blank (i)	Blank (ii)
a. palatable	d. vivacious
b. capricious	e. arduous
c. fallacious	f. lackadaisical

Questions 7–11 are based on the following passage.

The Middle Ages were a time of great superstition and theological debate. Many beliefs were developed and practiced, while some died out or were listed as heresy. Boethianism is a Medieval theological philosophy that attributes sin to gratification and righteousness with virtue and God's providence. Boethianism holds that sin, greed, and corruption are means to attain temporary pleasure, but that they inherently harm the person's soul as well as other human beings.

In *The Canterbury Tales,* we observe more instances of bad actions punished than goodness being rewarded. This would appear to be some reflection of Boethianism. In the "Pardoner's Tale," all three thieves wind up dead, which is a result of their desire for wealth. Each wrong doer pays with their life, and they are unable to enjoy the wealth they worked to steal. Within his tales, Chaucer gives reprieve to people undergoing struggle, but also interweaves stories of contemptible individuals being cosmically punished for their wickedness. The thieves idolize physical wealth, which leads to their downfall. This same theme and ideological principle of Boethianism is repeated in the "Friar's Tale," whose summoner character attempts to gain further wealth by partnering with a demon. The summoner's refusal to repent for his avarice and corruption leads to the demon dragging his soul to Hell. Again, we see the theme of the individual who puts faith and morality aside in favor for a physical prize. The result, of course, is that the summoner loses everything.

The examples of the righteous being rewarded tend to appear in a spiritual context within the *Canterbury Tales*. However, there are a few instances where we see goodness resulting in physical reward. In the Prioress' Tale, we see corporal punishment for barbarism *and* a reward for goodness. The Jews are punished for their murder of the child, giving a sense of law and order (though racist) to the plot. While the boy does die, he is granted a lasting reward by being able to sing even after his death, a miracle that marks that the murdered youth led a pure life. Here, the miracle represents eternal favor with God.

Again, we see the theological philosophy of Boethianism in Chaucer's *The Canterbury Tales* through acts of sin and righteousness and the consequences that follow. When pleasures of the world are sought instead of God's favor, we see characters being punished in tragic ways. However, the absence of worldly lust has its own set of consequences for the characters seeking to obtain God's favor.

7. What would be a potential reward for living a good life, as described in Boethianism?
   a. A long life sustained by the good deeds one has done over a lifetime.
   b. Wealth and fertility for oneself and the extension of one's family line.
   c. Vengeance for those who have been persecuted by others who have a capacity for committing wrongdoing.
   d. The act of reaching Sainthood.
   e. God's divine favor for one's righteousness.

8. What might be the main reason why the author chose to discuss Boethianism through examining *The Canterbury Tales*?

    a. *The Canterbury Tales* is a well-known text.

    b. *The Canterbury Tales* is the only known fictional text that contains use of Boethianism.

    c. *The Canterbury Tales* presents a manuscript written in the medieval period that can help illustrate Boethianism through stories and show how people of the time might have responded to the idea.

    d. Within each individual tale in *The Canterbury Tales*, the reader has the opportunity to read about different levels of Boethianism and how each level leads to greater enlightenment.

    e. Chaucer, who wrote *The Canterbury Tales,* was a devoted Boethianist.

9. What "ideological principle" is the author referring to in the middle of the second paragraph when talking about the "Friar's Tale"?

    a. The principle that the act of ravaging another's possessions is the same as ravaging one's soul.

    b. The principle that thieves who idolize physical wealth will be punished in an earthly sense as well as eternally.

    c. The principle that fraternization with a demon will result in one losing everything, including their life.

    d. The principle that a desire for material goods leads to moral malfeasance punishable by a higher being.

    e. The principle that wealth is impossible to enjoy when one has been corrupted in the pursuit of it.

10. Which of the following words, if substituted for the word *avarice* in paragraph two, would LEAST change the meaning of the sentence?

    a. Perniciousness

    b. Pithiness

    c. Covetousness

    d. Pompousness

    e. Capriciousness

11. Based on the passage, what view does Boethianism take on desire?

    a. Desire does not exist in the context of Boethianism.

    b. Desire is a virtue and should be welcomed.

    c. Having desire is evidence of demonic possession.

    d. Desire for pleasure can lead toward sin.

    e. Desire is the result of original sin.

For questions 12-15, select the <u>two</u> answer choices that can complete the sentence and create sentences that have complementary meaning.

12. There was one particular NFL football player who consistently delivered abrupt and _____ answers when the media approached him after the game.

    a. Loquacious

    b. Laconic

    c. Verbose

    d. Bombastic

    e. Terse

    f. Ranting

13. Janet is an exemplary kindergarten teacher due to her _____ character.
    a. audacious
    b. benign
    c. benevolent
    d. professional
    e. stoic
    f. whimsical

14. Once she smelled the barbeque chicken, our puppy knocked the plate off the table and wolfed it down. Then she responded to our scolding with the most _____ look I've ever seen.
    a. brazen
    b. credulous
    c. despondent
    d. irreproachable
    e. painstaking
    f. unabashed

15. Given their critical role in upholding the justice system, lawyers are required to always be completely _____ when responding to a judge's questions, even if it means harming their case.
    a. adept
    b. banal
    c. candid
    d. forthright
    e. munificent
    f. stolid

Questions 16–20 are based on the following two passages. Select only one answer choice for each question.

Passage I

Excerpt from Thomas Henry Huxley, "Science and Culture"

The representatives of the humanists in the nineteenth century take their stand upon classical education as the sole avenue to culture, as firmly as if we were still in the age of Renaissance. Yet, surely, the present intellectual relations of the modern and the ancient worlds are profoundly different from those which obtained three centuries ago. Leaving aside the existence of a great and characteristically modern literature, of modern painting, and, especially, of modern music, there is one feature of the present state of the civilized world which separates it more widely from the Renaissance than the Renaissance was separated from the Middle Ages.

This distinctive character of our own times lies in the vast and constantly increasing part which is played by natural knowledge. Not only is our daily life shaped by it, not only does the prosperity of millions of men depend upon it, but our whole theory of life has long been influenced, consciously or unconsciously, by the general conceptions of the universe, which have been forced upon us by physical science.

In fact, the most elementary acquaintance with the results of scientific investigation shows us that they offer a broad and striking contradiction to the opinions so implicitly credited and taught in the Middle Ages.

Passage II

Excerpt from Matthew Arnold, "Literature and Science"

When I speak of knowing Greek and Roman antiquity, therefore, as a help to knowing ourselves and the world, I mean more than a knowledge of so much vocabulary, so much grammar, so many portions of authors in the Greek and Latin languages. I mean knowing the Greeks and Romans, and their life and genius, and what they were and did in the world; what we get from them, and what is its value. That, at least, is the ideal; and when we talk of endeavoring to know Greek and Roman antiquity, as a help to knowing ourselves and the world, we mean endeavoring so to know them as to satisfy this ideal, however much we may still fall short of it.

The same also as to knowing our own and other modern nations with the like aim of getting to understand ourselves and the world. To know the best that has been thought and said by the modern nations, is to know, says Professor Huxley, "only what modern *literatures* have to tell us; it is the criticism of life contained in modern literature." And yet "the distinctive character of our times," he urges, "lies in the vast and constantly increasing part which is played by natural knowledge." And how, therefore, can a man, devoid of knowledge of what physical science has done in the last century enter hopefully upon a criticism of modern life?

16. The authors of the passages differ in their attitudes toward humanities in that the author of passage II is:

   a. an advocate of the study of science as it relates to classical text only, namely the writings of Greek and Roman text.

   b. an advocate of the study of science as it relates to natural knowledge only, namely the importance of it and how we are shaped by it.

   c. a defender of the study of humanities in "modern" schooling as it relates to both literature and science.

   d. a defender of the study of humanities in "modern" schooling as it relates to the study of literature only, namely Greek and Roman texts.

   e. a defender of the study of humanities in "modern" schooling as it relates to the axioms of Professor Huxley.

17. Which one of the following most accurately characterizes the relationship between the two passages?

   a. Passage B is written in response to passage A; passage B uses textual evidence from passage A to contradict passage A's argument.

   b. Passage B is written in response to passage A; passage B uses textual evidence from passage A to enthusiastically agree with its argument.

   c. Passage A is written in response to passage B; passage A offers a critique of passage B's views on classical literature in relation to the study of science, or natural knowledge.

   d. Passage A is written in response to passage B; passage A offers a concession of passage B's argument by showing that Greek and Roman literature can be studied alongside natural knowledge.

   e. Passage A is written in response to passage B; passage A is supportive of the argument of passage B with a few exceptions.

18. The authors of the passages would be most likely to disagree over whether:
    a. the process of evolution is considered an area of science or not.
    b. Eastern literature is more formidable than Western literature.
    c. science should be given a place in academia within this time period.
    d. whether art should be used for its intrinsic nature or for political purposes.
    e. classical literature lends itself to the progression of future generations.

19. The author of passage II thinks that knowing Greek and Roman culture is valuable because:
    a. scholars consider Greek and Roman literature the best in the world.
    b. it is a culture that offers foundation and experience on an array of subjects that we can learn from in the present.
    c. Latin is an important language to study in order to have a firm understanding of the natural sciences.
    d. Greek and Roman culture were far superior to the culture of the authors' time period.
    e. the Greeks and Romans placed more importance on the humanities than on science, which is what the author of passage B is arguing for.

20. What does the author of passage I mean by the last paragraph?
    a. That the Middle Ages was a formidable period of scientific progress and that modern science would do well to follow after it.
    b. That those with little acquaintance of scientific investigation are synonymous with those who lived during the Middle Ages.
    c. That an elementary knowledge of the Middle Ages is not conducive to the knowledge of scientific investigation.
    d. That what was studied and valued in the Middle Ages is in stark contrast to the scientific process valued in the author's period.
    e. That the opinions taught in the Middle Ages are superior to those opinions taught centuries later.

Section 3: Quantitative Reasoning

For questions 1-9, compare Quantity A to Quantity B, using additional information presented above the two quantities.

1.

Quantity A	Quantity B
The area of a circle whose radius is 20.	The area of a circle whose diameter is 43.

    a. Quantity A is greater.
    b. Quantity B is greater.
    c. The two quantities are equal.
    d. The relationship cannot be determined from the information given.

2.

Quantity A	Quantity B
60% of 30	30% of $\left(\frac{5}{12} \times 144\right)$

a. Quantity A is greater.
b. Quantity B is greater.
c. The two quantities are equal.
d. The relationship cannot be determined from the information given.

3.   1 foot is equal to 12 inches.

Quantity A	Quantity B
500 square inches	The area of a square with a side length of 4 feet

a. Quantity A is greater.
b. Quantity B is greater.
c. The two quantities are equal.
d. The relationship cannot be determined from the information given.

4.   A dog ate 2 less than 65% of the 120 bones his owner purchased.

Quantity A	Quantity B
The number of bones the dog ate	80

a. Quantity A is greater.
b. Quantity B is greater.
c. The two quantities are equal.
d. The relationship cannot be determined from the information given.

5.   A line in the Cartesian plan has the equation $6x + 4y = 0$.

Quantity A	Quantity B
The x- intercept of the line	The y- intercept of the line

a. Quantity A is greater.
b. Quantity B is greater.
c. The two quantities are equal.
d. The relationship cannot be determined from the information given.

6. $$8x^2 - 8(x + 6) = 0$$

Quantity A	Quantity B
41	x^3

a. Quantity A is greater.
b. Quantity B is greater.
c. The two quantities are equal.
d. The relationship cannot be determined from the information given.

7. The volume of a cylinder with a radius equal to 6 units is 360π.

Quantity A	Quantity B
8 units	The height of the cylinder

a. Quantity A is greater.
b. Quantity B is greater.
c. The two quantities are equal.
d. The relationship cannot be determined from the information given.

8.

Quantity A	Quantity B
The number of distinct prime factors of 44	The number of distinct prime factors of 52

a. Quantity A is greater.
b. Quantity B is greater.
c. The two quantities are equal.
d. The relationship cannot be determined from the information given.

9. $$(9a - 5b)(9a + 5b) = 3$$

Quantity A	Quantity B
$81a^2 - 25b^2$	9

a. Quantity A is greater.
b. Quantity B is greater.
c. The two quantities are equal.
d. The relationship cannot be determined from the information given.

10. How many distinct positive odd factors does 648 have?

a. 0
b. 1
c. 2
d. 3
e. 4

11. The length of a given rectangle is one half its width. If the rectangle's perimeter is 213 inches, what is its area?

    a. 71 square inches
    b. 5041 square inches
    c. 2520.5 square inches
    d. 252 square inches
    e.1260.25 square inches

12. Kelly is selling cookies to raise money for the chorus. She has 500 cookies to sell. She sells 45% of the cookies to the sixth graders. At the second lunch, she sells 40% of what's left to the seventh graders. If she sells 60% of the remaining cookies to the eighth graders, how many cookies does Kelly have left at the end of all lunches?

    ☐ cookies

13. A line passes through the point (5,6) and has slope $m = -\frac{1}{4}$. Which of the following points does the line also pass through?

    a. (0, 0)
    b. (6, 10)
    c. (-5, -6)
    d. (6, 2)
    e. (4, 2)

14. If $\sqrt[3]{m} = 2$ and $m = \sqrt{n}$, what is the value of n?

    ☐

15. 16 miles per hour is equivalent to how many feet per second?

    a. 23.5
    b. 10.9
    c. 1,408
    d. 27.5
    e. 160

16. $6,250 is invested in a bank account that earns 2.5% annual interest which is compounded monthly. How much is in the account after two months?

    a. $6,263.02
    b. $6,276.07
    c. $6,406.25
    d. $6,566.41
    e. $6,500.00

17. A fair, six-sided die is rolled three times. What is the probability that the result of exactly one of the three rolls will be a five?

    a. 0.0008

    b. 0.0463

    c. 0.1667

    d. 0.4629

    e. 0.0046

18. Find the value of x.

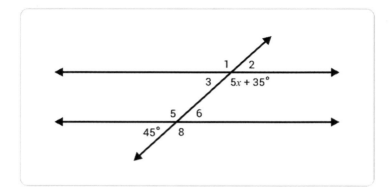

19. Which of the following is the result of simplifying the expression:

$$\frac{4a^{-1}b^3}{a^4b^{-2}} \times \frac{3a}{b}$$

    a. $12a^3b^5$

    b. $12\frac{b^4}{a^4}$

    c. $\frac{12}{a^4}$

    d. $7\frac{b^4}{a}$

    e. $4\frac{7b}{a}$

20. The graph shows the position of a car over a 10-second time interval. Which of the following is the correct interpretation of the graph for the interval 1 to 3 seconds?

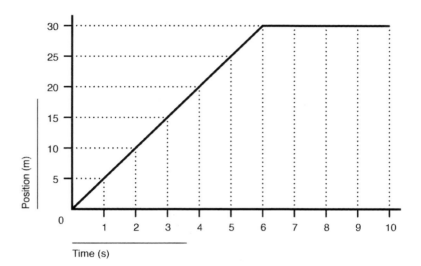

a. The car remains in the same position.
b. The car is traveling at a speed of 5 m/s.
c. The car is traveling up a hill.
d. The car is traveling at 5 mph.
e. The car is traveling at a speed of 10 m/s.

Section 4: Verbal Reasoning

For questions 1-6, select the best word from the corresponding column of choices that most clearly completes the passage:

1. The actor's (i) _____ of famous actors such as Marlon Brando and Al Pacino made him the life of the party.

Blank (i)
a. empathy
b. anecdotes
c. hypothesis
d. jubilation
e. vindication

2. The old woman's (i) _____ made her a pillar of her community and everyone's (ii) _____ way of obtaining advice.

Blank (i)	Blank (ii)
a. enmity	d. myopic
b. sagacity	e. preferred
c. impetuosity	f. variegated

3. We wanted to (i) _____ the flavor of the watermelon, so we added salt to it.

Blank (i)
a. enhance
b. discount
c. disdain
d. abbreviate
e. suppress

4. The athlete displayed remarkable (i) _____ after her injury. In fact, during her (ii) _____, the doctor told her that she was the most (iii) _____ patient he had ever seen.

Blank (i)	Blank (ii)	Blank (iii)
a. prosperity	d. expedition	g. befuddled
b. opulence	e. bereavement	h. deranged
c. resilience	f. convalescence	i. tenacious

5. After the huge disagreement we had the night before, we agreed to settle on a (i) _____ in order to keep the peace.

Blank (i)
a. altercation
b. prescription
c. fetter
d. compromise
e. pyre

6. The South American dictator was considered a (i) _____ who tormented his citizens and created unprecedented (ii) _____ in the surrounding areas.

Blank (i)	Blank (ii)
a. despot	d. exorbitance
b. novice	e. adversity
c. martyr	f. affluence

Questions 7 – 10 refer to the following passage, titled "Education is Essential to Civilization." Select only one answer choice for each question.

Early in my career, a master teacher shared this thought with me, "Education is the last bastion of civility." While I did not completely understand the scope of those words at the time, I have since come to realize the depth, breadth, truth, and significance of what he said. Education provides society with a vehicle for raising its children to be civil, decent, human beings with something valuable to contribute to the world. It is really what makes us human and what distinguishes us as civilized creatures.

Being "civilized" humans means being "whole" humans. Education must address the mind, body, and soul of students. It would be detrimental to society if our schools were myopic in their focus, only meeting the needs of the mind. As humans, we are multi-dimensional, multi-faceted beings who need more than head knowledge to survive. The human heart and psyche have to be fed in order for the mind to develop properly, and the body must be maintained and exercised to help fuel the working of the brain.

Education is a basic human right, and it allows us to sustain a democratic society in which participation is fundamental to its success. It should inspire students to seek better solutions to world problems and to dream of a more equitable society. Education should never discriminate on any basis, and it should create individuals who are self-sufficient, patriotic, and tolerant of other's ideas.

All children can learn, although not all children learn in the same manner. All children learn best, however, when their basic physical needs are met and they feel safe, secure, and loved. Students are much more responsive to a teacher who values them and shows them respect as individual people. Teachers must model at all times the way they expect students to treat them and their peers. If teachers set high expectations for their students, the students will rise to that high level. Teachers must make the well-being of their students their primary focus and must not be afraid to let their students learn from their own mistakes.

In the modern age of technology, a teacher's focus is no longer the "what" of the content, but more importantly, the "why." Students are bombarded with information and have access to ANY information they need right at their fingertips. Teachers have to work harder than ever before to help students identify salient information and to think critically about the information they encounter. Students have to read between the lines, identify bias, and determine who they can trust in the milieu of ads, data, and texts presented to them.

Schools must work in consort with families in this important mission. While children spend most of their time in school, they are dramatically and indelibly shaped by the influences of their family and culture. Teachers must not only respect this fact, but must strive to include parents in the education of their children and must work to keep parents informed of progress and problems. Communication between classroom and home is essential for a child's success.

Humans have always aspired to be more, do more, and to better ourselves and our communities. This is where education lies, right at the heart of humanity's desire to be all that we can be. Education helps us strive for higher goals and better treatment of ourselves and others. I shudder to think what would become of us if education ceased to be the "last bastion of civility." We must be unapologetic about expecting excellence from our students—our very existence depends upon it.

7. Which of the following best summarizes the author's main point?
   a. Education as we know it is over-valued in modern society, and we should find alternative solutions.
   b. The survival of the human race depends on the educational system, and it is worth fighting for to make it better.
   c. The government should do away with all public schools and require parents to home school their children instead.
   d. While education is important, some children simply are not capable of succeeding in a traditional classroom.
   e. All children must be given equal opportunity to participate in the education system without fear of discrimination.

8. Based on this passage, which of the following can be inferred about the author?
   a. The author feels passionately about education.
   b. The author does not feel strongly about his point.
   c. The author is angry at the educational system.
   d. The author is unsure about the importance of education.
   e. The author is against the use of technology in schools.

9. Based on this passage, which of the following conclusions could be drawn about the author?
   a. The author would not support raising taxes to help fund much needed reforms in education.
   b. The author would support raising taxes to help fund much needed reforms in education, as long as those reforms were implemented in higher socio-economic areas first.
   c. The author would support raising taxes to help fund much needed reforms in education for all children in all schools.
   d. The author would support raising taxes only in certain states to help fund much needed reforms in education.
   e. The author would support raising taxes to fund much needed reforms only for minority students who may lack certain advantages.

10. According to the passage, which of the following is not mentioned as an important factor in education today?
   a. Parent involvement
   b. Communication between parents and teachers
   c. Impact of technology
   d. Cost of textbooks
   e. High teacher expectations

For questions 11-16, select the <u>two</u> answer choices that can complete the sentence and create sentences that have complementary meaning.

11. I sympathize with Uncle Kevin's financial troubles, but asking our grandmother for a loan at her birthday party couldn't have been more _____.
   a. flamboyant
   b. gauche
   c. imperturbable
   d. pervasive
   e. tactless
   f. tortuous

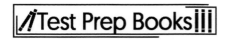

12. Lacking access to basic social services, many people rely on charitable organizations funded by _____ private citizens.
   a. beneficent
   b. craven
   c. intrepid
   d. magnanimous
   e. preeminent
   f. prescient

13. Eating only fruits and vegetables isn't a sustainable diet, but an occasional juice cleanse can be quite _____.
   a. delectable
   b. ebullient
   c. salubrious
   d. verdant
   e. wholesome
   f. winsome

14. The most effective presentations _____ key takeaways with a visual cue.
   a. accentuate
   b. bolster
   c. delineate
   d. offset
   e. rationalize
   f. underscore

15. A certain feeling of _____ descended on the group when they heard about the uncertain future of the start-up company where they worked; no one moved while the new information was presented during the meeting.
   a. Malaise
   b. Angst
   c. Chicanery
   d. Deference
   e. Quiescence
   f. Turpitude

16. Four roommates were looking for a simple, affordable apartment near the school; however, the agent insisted on showing them apartments that were _____ and expensive.
   a. Portentous
   b. Extravagant
   c. Loquacious
   d. Austere
   e. Obsequious
   f. Palatial

Questions 17 – 20 refer to the following passage. Select only one answer choice for each question.

Although many Missourians know that Harry S. Truman and Walt Disney hailed from their great state, probably far fewer know that it was also home to the remarkable George Washington Carver. At the end of the Civil War, Moses Carver, the slave owner who owned George's parents, decided to keep George and his brother and raise them on his farm. As a child, George was driven to learn and he loved painting. He even went on to study art while in college but was encouraged to pursue botany instead. He spent much of his life helping others by showing them better ways to farm; his ideas improved agricultural productivity in many countries. One of his most notable contributions to the newly emerging class of Black farmers was to teach them the negative effects of agricultural monoculture, i.e. growing the same crops in the same fields year after year, depleting the soil of much needed nutrients and resulting in a lesser yielding crop. Carver was an innovator, always thinking of new and better ways to do things, and is most famous for his over three hundred uses for the peanut. Toward the end of his career, Carver returned to his first love of art. Through his artwork, he hoped to inspire people to see the beauty around them and to do great things themselves. When Carver died, he left his money to help fund ongoing agricultural research. Today, people still visit and study at the George Washington Carver Foundation at Tuskegee Institute.

17. Which of the following describes the kind of writing used in the above passage?
    a. narrative
    b. persuasive
    c. technical
    d. expository
    e. descriptive

18. According to the passage, what was George Washington Carver's first love?
    a. plants
    b. peanuts
    c. animals
    d. soil
    e. art

19. According to the passage, what is the best definition for agricultural monoculture?
    a. The practice of producing or growing a single crop or plant species over a wide area and for a large number of consecutive years
    b. The practice of growing a diversity of crops and rotating them from year to year
    c. The practice of growing crops organically to avoid the use of pesticides
    d. The practice of charging an inflated price for cheap crops to obtain a greater profit margin
    e. The practice of planting the same crop at several farms to establish a monopoly on that crop

20. Which of the following is the best summary of this passage?
    a. George Washington Carver was born at a time when scientific discovery was at a virtual standstill.
    b. Because he was African American, there were not many opportunities for George Washington Carver.
    c. George Washington Carver was an intelligent man whose research and discoveries had an impact worldwide.
    d. George Washington Carver was far more successful as an artist than he was as a scientist.
    e. George Washington Carver was the person who first discovered peanuts.

Section 5: Quantitative Reasoning

For questions 1-9, compare Quantity A to Quantity B, using additional information presented above the two quantities.

1. Sierra rides her bike to the park at an average speed of 15 mph. On the way home, using the same route, she rides with her friend Kristen in a car traveling 25 mph.

Quantity A	Quantity B
20 mph	The average speed for Sierra's ride to and from the park

a. Quantity A is greater.
b. Quantity B is greater.
c. The two quantities are equal.
d. The relationship cannot be determined from the information given.

2.

Quantity A	Quantity B
The standard deviation of the set {1,4,7}	The standard deviation of the set {11,14,17}

a. Quantity A is greater.
b. Quantity B is greater.
c. The two quantities are equal.
d. The relationship cannot be determined from the information given.

3.   For any nonnegative integer a, let $a^* = a + 1$.

Quantity A	Quantity B
$\dfrac{14^*}{3^*}$	5^*

a. Quantity A is greater.
b. Quantity B is greater.
c. The two quantities are equal.
d. The relationship cannot be determined from the information given.

4. x, y and z are positive integers such that $xyz > 15$

Quantity A	Quantity B
$\dfrac{xy}{6}$	$\dfrac{4}{z}$

a. Quantity A is greater.
b. Quantity B is greater.
c. The two quantities are equal.
d. The relationship cannot be determined from the information given.

5.

Quantity A	Quantity B
$6x^2 - 3x + 9$	$3(x^2 - x + 2)$

a. Quantity A is greater.
b. Quantity B is greater.
c. The two quantities are equal.
d. The relationship cannot be determined from the information given.

6.
$$2x = 2y + 10$$

$$3x + 2y = 5$$

Quantity A	Quantity B
y	x

a. Quantity A is greater.
b. Quantity B is greater.
c. The two quantities are equal.
d. The relationship cannot be determined from the information given.

7.
$$x > 1$$

Quantity A	Quantity B
$\frac{x+2}{x}$	$\frac{x}{x+2}$

a. Quantity A is greater.
b. Quantity B is greater.
c. The two quantities are equal.
d. The relationship cannot be determined from the information given.

8.

Quantity A	Quantity B
The arithmetic mean (average) of 55, 56, and 58	The median of 55, 56, and 58

a. Quantity A is greater.
b. Quantity B is greater.
c. The two quantities are equal.
d. The relationship cannot be determined from the information given.

9. The original cost of a car is c dollars.

Quantity A	Quantity B
The cost of the car if the original cost was decreased by 15% and then increased by 15%	c

a. Quantity A is greater.
b. Quantity B is greater.
c. The two quantities are equal.
d. The relationship cannot be determined from the information given.

10. What are the zeros of the function: $f(x) = x^3 + 4x^2 + 4x$?
   a. -2
   b. 0, -2
   c. 2
   d. 0, 2
   e. 0, 0

11. If $g(x) = x^3 - 3x^2 - 2x + 6$ and $f(x) = 2$, then what is $g(f(x))$?
   a. -26
   b. 6
   c. $2x^3 - 6x^2 - 4x + 12$
   d. -2
   e. $2x^2 + 3x + 6$

12. What is the value of x in the diagram below?

---

13. Which of the following shows the correct result of simplifying the following expression?

$$(7n + 3n^3 + 3) + (8n + 5n^3 + 2n^4)$$

   a. $9n^4 + 15n - 2$
   b. $2n^4 + 5n^3 + 15n - 2$
   c. $9n^4 + 8n^3 + 15n$
   d. $2n^4 + 8n^3 + 15n + 3$
   e. $3n^4 + 4n^3 + 15n - 4$

14. What is the least positive three-digit multiple of 7?

15. What is the product of the following expression?

$$(4x - 8)(5x^2 + x + 6)$$

   a. $20x^3 - 36x^2 + 16x - 48$
   b. $6x^3 - 41x^2 + 12x + 15$
   c. $20x^4 + 11x^2 - 37x - 12$
   d. $2x^3 - 11x^2 - 32x + 20$
   e. $10x^3 + 2x^2 - 8x + 48$

16. Mom's car drove 72 miles in 90 minutes. How fast did she drive in feet per second?
   a. 0.8 feet per second
   b. 48.9 feet per second
   c. 0.009 feet per second
   d. 70.4 feet per second
   e. 55 feet per second

17. What is the solution for the following equation?

$$\frac{x^2 + x - 30}{x - 5} = 11$$

   a. $x = -6$
   b. There is no solution.
   c. $x = 16$
   d. $x = 5$
   e. $x = 6$

18. The following chart shows the birth month of 100 famous Americans. What is the percent chance of randomly selecting a famous American not born in January, April, or July?

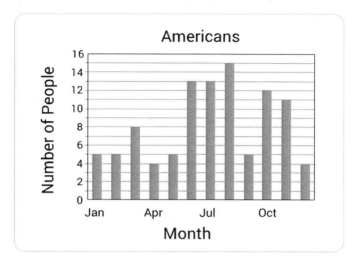

☐ Percent

19. If Sarah reads at an average rate of 21 pages in four nights, how long will it take her to read 140 pages?
   a. 6 nights
   b. 26 nights
   c. 8 nights
   d. 12 nights
   e. 27 nights

20. Dwayne has received the following scores on his math tests: 78, 92, 83, 97. What score must Dwayne get on his next math test to have an overall average of 90?
   a. 89
   b. 98
   c. 95
   d. 100
   e. 96

Answer Explanations #3

Section 2: Verbal Reasoning

1. B: *Munificent* is the best answer choice here because it means "very generous." The writer had a generous year because she was able to give to charities due to her increase in sales. The word *noxious* means deadly or injurious. The word *inveterate* means long-standing or established. The word *inimical* means not friendly. Finally, *deceptive* means false or wrong. The main implication of the sentence was that she had a prosperous, giving year, and none of the answer choices fit in this context.

2. C, D: For **i**, the best answer choice is *acceded*, which means agree or consent. We see the coworker agreeing to her suggestions because he find out that she *procured*, or won, the account last year, the answer for **ii**. *Admonished* is incorrect because it means to reprimand, and we can see that the coworker admired her. *Swooned* is in the wrong context because it means to faint. For **ii**, *aggregate* means to combine into a collection. While this isn't necessarily wrong, the word *procured* is a better choice because it fits into the entirety of the sentence and its meaning. *Precipitated* means to hurry or speed, so this is incorrect.

3. E: Choice *E*, *rife*, is the best answer choice because it means *abundant*. The island would be *abundant* with turmoil after a hurricane. Choice *A*, sanguine, means optimistic and cheerful; the island would not have been "optimistic with turmoil" after a hurricane, so this is incorrect. Choice *B*, *obdurate*, does have a negative connotation, but it's not the best answer choice because it means stubborn. Choice *C*, *mawkish*, means sentimental or emotional, which doesn't fit as well as *rife* in the preposition "with turmoil." Choice *D* means *careful*, and to be *careful with turmoil* doesn't quite fit here, making it incorrect.

4. A, D: The best answer for **i** is *leery*, Choice *A*, because it means suspicious. Since they are camping out at night and there has been a recent bear attack, they would be *suspicious* or *leery* of any noises. For **ii**, the word *cognizant* is the best choice because it means to be aware. The rangers would have to be *aware* or *cognizant* of any threats since they are out patrolling the woods. *Elated* and *assuaged* mean excited and comforted, so these do not fit in with the threatening tone of the sentence. *Oblivious* is an antonym to *cognizant*. *Quarantined* means isolated. The rangers would not be isolated of any threat while on patrol; they would be aware of any threat.

5. C: The correct word here is *premonition* because it means a feeling that something is about to happen. The captain had a feeling about the storm—that it would be worse than the authorities imagined. *Dialect* means local speech, visage means appearance, psyche means personality or inner self, and prestige means influence; none of these words indicates being able to anticipate a violent storm.

6. C, E: *Fallacious* means based on incorrect reasoning. To set a question right, the student would have to be confronted with *false* or *fallacious* reasoning on the exam. *Palatable* means delicious or agreeable, and we don't normally talk about argumentation as being either of these things. *Capricious* means a sudden behavior change and is used to describe people, not argumentation. For **ii**, *arduous* is the best choice because it means difficult. Usually if we see that something "pays off" in the end, it means that it was difficult to endure. *Vivacious* means lively or spirited, so this would not be used to describe years in law school. Neither would the word *lackadaisical*, which means careless or indifferent.

7. E: The author explains that Boethianism is a Medieval theological philosophy that attributes sin to temporary pleasure and righteousness with virtue and God's providence. Besides Choice *E*, the choices listed are all physical things. While these could still be divine rewards, Boethianism holds that the true reward for being virtuous is in God's favor. It is also stressed in the article that physical pleasures cannot be taken into the afterlife. Therefore, the best choice is *E*, God's favor.

8. C: *The Canterbury Tales* presents a manuscript written in the medieval period that can help illustrate Boethianism through stories and show how people of the time might have responded to the idea. Choices *A* and *B* are generalized statements, and we have no evidence to support Choice *B*. There is also no evidence that Chaucer was a devoted Boethianist, so Choice *E* is wrong. Choice *D* is very compelling, but it looks at Boethianism in a way that the author does not. The author does not mention "different levels of Boethianism" when discussing the tales, only that the concept appears differently in different tales. Boethianism also doesn't focus on enlightenment.

9. D: The author is referring to the principle that a desire for material goods leads to moral malfeasance punishable by a higher being. Choice *A* is incorrect; while the text does mention thieves ravaging others' possessions, it is only meant as an example and not as the principle itself. Choice *B* is incorrect for the same reason as Choice *A*. Choice *C* is mentioned in the text and is part of the example that proves the principle, and also not the principle itself. Choice *E* might be something the author holds to be true; however, it is not the main principle laid out in the two examples.

10. C: The word *avarice* most nearly means *covetousness*, or extremely desirous of money or wealth. Choice *A* means *evil* or *mischief* and does not relate to the context of the sentence. Choice *B* is also incorrect, because *pithiness* means *shortness* or *conciseness*. Choice *D*, *pompousness*, means someone is arrogant, which is also irrelevant to the context of the sentence. Choice *E* is close because *capriciousness* means erratic or unstable, which goes well with the context. However, we are told of the summoner's specific characteristic of greed, which makes Choice *C* the best answer.

11. D: Desire for pleasure can lead toward sin. Boethianism acknowledges desire as something that leads out of holiness, so Choice *A* is incorrect. Choice *B* is incorrect because in the passage, Boethianism is depicted as being wary of desire and anything that binds people to the physical world. Choices *C* and *E* can be eliminated because the author never says that desire indicates demonic possession or that it is the result of original sin.

12. B, E: Readers might recognize that the tone of the sentence is negative and short, as the writer used the word "abrupt." The two synonyms that best complete the meaning of the sentence are *laconic* and *terse*, which reflect a player's annoyance with the post-game media interview process.

13. B, C: *Benign* and *benevolent* both denote gentle kindness, which would both logically explain why Janet is an exemplary kindergarten teacher. Thus, Choices *B* and *D* are the correct answer choices. *Professional* fits logically, but no other answer choice would create sentences with complementary meaning, so Choice *D* is incorrect. Similarly, *whimsical* would make sense because an exemplary kindergarten teacher might be fanciful or playful. However, no other answer choice would create sentences with complementary meaning. Choices *A* and *E* are incorrect because they don't naturally fit the context or have a complementary answer choice. *Audacious* means someone is acting so boldly it's borderline disrespectful, and *stoic* denotes a lack of emotion or passion.

14. A, F: *Brazen* and *unabashed* both mean acting without any shame, and they create sentences with a complementary meaning since stealing barbeque chicken wouldn't necessarily make a puppy feel shame. Thus, Choices *A* and *F* are the correct answers. *Credulous* neither fits the context nor has a complementary answer choice. The puppy wouldn't be looking at her owner with a naïve willingness to believe anything. Thus, Choice *B* is incorrect. Choices *C, D,* and *E* could each individually complete the sentence logically, but they don't have a complementary answer choice. *Despondent* denotes feeling dejected or depressed; *irreproachable* means being faultless or beyond criticism; and *painstaking* involves trying to be diligent or thorough.

15. C, D: Candid and forthright both denote sincerity and honesty, which fit the context and create sentences with complementary meanings. Thus, Choices *C* and *D* are the correct answers. Choices *A* and *F* logically complete the sentence, but they have no complement. *Adept* denotes skillfulness, and *stolid* refers to someone who's calm and dependable; therefore, Choices *A* and *F* are incorrect. Choices *B* and *E* are incorrect because they neither have a complement nor fit logically. *Banal* denotes a lack of originality, and *munificent* means being overly generous.

16. C: A defender of the study of humanities in "modern" schooling as it relates to both literature and science. Choice *A* is incorrect; the author of passage B isn't advocating for the study of science, but defending the study of humanities. Choice *B* is also incorrect; this position is a characteristic of the author of passage A. Choice *D* is incorrect; a good portion of the argument is focused on the advantages of Greek and Roman antiquity. However, we see in the conclusion of passage B that Matthew Arnold, the author, uses the knowledge of classical texts as a proponent to the knowledge of both literature and science; that classical texts aid in the knowledge of both areas of studies and a broader "criticism of modern life." Finally, Choice *E* is incorrect; passage B uses the quotes from Huxley not as axioms, but to discredit the argument of passage A.

17. A: Passage B is written in response to passage A; passage B uses textual evidence from passage A to contradict passage A's argument. Choice *B* is incorrect; passage B does not enthusiastically agree with passage A. We see passage B use passage A's own rhetoric to contradict itself. Choices *C, D,* and *E* are also incorrect; we know that passage B was written in response to passage A because passage B uses quoted phrases from passage A.

18. E: The authors of the passages would be most likely to disagree over whether classical literature lends itself to the progression of future generations. Choice *A* is incorrect; the framework of the two arguments doesn't touch on what areas science consists of. Choice *B* is also incorrect; there is not enough information in the two passages to discern whether the authors would disagree over Eastern and Western literature. Choice *C* is incorrect; the passages seemingly disagree over science and its place in academia; however, passage B only argues for the place of Greek and Roman antiquity in academia, and not against the implementation of science. Choice *D* is incorrect; the authors might possibly disagree over this choice. The author of passage A would be more prone to agree that art should have a justified end, and would perhaps thus argue for political purposes. However, this isn't the *best* choice.

19. B: The author of passage B thinks that knowing Greek and Roman culture is valuable because it is a culture that offers foundation and experience on an array of subjects that we can learn from in the present. The author of passage B begins his second paragraph by saying "The same also as to knowing our own and other modern nations with the like aim of getting to understand ourselves and the world." The author of passage B thinks a key to understanding the building blocks of humanity is to know a wide array of subjects and past that contribute to humanity as a whole.

20. D: That what was studied and valued in the Middle Ages is in stark contrast to the scientific process valued in the author's period. Choices *A* and *E* are incorrect; the author is not saying that the Middle Ages were a "formidable period of scientific progress" or "superior to those opinions taught centuries later." Choices *B* and *C* are also incorrect; they both use the same language as presented in the last paragraph; however, they twist the words around and do not offer a truthful summary of the last paragraph.

Section 3: Quantitative Reasoning

1. B: The radius of a circle is half of its diameter, so the radius of the circle in Quantity B is equal to 21.5. The radius of the circle in Quantity B is larger than the one given in Quantity A. Therefore, the area of the circle in Quantity B is greater than the area of the circle in Quantity A.

2. C: Quantity A can be simplified. 60% can be expressed in decimal form as 0.6. Therefore, $0.6 \times 30 = 18$. Quantity B can be simplified as well.

$$\frac{5}{12} \times 144 = \frac{720}{12} = 60$$

30% can be expressed as 0.3. Therefore, $0.3 \times 60 = 18$. The two quantities are always equal.

3. B: Because 1 foot is equal to 12 inches, the square has a side length of $4 \times 12 = 48$ inches. The square is a 48 by 48-inch square, so the area of the square is equal to $48 \times 48 = 2,304$ square inches. This quantity is larger than a square with an area of 500 square inches. Quantity B is larger than Quantity A.

4. B: First, find 65% of 120. 65% can be expressed in decimal form as 0.65. Therefore, 65% of 120 is $0.65 \times 120 = 78$. Two less than this amount is 76. Therefore, Quantity B, 80, is greater.

5. C: In order to find the *x*- intercept of the line, plug 0 in for *y*. Therefore,

$$6x + 4(0) = 6x + 0 = 6x = 0$$

Divide both sides by 6 to obtain $x = 0$. The line runs through the origin, so both the *x* and *y*-intercepts must be 0. Therefore, the quantities are equal.

6. A: First, solve the given equation. Distribute the 8 to obtain $8x^2 - 8x - 48 = 0$, which can be factored as:

$$8(x - 3)(x + 2) = 0$$

Setting each factor equal to zero results in two solutions: $x = 3$ and $x = -2$. Therefore, x^3 can be equal to either $3^3 = 27$ or $(-2)^3 = -8$. Quantity A, which is 41, is greater than either of those two values.

7. B: The formula for the volume of a cylinder is $\pi r^2 h$, where r is the radius and h is the height. In this example, $r = 6$, so the volume is $\pi(6^2)h = 36\pi h$. It is given that the volume is 360π, so $h = 10$. The height of this cylinder is 10 units, which is greater than Quantity A.

8. C: The prime factorization of 44 is $2 \times 2 \times 11$, so there are three distinct prime factors of 44. The prime factorization of 52 is $2 \times 2 \times 13$, so there are three distinct prime factors of 52. The two values are equal and therefore, Quantity A is equal to Quantity B.

9. B: FOIL the left-hand side of the given equation to obtain:

$$(9a - 5b)(9a + 5b) = 81a^2 + 45ab - 45ab - 25b^2 = 81a^2 - 25b^2 = 3$$

Therefore, $81a^2 - 25b^2 = 3$, which is less than 9. Therefore, Quantity B is greater.

10. C: 648 can be written as $3 \times 3 \times 3 \times 3 \times 2 \times 2 \times 2 \times 1$. Note that 1 is always an odd factor of any number. In this example, 3 is the other distinct odd factor. Therefore, there are two distinct odd factors of 648.

11. C: If the length of the rectangle is L and the width is W, then the problem tells us that $L = 0.5W$. The perimeter of a rectangle is $2L + 2W$, and $2L + 2W = 213$ for this rectangle. Using the substitution $L = 0.5W$ results in the equation:

$$2(0.5W) + 2W = 1W + 2W = 3W = 213$$

Dividing by 3 results in $W = 71$, so the width of the rectangle is 71 inches. The length is $L = 0.5(71) = 35.5$ inches. The area of a rectangle is $L \times W$, so the area of this rectangle is:

$$71 \times 35.5 = 2,520.5 \text{ square inches}$$

12. 66: If the sixth graders bought 45% of the cookies, the number they bought is found by multiplying 0.45 by 500. They bought 225 cookies. The number of cookies left is $500 - 225 = 275$. During the second lunch, the seventh graders bought 40% of the cookies, which is found by multiplying 0.40 by the remaining 275 cookies. The seventh graders bought 110 cookies. This leaves 165 cookies to sell to the eighth graders. If they bought 60% of the remaining cookies, then they bought 99 cookies. Subtracting 99 from 165 cookies leaves Kelly with 66 cookies remaining after the three lunches.

13. D: Because the slope is equal to $m = -\frac{1}{4}$, for every unit increase in x, y decreases by 4 units. Therefore, starting from (5, 6), if the x −coordinate is increased by 1 and the y −coordinate is decreased by 4, another point on the line is (6, 2).

14. 64: The first step is to find the value of m. Recall that roots of numbers are the same as fractional exponents:

$$\sqrt[3]{m} = m^{\frac{1}{3}} = 2$$

Both sides of the equation can be raised to the power of 3 to solve for m. Using the power rule, an exponent on an exponent results in multiplying the exponents, cancelling out the cube root:

$$\left(m^{\frac{1}{3}}\right)^3 = m^{\frac{1}{3} \times 3} = m = 2^3$$

$$m = 8$$

Using the value of m, solve the second equation for n:

$$m = 8 = \sqrt{n}$$

$$n = 8^2$$

$$n = 64$$

Thus, n is equal to 64.

15. A: Use the following relationships to calculate this conversion: 1 hour $= 3,600$ seconds and 1 mile $= 5,280$ feet.

$$16\frac{mi}{hr} = \left(16\frac{mi}{hr}\right)\left(\frac{1hr}{3600s}\right)\left(\frac{5,280ft}{mi}\right) \approx \frac{23.5ft}{s}$$

16. B: After one month, the total value in the account is $6250\left(1 + \frac{.025}{12}\right) \approx \$6,263.02$. Therefore, after the second month, the total value in the account is:

$$6263.02\left(1 + \frac{.025}{12}\right) \approx \$6,276.07$$

17. D: On a single roll, there is one desired outcome, which is rolling a 5. Therefore, the probability of obtaining a 5 on a single roll is $\frac{1}{6}$. On three rolls, the probability is therefore $\left(\frac{1}{6}\right)^3 \approx 0.0046$.

18. 20: Because these are 2 parallel lines cut by a transversal, the angle with a measure of 45 degrees is equal to the measure of angle 6. Angle 6 and the angle labeled $5x + 35$ are supplementary to one another. The sum of these angles should be 180, so the following equation can be generated: $5x + 35 + 45 = 180$. Solving for x, the sum of 35 and 45 is 80, which is then subtracted from 180 to yield 100. Dividing 100 by 5 gives the value of x, which is 20.

19. B: To simplify the given equation, the first step is to make all exponents positive by moving them to the opposite place in the fraction. This expression becomes:

$$\frac{4b^3b^2}{a^1a^4} \times \frac{3a}{b}$$

Then the rules for exponents can be used to simplify. Multiplying the same bases means the exponents can be added. Dividing the same bases means the exponents are subtracted. Thus, after multiplying the exponents in the first fraction, the equation becomes:

$$\frac{4b^5}{a^5} \times \frac{3a}{b}$$

Therefore, we can first multiply to get:

$$\frac{12ab^5}{a^5b}$$

Then, simplifying yields:

$$12\frac{b^4}{a^4}$$

20. B: The car is traveling at a speed of five meters per second. On the interval from one to three seconds, the position changes by ten meters. By making this change in position over time into a rate, the speed becomes ten meters in two seconds or five meters in one second.

Section 4: Verbal Reasoning

1. B: The correct answer here is *anecdotes*, Choice *B*, because it means a short account of an event or events, or a story. The actor telling stories about other famous actors would make him the life of the party. *Empathy* means to share feelings with another; this word doesn't fit here because the actor empathizing with celebrities wouldn't necessarily make him popular at a party. The same goes with the words hypothesis (theory requiring proof), jubilation (joy), and vindication (to clear from blame).

2. B, E: For **i**, the best answer choice is *sagacity*, because it means wisdom. Wisdom would make one a pillar of one's community as well as an advice-giver. *Enmity* means hatred, so this would not make her a pillar of the community, and neither would *impetuosity*, which means rashness. For **ii**, *preferred* is the best answer choice because it means favorite or chosen. It was their *favorite* way of obtaining advice. *Myopic* means nearsighted, so this isn't the right word to used for a way of obtaining advice. Neither is *variegated*, which means diversified.

3. A: *Enhance* is the best answer choice here because it means to improve. They want to *improve* or *boost* the flavor of the watermelon by adding salt to it. *Discount* is incorrect because it usually pertains to sales economy, not taste. *Disdain* means to regard with scorn, which doesn't quite fit the context here. *Abbreviate* means to shorten and is usually used in context with shortening words, not flavor. *Suppress* means to restrain; one wouldn't try to *suppress* flavor with salt. Salt tends to enhance the flavor of food.

4. C, F, I: For **i**, we would say that the athlete displayed remarkable *resilience* after her injury, because resilience means the ability to recover quickly. *Prosperity* (wealth) and *opulence* (affluence) aren't usually things someone would display after an injury. For **ii**, *convalescence* is the best answer choice here because it means the gradual period of returning back to health. *Bereavement* means a period of grief or mourning, so this is incorrect. *Expedition* is also incorrect because it means a group of people going on a journey. For **iii**, *tenacious* is the best answer choice because it means strong or unyielding. She would be a *strong* patient due to her fast recovery. *Deranged* means mentally ill or insane, so this does not fit in with the context of recovering from a sports injury. *Befuddled* means confused, so this is also not appropriate here because there is no indication in the sentence that the patient is confused.

5. D: The best answer choice here is *D, compromise*, which means to settle differences. *Altercation* is incorrect because it means a fight, and two people wouldn't settle a fight with a fight. *Prescription* means formula or medicine, and this also doesn't make sense in settling a disagreement. *Fetter* means shackle, so this does not fit into the context. *Pyre* means a heap of wood, and like the others, one wouldn't use a heap of wood to settle an argument.

6. A, E: For **i**, *despot* is the best answer choice because it means a cruel and oppressive dictator. The term *novice* means someone who is new at something, and someone who is new or a beginner at leadership would probably not have enough experience to be considered a dictator. *Martyr* is also incorrect; this word often denotes a saint of some sort who suffers or dies in order to stand up for something they believe in. This does not fit in the context of a leader who torments his citizens. For **ii**, the best word is *adversity* because it means bad fortune or circumstance. The words *exorbitance* and *affluence* have to do with wealth, so these are incorrect.

7. B: The author clearly states that education is crucial to the survival of the human race, and it can be easily inferred that if this is true, then improvements to our educational system are certainly worth fighting for. Choices *A* and *C* are incorrect because there is nothing in the passage that relates to these statements. Choice *D* is incorrect because it directly contradicts what the author states about all children's ability to learn. Choice *E* is a point made in the passage, but it is not the overall main point.

8. A: Clearly, this author feels passionately about the importance of education. This is evident especially in his word choices. For this reason, all the other answer choices are incorrect.

9. C: Based on the author's passionate stance about the importance of education for all children, this answer choice makes the most sense. For this reason, all the other answer choices are incorrect.

10. D: The author mentions the importance of parent involvement and communication between school and home. He also devotes one full paragraph to the impact of technology on education. The issue of teachers having high expectations for students is also discussed. Nowhere in the passage does the author mention the cost of textbooks, so Choice *D* is correct.

11. B, E: *Gauche* and *tactless* both mean acting without social grace in an inappropriate manner. They both fit the context and create sentences with complementary meanings. Thus, Choices *B* and *E* are the correct answers. Choices *A* and *F* can complete the sentence logically. In this context, *flamboyant* could mean Kevin attracted attention due to overconfidence, and *tortuous* could refer to his request being convoluted. However, neither has a complementary answer choice, so Choices *A* and *F* are both incorrect. Choices *C* and *D* don't coherently complete the sentence or have a complement. *Imperturbable* means staying calm, and *pervasive* denotes spreading across an area.

12. A, D: *Beneficent* and *magnanimous* both describe someone being generous, like a private citizen who funds charitable organizations that provide basic social services. Since they create sentences with complementary meanings, Choices *A* and *D* are the correct answers. Preeminent somewhat makes sense because a private citizen wealthy enough to fund a charitable organization would be very distinguished; however, it has no complementary answer choice, so Choice *E* is incorrect. Choices *B*, *C*, and *F* are all incorrect because they don't fit logically or create complementary sentences. *Craven* means totally lacking courage; *intrepid* denotes fearlessness or adventurousness; and *prescient* relates to having knowledge of future events.

13. C, E: *Salubrious* and *wholesome* both denote healthy living. Since the first clause describes a diet that's unsustainable, the modified second clause is likely something that's healthy. So, *salubrious* and *wholesome* fit logically and create sentences with complementary meanings; thus, Choices *C* and *E* are the correct answers. *Delectable* means delicious, which would make sense in context, but it has no complement, so Choice *A* is incorrect. Choices *B* and *E* could both denote enthusiasm, creating sentences with complementary meanings, but they wouldn't fit logically in context. Therefore, Choices *B* and *E* are incorrect. Choice *D* is incorrect because it refers to a green countryside.

14. A, F: *Accentuate* and *underscore* both mean emphasize, which matches the sentence's context. Emphasizing takeaways with a visual cue would improve a presentation. Thus, Choices *A* and *F* are the correct answers. *Bolster* and *delineate* are both strong logical fits, but they don't have a complementary answer choice. *Bolster* means to strengthen, and *delineate* involves describing something with details. Therefore, Choices *B* and *C* are incorrect. Choices *D* and *E* are incorrect because they don't create coherent or complementary sentences. *Offset* means to counteract, and to *rationalize* is to make a logical argument even if it's not necessarily true or factual.

15. A, B: Several words work well in this sentence; however, not all words have a synonym partner that would complete the meaning of the sentence except for *malaise* and *angst*. The other words are nouns, but they do not clarify the meaning of the sentence provided.

16. B, F: If readers know that the root part of *palatial* means "like a palace," they may see an immediate connection between *palatial* and *extravagant*. Both words fit the meaning of the sentence that suggests the agent is showing places that are not simple and affordable.

17. D: This is the correct answer choice because expository writing involves straightforward, factual information and analysis. It is unbiased and does not rely on the writer's personal feelings or opinions. Choice *A* is incorrect because narrative writing tells a story. Choice *B* is incorrect because persuasive writing is intended to change the reader's mind or position on a topic. Choice *C* is incorrect because technical writing attempts to outline a complex object or process. Choice *E* is incorrect because descriptive writing appeals to the senses to create a picture for the reader.

18. E: This is the correct answer choice because the passage begins by describing Carver's childhood fascination with painting and later returns to this point when it states that at the end of his career, "Carver returned to his first love of art." For this reason, all the other answer choices are incorrect.

19. A: This is the correct answer choice because the passage contains a definition of the term, *agricultural monoculture*, which is very similar to this answer; therefore, all the other answer choices are incorrect.

20. C: This is the correct answer choice because there is ample evidence in the passage that refers to Carver's brilliance and the fact that his discoveries had a far-reaching impact both then and now. There is no evidence in the passage to support any of the other answer choices; therefore, they are all incorrect.

Section 5: Quantitative Reasoning

1. A: Sierra spends more time riding her bike at 15 mph than the car spends at 25 mph because both travel the same distance. The car is faster than the bike. Therefore, the average speed is closer to 15 mph than 25 mph. Hence, the average speed is less than 20 mph, and Quantity A is larger than Quantity B.

2. C: The standard deviation is calculated from the distance of each number in the set from the mean. The set in Quantity A has a mean of $\frac{1+4+7}{3} = 4$, and the distance from each number in the set is 3, 0, and 3. The set in Quantity B has a mean of $\frac{11+14+17}{3} = 14$ and the distance from each number in the set is 3, 0, and 3. The distances from the means in each set are the same, and therefore, the standard deviations of each set are the same. Quantity A is equal to Quantity B.

3. B: $14^* = 14 + 1 = 15$, and $3^* = 3 + 1 = 4$. Therefore, Quantity A is equal to $\frac{15}{4} = \frac{7}{2} = 3.5$. Quantity B is equal to $5^* = 5 + 1 = 6$. Quantity B is greater than Quantity A.

4. D: Multiplying Quantity A by $6z$ results in xyz, and multiplying Quantity B times $6z$ results in 24. Because it is given that $xyz > 15$, Quantity A could be either less than 24 or greater than 24. There is not enough information given to determine a relationship.

5. A: Factoring Quantity A results in $3(2x^2 - x + 3)$. Comparing this expression to Quantity B shows that there is only a difference in the last term. The last term in Quantity A is 3, and the last term in Quantity B is 2. 3 is always greater than 2, so Quantity A is greater than Quantity B.

6. B: The system of equations can be solved through substitution. Because $2x = 2y + 10 = 2(y + 5)$, we can divide both sides by 2 to obtain $x = y + 5$. This can be substituted into the second equation to obtain:

$$3(y + 5) + 2y = 5$$

Therefore, $3y + 15 + 2y = 5$ and $5y + 15 = 5$. Subtracting 15 off of both sides and dividing by 5 results in $y = -2$. Plugging this into $x = y + 5$ results in $x = 3$. Because Quantity A is $y = -2$ and Quantity B is $x = 3$, Quantity B is greater than Quantity A.

7. A: Quantity A can be rewritten as $1 + \frac{2}{x}$. If $x = 1$, it is equivalent to $1 + \frac{2}{1} = 3$. However, this quantity is always greater than 3 because $x > 1$. Quantity B is always less than 1. Because $x > 1$, the numerator is always less than the denominator. Therefore, Quantity A is greater than Quantity B.

8. A: In a set containing an odd number of values, the median is the value that falls in the middle when placed in numerical order. Therefore, the median of these three numbers is 56. The mean is calculated by adding the three numbers together and dividing by 3. The mean is:

$$\frac{55 + 56 + 58}{3} = \frac{169}{3} \approx 56.3$$

Therefore, the mean is larger, and Quantity A is greater than Quantity B.

9. B: Choose a value for c and compare the two quantities. Let c be equal to $10,000, the original cost of the car. In Quantity A it was first decreased by 15%. Therefore, the cost was $(1 - 0.15) \times 10,000 = 8,500$ after the decrease. Then, it was increased by 15%, so Quantity A is equal to:

$$(1 + 0.15) \times 8,500 = \$9,775$$

This amount is less than the original cost of the car, so Quantity B is larger than Quantity A.

10. B: There are two zeros for the function $x = 0, -2$. The zeros can be found several ways, but this particular equation can be factored into:

$$f(x) = x(x^2 + 4x + 4) = x(x + 2)(x + 2)$$

By setting each factor equal to zero and solving for x, there are two solutions. On a graph, these zeros can be seen where the line crosses the x-axis.

11. D: This problem involves a composition function, where one function is plugged into the other function. In this case, the $f(x)$ function is plugged into the $g(x)$ function for each x-value. The composition equation becomes:

$$g(f(x)) = 2^3 - 3(2^2) - 2(2) + 6$$

Simplifying the equation gives the answer:

$$g(f(x)) = 8 - 3(4) - 2(2) + 6$$

$$8 - 12 - 4 + 6 = -2$$

12. 30: A complete circle measures 360 degrees. This circle is broken up into 4 different parts with different measures for each part. Adding these parts should give a total of 360 degrees. The equation generated from this diagram is:

$$4x + 5x + x + 2x = 360$$

Collecting like terms gives the equation $12x = 360$, which can be solved by dividing by 12 to give $x = 30$. The value of x in the diagram is 30.

13. D: The expression is simplified by collecting like terms. Terms with the same variable and exponent are like terms, and their coefficients can be added.

14. 105: The least positive three-digit number is 100. Dividing 100 by 7 yields a value of 14 with a remainder of 2. Since 100 is not itself divisible by 7, given a remainder of 2, the remainder amount can be used to calculate the least three-digit number divisible by 7. Since the remainder is 2, a value of 5 can be added to the total of 100 to ensure there is not a remainder when you divide by 7. This number is 105. This number is a multiple of 7 because 7 times 15 is 105.

15. A: Finding the product means distributing one polynomial onto the other. Each term in the first must be multiplied by each term in the second. Then, like terms can be collected. Multiplying the factors yields the expression:

$$20x^3 + 4x^2 + 24x - 40x^2 - 8x - 48$$

Collecting like terms means adding the x^2 terms and adding the x terms. Then, simplify:

$$20x^3 - 36x^2 + 16x - 48$$

16. D: This problem can be solved by using unit conversion. The initial units are miles per minute. The final units need to be feet per second. Converting miles to feet uses the equivalence statement 1 mi = 5,280 ft. Converting minutes to seconds uses the equivalence statement 1 min = 60 s. Setting up the ratios to convert the units is shown in the following equation:

$$\frac{72 \text{ mi}}{90 \text{ min}} \times \frac{1 \text{ min}}{60 \text{ s}} \times \frac{5,280 \text{ ft}}{1 \text{ mi}} = 70.4 \frac{\text{ft}}{\text{s}}$$

The initial units cancel out, and the new units are left.

17. B: The equation can be solved by factoring the numerator into $(x + 6)(x - 5)$. Since that same factor exists on top and bottom, that factor $(x - 5)$ cancels. This leaves the equation:

$$x + 6 = 11$$

Solving the equation gives the answer $x = 5$. When this value is plugged into the equation, it yields a zero in the denominator of the fraction. Since this is undefined, there is no solution.

18. 78: From the information provided in the problem, the total number of people whose birthdays are given is 100. The number of birthdays in January is 5, the number in April is 4, and in July there are 13. The sum of birthdays in these months is 22. Thus, there are $100 - 22 = 78$ birthdays not in those months. By taking 78 and dividing by the total of 100, the decimal 0.78 is found. Multiplying this number by 100 turns it into 78%. Therefore, there is a 78 percent chance of selecting a famous American not born in January, April, or July.

19. E: This problem can be solved by setting up a proportion involving the given information and the unknown value. The proportion is:

$$\frac{21 \text{ pages}}{4 \text{ nights}} = \frac{140 \text{ pages}}{x \text{ nights}}$$

Solving the proportion by cross-multiplying, the equation becomes $21x = 4 \times 140$, where $x = 26.67$. Since it is not an exact number of nights, the answer is rounded up to 27 nights. Twenty-six nights would not give Sarah enough time.

20. D: To find the average of a set of values, add the values together and then divide by the total number of values. In this case, include the unknown value of what Dwayne needs to score on his next test, in order to solve it.

$$\frac{78 + 92 + 83 + 97 + x}{5} = 90$$

Add the unknown value to the new average total, which is 5. Then multiply each side by 5 to simplify the equation, resulting in:

$$78 + 92 + 83 + 97 + x = 450$$
$$350 + x = 450$$
$$x = 100$$

Dwayne would need to get a perfect score of 100 in order to get an average of at least 90.

Test this answer by substituting back into the original formula.

$$\frac{78 + 92 + 83 + 97 + 100}{5} = 90$$

Dear GRE Test Taker,

We would like to start by thanking you for purchasing this study guide for your GRE exam. We hope that we exceeded your expectations.

Our goal in creating this study guide was to cover all of the topics that you will see on the test. We also strove to make our practice questions as similar as possible to what you will encounter on test day. With that being said, if you found something that you feel was not up to your standards, please send us an email and let us know.

We would also like to let you know about other books in our catalog that may interest you.

Test Name	Amazon Link
MCAT	amazon.com/dp/1637752997
GMAT	amazon.com/dp/1637753829

We have study guides in a wide variety of fields. If the one you are looking for isn't listed above, then try searching for it on Amazon or send us an email.

Thanks Again and Happy Testing!
Product Development Team
info@studyguideteam.com

FREE Test Taking Tips Video/DVD Offer

To better serve you, we created videos covering test taking tips that we want to give you for FREE. **These videos cover world-class tips that will help you succeed on your test.**

We just ask that you send us feedback about this product. Please let us know what you thought about it—whether good, bad, or indifferent.

To get your **FREE videos**, you can use the QR code below or email freevideos@studyguideteam.com with "Free Videos" in the subject line and the following information in the body of the email:

     a. The title of your product

     b. Your product rating on a scale of 1-5, with 5 being the highest

     c. Your feedback about the product

If you have any questions or concerns, please don't hesitate to contact us at info@studyguideteam.com.

Thank you!